# Olympic Turnaround

# OLYMPIC TURNAROUND

How the Olympic Games stepped back
from the brink of extinction
to become the world's best known brand
– and a multi-billion dollar global franchise

Michael Payne

London
Business
Press

First published in 2005
Reprinted 2006

London Business Press
Editorial Offices
23 Ruscombe Road
Twyford
Berkshire RG10 9JL
UK

00 44 (0)1342-825328
www.londonbusinesspress.com

ISBN 0-9550085-0-6

Text design and typesetting by Sparks – www.sparks.co.uk
Cover design by Iconologic – www.iconologic.com
Cover photograph © Getty Images

Printed and bound in Great Britain by Cambrian Printers Ltd, Aberystwyth

For Marta and our three children –
Christopher, Sofia and Andres.

# CONTENTS

*The plate section appears between pages 108 and 109*

# FOREWORD

There is no higher prize in the sporting world than to be an Olympic champion. No other event combines the very best of our sporting and cultural ideals. Yet, the power of the Olympics goes beyond sport: they are a celebration of humanity.

Today, we tend to take the Olympics for granted. We are not surprised that so many of the greatest cities in the world now want to host the Olympic Games, or that children grow up just dreaming of competing – let alone winning – at the Games. But it wasn't always so. Just 25 years ago, one of the world's greatest institutions was on the brink of extinction. That it survived at all is due to the vision and hard work of a few individuals. *Olympic Turnaround* recounts their story and also provides an inside view of the creation of the sports marketing industry.

No one is better positioned to tell this story than Michael Payne. Under the leadership of IOC president Juan Antonio Samaranch, Michael was one of those responsible for creating the Olympic marketing programme that took the Olympics from a cash-strapped amateur event, on the brink of bankruptcy, to the greatest sports spectacle in the world. More recently, he was responsible for negotiating the multi-billion TV rights deals up to 2012.

I first met Michael in the early 1990s, in the run up to the Barcelona Olympic Games. At the time, he was the IOC's marketing director – a role that did not exist until his appointment. Not only was Michael integral to the creation of TOP, the Olympic sponsorship programme that, together with sales of the TV rights, allowed the Olympics to break free of its political purse strings, he was also the IOC's brand champion – and chief enforcer.

From the start, Michael recognised the emotional, human and financial worth of the Olympic Movement. The five Olympic rings are one of the most powerful images in the world; they epitomise the aspiration and ambition of athletes everywhere. The personal endeavours and stories of these athletes also touch all who watch them. Over the years, they have provided many unforgettable moments: moments that define the indomitable Olympic spirit.

From a marketing point of view, too, the Olympic Games are beyond value. No wonder, then, that companies are prepared to go to enormous lengths to be associated with the Olympic rings. For the official sponsors and the TV companies that possess the broadcast rights to the Games, the rewards can be spectacular. An Olympic year can, and does, transform the financial health of the advertising industry.

But it is because they remain true to the Olympic ideal that the rings retain their magical aura. The Olympic brand, in all its associations, has to strike a delicate balance between financial stability and selling out to the god of Mammon. That it has managed to do so is a testament to the way the brand has been developed, nurtured and protected over the past two decades.

This is Michael's account of a remarkable period of Olympic and sports marketing history. Packed with previously untold stories and case studies, it is a unique business story – but one with universal applications. It offers important insights into the future of the Olympic franchise and branding in general. The lessons – and mistakes – are here for all to learn from. It is also a fascinating historic account, written by someone who was there.

As someone who advises companies on their marketing and communications strategies, I can testify to the continuing power of the Olympic brand. There is perhaps no better case study than that of Samsung, one of our clients: the Olympics helped to catapult the brand to global market leadership in less than eight years.

I can personally testify to the unique emotional symbolism of the Olympics. I have been one of the very fortunate few to carry the Olympic torch on its journey to the Games. It is a deeply moving experience – and one I will never forget. Michael calls the torch the 'magic wand' of the Olympic brand – guaranteed to move even the most hardened CEO. I can attest to its power.

As the world turns its attention to China, and the prospect of the Beijing Games in 2008, *Olympic Turnaround* could not be more timely. With China emerging from isolation to take its rightful place on the world stage, the

Beijing Games mark a watershed in global commerce and international relations.

China's ambition to host the Games will have taken over a century to be realised, but a no less remarkable achievement will also be celebrated in Beijing: the triumphant resurgence of the Olympic Movement itself.

*Sir Martin Sorrell*
*London, March 2005*

# PREFACE

I grew up, like many young boys, dreaming about what it would be like to compete in the Olympic Games. I soon realised that the likelihood of me ever becoming an Olympic athlete was slim. I enjoyed a brief career as a professional freestyle skier – a *hotdogger* – in the 1970s. But I did a far better job finding sponsors for the team than winning any of the competitions. So, I entered the brave and, at the time, very new world of sports management and event marketing.

After a few years working on a diverse portfolio of events – everything from launching the London Marathon to test match cricket and a round Britain tall ship race – I was hired by a start-up sports marketing agency in 1983. The brief was startlingly simple: to create a marketing strategy for the Olympic Games. Six months later, I found myself driving across the Alps to Sarajevo, with a Japanese advertising executive as co-driver, for the 1984 Winter Olympic Games. We were to give a presentation to the Executive Board of the International Olympic Committee, on the development of a marketing strategy for the Olympic Movement.

Understandably, I was nervous. I wasn't the only one. Before the Sarajevo opening ceremony, storm clouds loomed over the Olympic Movement. With the death of the Russian leader Yuri Andropov, the Russians were contemplating a boycott of the Los Angeles Games later that year. Peter Ueberroth, the president of the Los Angeles Organising Committee, sat in the lobby of the Sarajevo Hilton, wondering whether his vision of a privately funded Olympic Games was about to come to a grinding halt.

For the next twenty years, the storm clouds came and went. As the IOC's first ever marketing director, and then as its first director of global broadcast and new media rights, I was at the heart of a remarkable and unique commercial adventure. The goal was to design a marketing strategy for the Olympic Games that would save the IOC and the Olympic Movement from bankruptcy and, in the process, avoid selling the Olympic soul to Mammon.

The turnaround of the Olympics is a remarkable business story. It is the story of how the nearly bankrupt Olympic Movement, effectively written off by most commentators, was led away from the abyss by visionary, and sometimes hard-headed, leadership and the creation of a unique corporate marketing platform. It is the story of how the future of one of the world's iconic institutions was secured. It is the story of a fine balancing act as an amateur organisation struggled with and eventually embraced the business world. But it did so on its own terms, maintaining its identity, not compromising its core values and, in the process, establishing many of the ground rules of today's sports marketing industry.

This is also the story of the broadcast industry's love affair with sport. It charts how companies began to understand the power of sport as a marketing and promotional tool. It is also a cautionary tale of success and failure; how some nations learned to embrace the potential of hosting the world, while others, through short-sighted local political agendas, failed to see the bigger picture.

This is the business story of the world's most valuable and important franchise, the largest event in the world, the Olympic Games.

# ACKNOWLEDGEMENTS

There have been many books written on the history of the Olympic Games. Yet, few have tried to tell the behind the scenes story of the business of the Games. Each organising committee president has told his own story of the challenges and the adventure of putting on their Games. Each represents a moment in time, but offers only limited perspective on the broader on-going business agenda.

In addition, there are books concerned with the political process – and, of course, there is a regular supply of tabloid newspaper articles with their large headlines and appetite for scandal. But there is scant in-depth research and analytical perspective.

Although I did not keep a detailed diary during my two decades at the IOC, I have had access to the resources of the Olympic Museum and its press archives. I have also compared my own notes and memories with media reports of the time. The balance between my first-hand experience and that of informed – and occasionally not quite so informed – observers, hopefully provides accurate and new insights into the story.

The turnaround of the Olympics was a team effort. It involved numerous business executives and thousands of volunteers. The two most influential characters were Juan Antonio Samaranch and Dick Pound. Samaranch was the IOC president from 1980 until 2001, who provided the inspiration and vision to lead the Olympic Movement to its current standing. Pound was the IOC member from Canada who, as IOC vice president and chair of the IOC Marketing Commission and TV Negotiations Commission, provided the political direction and counsel to drive the business agenda. It should be remembered that Samaranch and Pound, like all IOC members, were also volunteers, unsalaried devotees to the Olympic cause.

The parallel story to this unique period in Olympic history is that it was also the time when the sports marketing industry came of age. Key to both was Horst Dassler, the president of Adidas. Sadly, he died before he could see his vision for the IOC's global marketing programme come to fruition. His early partner in the sport marketing agency West Nally, Patrick Nally, helped to pioneer many of the governing principles of rights packaging and sponsor category exclusivity. Together with the legendary American sports agent Mark McCormack, Nally had an influence still felt throughout the industry.

## Organising genius

Each Olympics is unique with a completely different team, a new set of personalities, agendas and egos. Each Olympic organising committee is challenged by the IOC to see how they can enhance the Olympic brand: how they can nurture it and pass it on healthier, and in better condition, to their successors. From Peter Ueberroth in Los Angeles and Josep Miguel Abad in Barcelona, through to Gianna Angelopoulos-Daskalaki in Athens, each organising committee president has led a team that has cared for and tried to cultivate the Olympic ideal.

The marketing bosses of each organising committee have always had to struggle with the conflicting agendas of respecting the Olympic ideal while following the dictate of local politicians to 'show me the money'. It is a political high wire act. Some, like Jomar Selvaag and Sigmund Thue in Lillehammer, John Moore in Sydney, Mark Lewis in Salt Lake City and George Bolos and Marton Simitsek in Athens, have managed the balance better than others. They understood that there was a broader agenda, and that their contribution to the Olympic brand went beyond pure dollars and cents.

The Olympic Games have always attracted the very best talent – both on and off the sporting field. They have provided each nation with an opportunity to showcase their best designers, their best architects, their best creative producers. Luis Bassatt in Barcelona, Petter Moshus in Lillehammer, George Hirthler and Brad Copeland in Atlanta, Scott Givens in Salt Lake City, and Theodora Mantzaris-Kindel in Athens are a few of the unsung heroes who did more for the design and image of the Olympic Games and their own countries than people will ever realise.

The Games have also attracted some of the world's greatest story tellers. Both Bud Greenspan, Olympic film-maker extraordinaire, and Stewart Binns, have brought their creative talents to the Olympic story. I am also indebted to Steve McCarthy and his team at ALEM for sharing some of the most powerful and poignant Olympic torch relay experiences.

Thousands of other people have made a significant contribution to the turnaround of the Olympic Games. I was very fortunate throughout my twenty years with the Olympic Movement to have been supported by a dedicated team of marketing professionals and fellow directors. Broadcasters and sponsors not only signed the cheques that provided much of the fuel for the turnaround, but in many cases provided a great deal of the inspiration to develop and cultivate the Olympic brand. Many are singled out in this book – but it has been impossible to list everyone. To the many I have missed, I apologise.

Finally, I would like to acknowledge a few people who have helped in the writing of the book. My sister, Vicky Payne, and my good friend Nick Grey ploughed through repeated drafts on their holidays to give me valuable feedback on what was interesting, and what was not. Lee Martin at Getty Images allowed me to raid the world's greatest sports photographic library and to borrow some of the unique images to help tell the story. Raymond Burki allowed me to reproduce one of his excellent cartoons. Brad Copeland and his team at Iconologic came up with the design of the book jacket. Tom Fryer and John Duggan at Sparks masterminded production. Stuart Crainer and Des Dearlove of London Business Press helped transform my rough draft, and then transformed themselves into publishers with the launch of London Business Press. And, last but not least, to my long-suffering wife Marta for all her love and support, and for not letting the kids drop the computer in the bath or wipe the memory clean.

*Michael Payne*
*Lausanne, March 2005*

## OLYMPIC WINTER AND SUMMER GAMES

1896    Athens, Greece
1900    Paris, France
1904    St Louis, USA
1908    London, UK
1912    Stockholm, Sweden
1916    Cancelled
1920    Antwerp, Belgium
1924    Chamonix, France/Paris, France
1928    St Moritz, Switzerland/Amsterdam, Netherlands
1932    Lake Placid, USA/Los Angeles, USA
1936    Garmisch-Partenkirchen, Germany/Berlin, Germany
1940    Cancelled
1944    Cancelled
1948    St Moritz, Switzerland/London, UK
1952    Oslo, Norway/Helsinki, Finland
1956    Cortina, Italy/Melbourne, Australia
1960    Squaw Valley, USA/Tokyo, Japan
1964    Innsbruck, Austria/Rome, Italy
1968    Grenoble, France/Mexico City, Mexico
1972    Sapporo, Japan/Munich, Germany
1976    Innsbruck, Austria/Montreal, Canada
1980    Lake Placid, USA/Moscow, USSR
1984    Sarajevo, Yugoslavia/Los Angeles, USA
1988    Calgary, Canada/Seoul, South Korea
1992    Albertville, France/Barcelona, Spain
1994    Lillehammer, Norway
1996    Atlanta, USA
1998    Nagano, Japan
2000    Sydney, Australia
2002    Salt Lake City, USA
2004    Athens, Greece

2006   Torino, Italy
2008   Beijing, China
2010   Vancouver, Canada

While the Games themselves are the chronological backbone of the book, it is worth noting that the Olympic Movement also has a parallel timeline. Host cities are chosen six to seven years in advance. Broadcasting and sponsorship rights are negotiated anywhere between four and ten years before the actual event. As there is now a Games every two years, this means a continual forward-looking schedule.

Over the course of the book's 25 year story, key executives obviously change. In the text they are given their job titles at the time. Similarly, some key statistics within the Olympic Movement evolved – the number of National Olympic Committees, for example, rose from 160 to over 200 in the wake of the collapse of the Soviet Union and the recognition of various new territories.

# Chapter 1

# RINGS SIDE SEAT

## Beijing, August 8th, 2008

Picture the scene: Chinese President Hu Jintao steps up to a podium in the spectacular new Beijing Olympic Stadium. Watched by more than four billion television viewers across 220 countries, he declares open the 29th Olympiad of the modern era.

Jintao's speech follows in a tradition. Over the last century, American Presidents Reagan, Clinton, and George W Bush; along with King George VI and Queen Elizabeth II of Great Britain; King Juan Carlos of Spain; President Mitterand of France; President Brezhnev of the Soviet Union; and Emperors Hirohito and Akihito of Japan have all opened the world's greatest sporting festival. As the speech concludes, the Olympic cauldron is ignited. China's spectacular party, firmly establishing its position on the world stage, can officially begin.

And what a celebration it will be! Over 10,500 athletes from 202 nations will be present. More than 20,000 media representatives will attend. More journalists will visit China during the 17 days of the Olympic Games than visited the country in the previous 100 years. The financial figures are equally impressive. By the time the 2008 Games are officially declared open, companies from around the world supporting China's Olympic effort will have invested more than $2 billion in the event and many more billions globally in advertising and promotional campaigns connected to the Olympics. Two hundred broadcasters from around the world will have paid around $2.5 billion to the International Olympic Committee (IOC) for exclusive broadcasting rights.

For China, the Beijing Olympics marks a symbolic turning point. At an estimated cost of $40 billion, the Chinese Government will transform the nation's capital. The new stadium will be the most visible sign of a huge capital investment programme in China's sporting, transportation and economic infrastructure. No expense will be spared. After decades of isolation, China's leaders see the Games as a key instrument of change, both symbolic and economic.[1]

For China it is a golden opportunity to enter the global community and open its gates to the future. China's pursuit of the Olympic dream started in 1908 when a news magazine called Tianjin Youth asked: 'When will it be possible for China to host the Olympic Games on its own territory?'[2] The dream took a century to become reality.

The 2008 Beijing Olympic Games will make history. It will usher in a new era in global commerce and relations. China's economic renaissance and desire to host the Games has quite rightly attracted huge media attention. But another remarkable transformation story will also be celebrated on the Beijing stage: the renaissance of the Olympic Movement itself.

Since the drably politicised Moscow Games of 1980, the Olympic Games have undergone a dramatic reversal of fortune, the result of a quiet revolution and unique business turnaround.

It is difficult, today, to fully appreciate quite how close the world came to losing the Olympics in the early 1980s. With the world's greatest cities now falling over themselves to host the Games; with media empires paying billions of dollars for the right to televise the event; and a roster of the world's most prestigious companies lining up to associate themselves with the Olympics, it is easy to forget that twenty five years ago, one of the great icons of global civilisation was very nearly lost due to lack of funding, political interference, and a general lack of interest.

What would it have meant to the world, if the Olympics had come to an end? What inspiration would have been denied to the children of the world? What aspiration would have been lost by mankind?

## The Olympic renaissance

The Olympic Games represents the highest summit of sporting achievement. Yet, the Olympic Games have always transcended sport. As individuals and nations, they raise us all – athletes and spectators alike – to a higher plain.

Nelson Mandela observed that: 'Sport reaches areas far beyond any sphere of political influence and has probably done more to unify nations than any politician has been capable of.'

No other sporting event embodies that aspiration in quite the way that the Olympic Games does. This is no coincidence. It was the intention of Baron Pierre de Coubertin when he founded the modern Olympic Movement more than 2,500 years after the original sporting festival in Ancient Greece.[3]

'Why did I restore the Games? To ennoble and strengthen sports, to ensure their independence and duration, and thus to enable them to fulfil the educational role incumbent upon them in the modern world. For the glorification of the individual athlete, whose muscular activity is necessary for the community and whose prowess is necessary for the maintenance of the spirit of competition,' de Coubertin said.

An educational theorist, de Coubertin believed that sport had a vital role to play in the development of the individual. At an international sports conference at the Sorbonne in Paris in 1892, he proposed that the Olympic Games be revived. Two years later, he founded the IOC and established the founding four principles of the modern Olympic Movement:

1    To promote the development of those physical and moral qualities which are the basis of sport.
2    To educate young people through sport in a spirit of mutual understanding and friendship, thereby helping to build a better and more peaceful world.
3    To spread the Olympic principles throughout the world, thereby creating international goodwill.
4    To bring together the athletes of the world in the Olympic Games every four years.

From these are derived the Olympic ideals of fraternity, friendship, peace and universal understanding.

Central to de Coubertin's creation was establishing the framework to run the Games. Taking the leading role was the International Olympic Committee, a non-profit international organisation. For want of a better word, the IOC is the 'owner' of the Olympic Games. The IOC was initially just a collection of individual members – until recently co-opted for life – who acted as trustees to the Olympic ideal. The members were selected from all corners of society – from heads of state, to industrialists and lawyers through to sports administrators and Olympic champions. The primary role of the IOC members was to select the site of the Games. Today, the 130

IOC members are supported by a professional administration of over 250 employees based on the shores of Lake Geneva in Lausanne, Switzerland. Next down from the IOC are the National Olympic Committees (NOCs), which administer the Olympic Movement in their respective country and send their teams to the Games. Finally, de Coubertin enlisted International Federations to manage the technical aspects of their sports at the Games. These three groups – the IOC, the NOCs and the International Federations – form what is loosely known as the Olympic Movement.

The first modern Games were held in 1896 in Athens. On April 6, King George of Greece opened the Games at the Acropolis in front of a crowd of 60,000. Two hundred and twenty men (women didn't participate until 1900) from 13 countries competed in nine sports: athletics, cycling, fencing, gymnastics, shooting, swimming, tennis, weight lifting and wrestling. There is some confusion over the exact number of competitors, as some tourists, who happened to be in Athens at the time, took part. The athletics took place at the Panathenaic Stadium, where the bends on the tracks were so tight the competitors had to slow down to stay in lane. The swimming events were held in the Bay of Zea. Only three competitors lined up for the 500m.

The first Winter Olympics were held over 11 days at Chamonix, France, in 1924. Originally titled the International Winter Sports Week it was only later designated the first Winter Olympics. Norway and Finland captured 27 out of the 43 medals available. One medallist had to wait a little longer than usual for his medal. US competitor Anders Haugen won a bronze medal in the ski jump, but a scoring error meant that no one realised. He didn't receive his medal until 1974 – when he was 83.

## Starting at the finishing line

By the 1970s, decay had set in. After the tragedies of the 1972 Munich Olympics, when Palestinian terrorists killed 11 members of the Israeli team, an air of resignation enveloped the entire Olympic Movement. As he handed over the symbolic keys to the IOC presidency in 1972, the American industrialist Avery Brundage reluctantly told his successor, Lord Killanin: 'You won't have much use for these; I believe the Olympic

Movement will not last more than another few years.' Indeed, Brundage forecast that the demise of the Olympic Movement would occur before the end of Killanin's presidency.

By July 1980, when the IOC gathered in Moscow for its 83rd session, and the election of a new president, Brundage's forecast looked as if it was about to come true.[4] The Olympic Movement's obituary was already being penned. Critics had come to view the Games as too political and too expensive to stage.

Writing about the IOC presidential elections, John Rodda, long-standing Olympic columnist for the UK's Guardian newspaper, observed that the presidential hopefuls were 'prepared to become king of a crumbling castle'. The candidates to replace the Irish aristocrat Killanin, and become the seventh president of the IOC, were Jim Worrall, a lawyer from Canada; Willi Daume, organiser of the 1972 Munich Games; Marc Hodler, the long standing International Ski Federation president from Switzerland; Sir Lance Cross, a New Zealand television executive; and Juan Antonio Samaranch.[5]

Samaranch was a little known 60-year-old Spanish industrialist and diplomat. He had spent three years from 1977 to 1980 serving as Spain's first Ambassador to Moscow.[6] Samaranch was co-opted onto the IOC by Brundage in 1966. At the time, this broke the IOC's own rules which limited countries that had not staged the Games to one member. Spain already had a member, but Brundage saw something in Samaranch. He believed that one day the Spaniard could lead the Olympic Movement.

A lot has been written about Samaranch in the intervening 25 years. Some of it has been misinformed, unfair, if not plain wrong. Not only did Samaranch go on to lead the Olympic Movement, but in many ways he saved it. Working alongside the IOC president for nearly two decades, I experienced first-hand his political and strategic skills. Through his vision, an extraordinary work ethic and dogged perseverance, he reunited the diverse factions within the organisation and built the stature of the IOC and the core foundations that led to the success enjoyed by the Olympic Games today.

Samaranch had, and continues to have, his critics, of course. My own view is unapologetically positive. It is informed by what I saw with my own eyes. This does not mean he was without flaws. For all of his strengths,

Samaranch was not a particularly good media communicator and was uncomfortable with the discipline of modern day public relations. Throughout his presidency he faced a largely unsympathetic Anglo-Saxon press who often had little knowledge of the broader political agenda he was pursuing.

Samaranch focused on long-term results, achieved through a fine-tuned diplomatic agenda and insight into the key issues. He rarely worried about what he regarded as petty operational or administrative details – although he maintained a remarkable attention to detail when he wanted. Samaranch was, paradoxically, a pragmatic idealist. His focus on uniting the Olympic Movement meant that, occasionally, he turned a blind eye to indiscretions within the Olympic family. Anyone faced with managing the agendas of 200 countries deals with similar issues. His own personal tastes were extremely modest. But, in his desire to build the stature of the IOC as a global international organisation that would be received on an equal basis by heads of state, he gained a reputation for a grandiose lifestyle. This is something for which he was often criticised.

The Samaranch presidency began in the famous Hall of Columns of Moscow's Central House of Trade Unions. After a secret ballot of IOC members, Lord Killanin stepped out in front of his colleagues to announce the Spaniard's elevation to the most political – and most fragile – position in the world of sport.[7]

## The cancer of politics

Taking over the leadership of an organisation which manages two events every four years should be comparatively straightforward. There is time, you would imagine, for leisurely contemplation; time to reach considered judgements. There are no investors eyeing quarterly results with a gimlet gaze.

But in 1980, when Samaranch took over the IOC presidency, the political problems were both pressing and depressing. From day one, Samaranch faced intense pressure and imminent bankruptcy. With the Moscow Games about to begin, the Olympic Movement was on the brink of its second serious boycott. The first boycott had occurred four years earlier in Montreal, when 17 African nations walked out over New Zealand's continued sporting links with the apartheid regime in South Africa.[8]

When the Moscow Games opened, a few days after Samaranch was elected IOC president (though his formal office began after the Games), 65 nations responded to US President Jimmy Carter's call for a boycott, in retaliation to the Soviet Union's invasion of Afghanistan. Some teams were forced to pull out because of financial pressures. This was one of the weaknesses in the way that the Olympic Movement was structured at the time. What many observers didn't realise was that once governments withdrew their support for the cost of sending the team to the Games, many National Olympic Committees had no other source of funding. Whether they agreed with the policy or not, they had no choice but to withdraw from the competition. Eighty-one nations finally did turn up but, without complete teams from the United States, Kenya, Canada, Japan, Germany and Norway, the sporting field was decimated. Moscow was the largest boycott in sports history. It plunged the event into crisis. The Olympic Movement was on the verge of unravelling.[9]

The idea of the Olympic Movement as a catalyst for promoting peace around the world – one of its founding principles – was sorely tested in Moscow. Doves of peace appeared incongruous when Russian tanks were rolling through Afghanistan. 'Russia is a country that tries so hard to impress but does so much to depress,' observed the BBC's sports commentator David Coleman. The depression seeped out from Moscow to the entire Olympic Movement. The threat of more boycotts was an Olympic cancer, eating away at the Movement's very survival. The political machinations undermined what the Olympic Games stood for.

With the Olympic Games a Cold War battleground, the United Nations had begun to debate whether it should even take over the Olympics, reasoning that the IOC had failed. And there were more clandestine threats, with rumours of Eastern Bloc nations, led by the Soviet Union, lobbying to shift control of the Games from the IOC to UNESCO, where every nation could have a vote. This was more manipulative than it now looks – the Soviets calculated that under UNESCO control, Third World countries would dominate the Games and they could, as a result, wrest control of the Games away from what they saw as Western dominance. With Los Angeles selected to host the 1984 Olympic Games, talk had already turned to whether the Soviets would seek their revenge for the American-led boycott of their Games.

## Running on empty

The other looming issue was financial. The Olympic Movement had not come to terms with the spiralling costs of organising a world event. Putting on the Games was increasingly costly and increasingly difficult for cities to justify. When Montreal was awarded the 1976 Games, the city's mayor, Jean Drapeau, was quoted as claiming that 'the Olympics could no more produce a deficit, than a man a baby'. He was wrong – and by a large margin. The original cost of hosting the Montreal Games was estimated at $310 million. But cost overruns on the construction of Montreal's Olympic stadium left the city burdened with debts of $1 billion. By the time these are cleared in 2006, the final cost will be about $2 billion.[10]

The Judge Malouf inquiry on the financing of the Montreal Games produced a scathing indictment of how they were organised and run. Quebec's then Prime Minister, Rene Levesque, described it as a massive abuse of funds. The citizens of Montreal when asked what should be done about the main stadium simply suggested the use of dynamite. Not surprisingly, this and other financial disasters made cities reluctant to host the Games, casting a shadow that remained over the Olympics for decades.

The finances of the Moscow Games were, as you'd expect at the height of the Cold War, shrouded in mystery. The official figure was that the Moscow Games cost $1.3 billion (861 million roubles). But unofficial figures mentioned sums of over $9 billion. The Winter Olympic Games in Lake Placid, a few months earlier in 1980, were also pushed to the edge of financial ruin thanks to a combination of administrative problems, insufficient revenue and poor publicity as a result of the Moscow boycott.[11]

To make matters worse, the IOC itself was also perilously close to bankruptcy. At the time of Samaranch's election to the presidency, the IOC had less than $200,000 in liquidity, and just $2 million in assets. What revenue potential did exist came from US broadcast rights. Total broadcast revenue from the 1980 Lake Placid and Moscow Games was $122 million, 83 per cent of which came from the US, and nearly all of which was pledged to the organising committees to try and help defray some of the costs.[12]

But even this revenue source was under threat. With the boycott of the Moscow Games underway, the US Department of Commerce placed an embargo on any payments by the American broadcaster NBC to the Moscow organisers. President Carter subsequently extended the embargo to the IOC.[13] It was estimated that even with Lloyds insurance cover, Moscow cost NBC between $20 and $40 million in lost advertising revenues – losses not covered by insurance.

The Moscow experience was also likely to make US networks reticent about bidding for future Olympic rights. Pundits forecast that TV rights fees would level off and, perhaps, decline. There was talk of the networks combining to place a single bid for the Games, thus killing any form of competitive bidding to drive up the price. The three networks – NBC, ABC and CBS – had already met with the US Justice Department to explore an anti-trust exemption and were discussing how to pool resources to bring the rights fees down and divide the coverage between them.

## Mission impossible

Given all this, many viewed Samaranch's task as the new IOC president as mission impossible. One of those looking pessimistically to the future was Dick Pound. Elected to the IOC in 1978, Pound was a former member of the Canadian Olympic swimming team at the 1960 Olympic Games in Rome, and went on to serve two terms as IOC vice president. Dick Pound was one of the most influential IOC members during Samaranch's presidency. He chaired many of the IOC's most important commissions and, in 2001, himself ran for the IOC presidency, losing to Jacques Rogge.[14]

Looking back on the early days of the Samaranch presidency, Pound reflected: 'In 1980, the Olympic Movement was under sustained attack from political powers and was, indeed, a virtual hostage to world tensions. It was disunited, well short of universal and had no financial resources to give it the autonomy and independence it needed to resist political pressures.'

Samaranch himself was far from optimistic. In an uncharacteristically frank analysis, he later recalled: 'I felt so alone that I couldn't cope with all the demands of the job, with the sizeable problems that I knew there were and had to be handled. It was a feeling that lasted maybe two weeks, during which it even crossed my mind how I might withdraw.'

Samaranch wasn't the only one with problems. The organisation of the 1984 Los Angeles Games was established on fragile foundations. Eighty three per cent of the population of Los Angeles had actually voted *against* providing any funding for the Games. For the first time, the Games were being staged by a private commercial group of individuals, led by Peter Ueberroth, rather than a city and national government. It was a step into the unknown.

Many IOC members were far from comfortable with Ueberroth's approach. Sir Reginald Alexander, the longstanding IOC member for Kenya, set the scene when he addressed Ueberroth, following his report to the IOC Session in Moscow: 'You, Mr Ueberroth represent the ugly face of capitalism... and its attempt to take over the Olympic Movement and commercialise the Olympic Games.'

And so, sitting in Moscow, facing the true impact of the US Government-led Moscow boycott, Peter Ueberroth was beginning to wonder whether the few sponsors that he had persuaded to sign up for Los Angeles would defect. 'Would all the TV negotiations come to a halt ... and would the IOC yank the Los Angeles Games?' he reflected. There was growing scepticism about whether Los Angeles would ever really happen.

## Gentlemen amateurs

Dealing with this cash flow crisis, apparently diminishing future returns and crumbling confidence was the IOC's administration in Lausanne, Switzerland. This was made up of one full-time director along with a small, and somewhat amateur, administrative staff. One story exemplifies the IOC's amateurish approach. In 1979, the IOC counsel was given a cheque for $25 million by Peter Ueberroth as the Olympic Movement's then share of the Los Angeles TV rights.[15] Rather than bank the proceeds and earn interest, he headed off for a few weeks' holiday with the cheque in his wallet.

The IOC was as inept at generating money as it was at looking after it. Despite having one of the world's best known brands, the limited marketing experiments undertaken by the IOC and Olympic organisers, more often than not, failed. In 1977, for example, the IOC entered into an agreement with a company called Interlicense for a 70-year term to license the pictograms – the graphic icons designed to depict each sport – from Montreal. By 1980 the contract was in dispute – a dispute that was not finally settled until 1990. At one stage, the Swiss courts ruled that the IOC should pay 60 million Swiss Francs in compensation. The IOC eventually settled the case for $2 million.

With the IOC impotent – or worse – Olympic organisers had begun to develop their own sponsorship and licensing programmes. But the revenue they generated did little more than cover the cost of administering the programmes. Montreal attracted the support of 628 companies, with 42 official sponsors paying an average of Can$50,000 each and generating a total of $5 million in cash and another $12 million in value in kind (products and services provided free) – just two per cent of the total receipts. Moscow issued some 6,972 certificates to manufacture over 17,500 different products but was unable to fill the yawning funding hole. Even Lake Placid, with the power and potential of the US market, could only generate $26.5 million in cash and $30 million in value in kind from some 200 companies. And, after the Games, organisers were faced with numerous lawsuits from companies who felt they had been cheated.

## Any takers?

At the start of the 1980s, the situation looked bleak. Given the political boycotts and an unappealing commercial proposition, it was little wonder that the IOC was having great difficulty in finding any city willing to stage the Games. The risks were simply too great. For many it was seen as commercial suicide to even apply to host the Games. In fact, Lake Placid was the only city prepared to host the Winter Games in 1980.

When the IOC met in 1978 to select the city to host the 1984 Games, things weren't much better. Tehran, Iran, had originally considered bidding but lost interest when the Shah's regime collapsed. Islamic fundamentalism and sport are unlikely bedfellows. 'Tehran had a management problem at the time,' Peter Ueberroth wryly noted. The shortage of willing candidates gave Los Angeles a strong bargaining position. The Los Angeles organisers simply demanded that the Games be staged on their terms. So difficult were the subsequent negotiations between the IOC and the organisers, that Lord Killanin began to explore whether there were any other potential host cities.[16] There were none.

Similarly, the queue of candidates in 1981 applying to host the 1988 Summer Games was short.[17] At the time of the Moscow Games, only one candidate had formally confirmed its intention to bid – Nagoya, an industrialised city in central Japan.

A possible second candidature came from Seoul in South Korea which was still a developing nation. Perhaps more worryingly, it was technically at war with neighbouring North Korea.[18] The demilitarised zone, one of the most volatile places on earth, was less than 50 kilometres from Seoul. Howard Cosell, the distinguished ABC TV sports commentator remarked: 'You can't hold an Olympics in the middle of a war zone.' The country bidding to host the world claimed diplomatic relations with only 60 of the 160 nations scheduled to participate in the Olympics.[19]

Although a nominal democracy, politically South Korea was precariously balanced. The nation's president, Chun Doo Hwan, a former army general, had assumed power in the latest of a series of military coups, just a few months before the 1981 IOC Session. Based on the country's track record of military coups, it was more than likely that there would be several more in the intervening period between election and the eventual hosting of the Games.

These were some of the worries Samaranch inherited. Most disturbing of all was a growing sense that the Olympic Movement was becoming a political football. Unless it could become financially independent and free itself from political interference, it risked losing the moral authority imbued in it by the Olympic ideals.

## Hostage to ill fortune

In the weeks after Moscow, Samaranch identified the priorities for building a solid foundation for the IOC. They were three-fold. First, he made it clear that the IOC needed to stand on its own two feet financially. Given the IOC's parlous financial state, there could be little debate about the need for it to become self-sufficient.

In his first letter to IOC members after election, Samaranch wrote, with typical understatement, that 'the financing of the IOC is a matter of some urgency'. For the next two decades Samaranch devoted all his considerable energies to building a solid financial base for the Olympic Movement, so that cities would want to and could afford to host the Olympic Games, and National Olympic Committees could afford to make their own decisions, and not be solely subject to the financial whims of their governments. Providing a firm financial foundation for the Games was Samaranch's primary focus throughout his time as IOC president.

From the moment that Samaranch took over the IOC presidency, he turned to his close friend Horst Dassler, president of Adidas, and began to explore how to create a global marketing strategy for the Olympic Movement.

Dassler was no stranger to the workings of large sports organisations. He was closely connected to Joao Havelange who became president of the Fédération Internationale de Football Association (FIFA) in 1974. He was also friends with Sepp Blatter who succeeded Havelange in 1998. Dassler eventually became FIFA's marketing partner handling its marketing rights.[20]

While there were prophets of doom aplenty, Dassler was an enthusiastic Olympic supporter and a voice of commercial sense and optimism. Dassler's vision for the Olympic franchise eventually provided the inspiration for its financial salvation. But all that was in the future. In the year after his election, Samaranch created a new commission, the New Sources of Financing Commission, with the specific mandate to explore additional revenue generating programmes for the Olympic Movement. It met for the first time in December 1981.[21]

The second element of Samaranch's turnaround strategy was to take control of the Olympic agenda. He would use his honed diplomatic skills to depoliticise the agenda, so that the term boycott could be banished from the Olympic lexicon and the Olympic cancer cured.

When he took over, the Olympic Movement was powerless in the face of politically motivated boycotts. Samaranch set out to change this by creating a dialogue with world leaders. His idea was to avoid problems by anticipating and engaging with issues at an early stage – rather than attempting to solve them at the last minute. No longer would the IOC trail behind politicians and others whose short-term focus meant they were only interested in tomorrow's newspaper headlines. Instead, the IOC would run its own race – with its own strategy. Samaranch invested time and energy in developing relationships with the world's political rulers.

To establish close relationships with the rulers of the world, Samaranch had to appear their equal. He set out to visit each and every country. He sat down and talked face-to-face with each head of state and a range of government leaders to explain the role of the Olympic Movement. He explained how the boycotts were not only hurting them, but undermining the potential of the Olympics as a tool for peace. With this personal contact and access, Samaranch calculated that next time there was a crisis he might be able to speak to world leaders in person, or enlist their support before the situation escalated. His priority was to create a dialogue so that at least political leaders would talk before they did anything to jeopardise the Olympics.

The third element in Samaranch's recovery strategy was unity. The entire Olympic Movement faced a crisis, he explained, and it was only by working together that it could get out of it. In this simple plea lay the insight that the Olympic brand is bigger than any one person or group. Perceived wisdom says that consensus can most easily be built on the lowest common denominator, but the Olympic Movement exemplifies the opposite. It is a cause that appeals to our aspirations, a brand that appeals to our highest instincts, one built on the *highest common denominator.* Samaranch understood this and used it to unify the Olympic family.

## Mission possible

Over the next two decades, Samaranch and the IOC set about achieving his objectives of unity, setting the agenda and establishing the Olympic Movement's financial independence and strength. Of course, in reality, the three are inextricably linked. Strong finances allow you to set the agenda and so on; and what was achieved was usually slightly different from the initial objective – such is organisational life – but what was achieved was substantial and significant.

On the financial side revenues were raised dramatically. By 2008, global broadcast revenues had increased over 30-fold to $3 billion, with NBC and the European Broadcasting Union paying a further 35 per cent increase in rights fees for the next quadrennial through 2012. This bucked the downward spiral that nearly all other sports events were facing. Coverage of the Olympic Games more than doubled to over 220 countries, with a global audience of close to four billion people – making it the largest broadcasting event in the world.

Increased broadcast revenues allowed the IOC to dramatically expand its funding support to the National Olympic Committees and International Sports Federations around the world.[22]

This was further boosted by the establishment of the premier global marketing programme of its kind – the TOP programme – which attracted the support of some of the world's leading blue-chip corporations, including Coca-Cola, Kodak, McDonald's, Visa, Samsung, Swatch, and Panasonic.

Cash began to flow into, instead of out of, the Olympic coffers. Sponsorship revenues grew from $56.5 million at Lake Placid to over $850 million at Salt Lake City in 2002. The first sponsor for Vancouver 2010 paid over $150 million, nearly triple the total amount generated in Lake Placid from 200 corporations.

Today, the Olympic marketing programmes are among the most powerful available. 'The Olympics provides companies with a marketing opportunity unlike any other,' noted the *Wall Street Journal*, 'The 17 days of competition, many of the Olympic sponsors and suppliers say, offer a unique chance to test new products, ideas, concepts and programmes.'

## Less is more

Paradoxically, this financial success was achieved with less commercial association, not more. There was a dramatic reduction in the number of marketing partners. It was also achieved without compromising the cherished Olympic ideals which make the Games unique and special.

The IOC was not seduced by higher offers from private broadcasters. Instead, it chose to keep the broadcast on free-to-air broadcast. This ensured that everyone in the world can afford to watch, and that economic access is not a barrier to following the Games. The Olympic stadiums and athlete bibs also remain free of any form of advertising. Tobacco and spirits sponsorship is also prohibited.

Maintaining the values and ethical principles of the Olympic ideals – and not selling out to Mammon – is a fine and continual balancing act. How to keep the Olympic soul and yet still provide the funding basis that allows the Olympic Movement to grow and thrive, is a formidable ongoing challenge. There is an obvious tension between the idealistic and commercial principles which resonate with modern Olympic philosophy and the need to finance the world's largest athletic and media event. More and more Olympic observers admit that this tension is no longer a conflictual one, but rather a dynamic balance where the identity of the Olympics, as the embodiment of a special set of values, engages in a delicate dance with commercial entities eager to use that identity to sell products.

It is important to remember that Baron de Coubertin's inspiring vision of the Olympic Movement contained one serious flaw: it paid little attention to financing the Games. Most Olympic Games in the twentieth century were made possible by imaginative scrimping and scraping – by athletes, NOCs, host cities and host governments. The ethics and ideas of the Olympic Movement were clear but their execution was built on a fragile commercial edifice. By 1980 this was teetering on the brink of collapse. The Olympic Movement had a choice: to continue on its amateurish and peripheral way into extinction or to reinvent its organisation and outlook for the modern age.

It chose the latter.

The journey began with the election of Samaranch to the IOC presidency. Just four years later, and despite all the predictions to the contrary, a bidding contest for TV rights offered the first glimmer of financial salvation. Yet, what seemed to be a massive shot in the arm for the Olympic Movement nearly killed it. The Scorpion Wars were about to begin, and for the IOC, the sting was in the tail.

## NOTES

1 The leaders of the biggest and most powerful companies will also be in Beijing. For many, China represents the company's fastest growing market. By 2008, it is estimated that China will have become the world's second largest advertising market. The rapidly expanding ranks of Chinese corporate executives will be equally transfixed; aware that the Games is a unique global platform to build an international profile and brand. According to Chinese State Council spokesman Ye Zhen, the 'Olympic Factor' could contribute between 0.3 and 0.4 of a percentage point to GDP growth. Wang Naisheng, an economist at the China Agricultural Academy forecast that the Olympics would create 1.3 million new jobs per annum in building new subway lines, roads, stadiums. Tourism is forecast to rise by at least 5 per cent per annum, with the number of starred hotels in Beijing doubling.

2 It also asked: when will it be possible for China to send an athlete to compete in the Olympic Games? The first Chinese athlete, Liu Changchun, participated at the 1932 Los Angeles Olympic Games unbeknown to the Chinese Government. He finished last in his heats for the 100 and 200 metres. Embarrassed by the fact that the world's most populous nation was represented by only one athlete, the Chinese government decided to create a special training fund with 200,000 Yuan (approximately $24,000) to prepare 36 athletes for the 1936 Games. The Chinese team returned from Berlin empty handed, prompting the delegation's official report to record that 'we were a far cry from many countries in the results and athletic abilities. We were ridiculed as having bought back nothing but a duck's egg.' The Chinese team did not return to the Olympic Games until Los Angeles 1984 – when, with a team of 225 athletes and 50 coaches, they won fifteen gold, eight silver and nine bronze medals, coming fourth in the national medal ranking table. Twenty years later, in Athens, the Chinese delegation won a record 32 gold medals, with second place in the global medal rankings. By 2008, the Chinese are expected to dominate the medal rankings.

3 The ancient Games were first staged in Olympia, Greece, in 760 BC. The Games survived over twelve centuries and 292 Olympiads until

AD 393, when the abolition of paganism by Christian Roman Emperor Theodosius I put a stop to them.

4  The IOC Session is the General Assembly of the IOC, much like a Parliament, and brings together all IOC members. Due to the boycott, only 77 members attended the IOC Session in Moscow. The Session normally meets once a year and reviews all matters of policy.

5  Sir Lance Cross was an early candidate but later withdrew from the race, giving his support to Samaranch.

6  Born in Barcelona in 1920, Samaranch showed an early interest in sports and sports administration. He studied at the Barcelona Higher Institute of Business Management. While there, he played roller hockey going on to organise the world roller hockey championships in Barcelona in 1951 (which Spain won). After college, he worked in the family business and also became involved in politics. He was a municipal councillor by 1954; a member of the Spanish Parliament by 1967; and served as Spain's national delegate for sport for three years. From 1967 to 1970 he served as president of the Spanish Olympic Committee. He was president of the Barcelona Provincial Council between 1973 and 1977, resigning to pursue his diplomatic career.

7  Moscow is a geographical thread running through the Olympic turnaround. In the same city, on July 13, 2001, Samaranch was handed an envelope by the election scrutineers following another secret ballot to decide which of Beijing, Istanbul, Osaka, Paris and Toronto could host the 2008 Games. Samaranch nervously fiddled with the envelope in front of IOC members and a barrage of TV cameras and then calmly announced: 'And the winner is Beijing.' It was also in the same Hall of Columns that, with perfect symmetry, the secret ballot results were announced that declared Jacques Rogge as Samaranch's successor.

8  Twenty-seven African nations were absent from Montreal – 10 never entered, and 17 withdrew, in addition to Iraq and Guyana. On the eve of the opening ceremony, a delegation of African NOCs asked to meet with Lord Killanin to avert a boycott. For whatever reason, IOC director, Monique Berlioux, refused the meeting. The Africans left Montreal on the next day.

9 President Carter even tried to stage an alternative event in Africa. Lord Killanin nearly repeated his Montreal African NOC mistake. The president of the American NOC organisation, Mario Vasquez Rana, rushed to meet Killanin to tell him that he had persuaded all South American NOCs to attend the Moscow Games. He was kept waiting for four hours and very nearly went back on his decision not to boycott.

10 The Montreal Organising Committee actually generated revenue of $430 million against operating expenses of $207 million, thereby technically making a profit on the Games operation of $223 million. The capital expenses of the Games, and the building programme charged against the Games budget dragged the overall operation into the red.

11 Lake Placid's attempts to get federal assistance to cover the $8.5 million shortfall were repeatedly rebuffed, and were only eventually covered the following year by the Governor of New York.

12 Total broadcast rights for Moscow were $101 million, with NBC paying $85 million for US rights. Total broadcast rights for Lake Placid were $21 million, with ABC paying $15.5 million.

13 NBC's contract for the rights fees for the Moscow Games was valued at $85 million – $50 million in technical fees payable to the Moscow Organising Committee, and $35 million in rights fees. Of this $22.3 million was payable to the organisers and $12.7 million to the IOC (for further distribution to the NOCs – Olympic Solidarity and International Federations). At the time the US Government issued its embargo on further rights fee payments, some $12.32 million was still due to the Moscow organisers, and $6 million to the IOC. In August 1981, NBC paid the amounts due to the IOC having recouped some of its losses from insurance coverage from Lloyds of London.

14 Dick Pound chaired numerous IOC Commissions including the IOC New Sources of Finance Commission (subsequently renamed the IOC Marketing Commission), IOC TV Rights Commission, IOC Co-Ordination Commission for the 1996 Centennial Olympic Games, IOC Centennial Working Group and the IOC Ad Hoc Commission into the Salt Lake affair. He is now chairman of the World Anti-Doping Agency (WADA).

15  While the IOC could bank the cheque and collect interest, it could not spend the capital until 1984 – once the Games had been successfully delivered.

16  On one occasion, when Killanin met with Mayor Tom Bradley, the mayor reportedly handed the Games back to the IOC president – noting that things had just become too difficult and the IOC's demands too burdensome.

17  The election of the host city for the 1988 Summer Games was scheduled for the IOC Session in Baden-Baden, Germany in 1981.

18  Seoul's bid nearly defaulted, as it failed to reply to the IOC questionnaire and make a presentation by the required date. The bid was only saved when Samaranch, now acting as President, insisted that the IOC evaluation commission visit Korea. Costs for the Games, even in the bid phase were already starting to escalate. The first budget analysis for the Government jumped from $237 million to over $900 million.

19  Seoul beat Nagayo by 52 votes to 27. The next seven years tested Samaranch's political skills to the limit.

20  Dassler's first role in a sports marketing agency was as the silent partner in the UK sports PR agency West Nally. West Nally was founded in the early 1970s by Patrick Nally, a young PR executive, and Peter West, the BBC sports commentator and presenter of the classic TV show, *Come Dancing*. West Nally rapidly became the foremost sports event marketing agency in the world. When Nally joined forces with Host Dassler, West Nally built up an international portfolio of sports properties (including soccer's World Cup and tennis' Davis Cup as well as helping establish new events like the Athletics World Championships and the Rugby World Cup). It also created the concept of event packaging, with product category exclusivity for sponsors. Many West Nally executives went on to hold leading positions in sports federations and agencies around the world, giving the agency the title 'the global sports marketing university'. In 1982, Dassler and Nally fell out, and Dassler established a new agency ISL – taking with him nearly all of the international federation clients. The Japanese advertising giant, Dentsu, was anxious to get back into

the sports sponsorship field, and unseat its rival Hackhudo which, through West Nally, had cornered the sports market in Japan and was poaching Dentsu clients. It aligned with Nally, helping Dassler build ISL quickly into the global force in event marketing. After Dassler's death in April 1987, following a short battle with cancer, his heirs inherited the company, with his brother-in-law Christoph Malms, a former McKinsey consultant, taking over day-to-day operations despite knowing nothing about the business. Soon all the experienced executives left: Klaus Hempel and Juegen Lenz created the Team agency that founded the Champions League; Stephen Dixon and Peter Sprogis founded Prisma to market the broadcast rights to the World Cup; and Andrew Craig left to run cart motor racing in the US. With no experienced executives left, ISL soon lost its way and was eventually declared bankrupt in May 2001.

21  The New Sources of Financing Commission was officially approved at the IOC Executive Board Meeting in Sarajevo, December 1981. Its chairman was Louis Guirandou-N'Diaye, the IOC member from Ivory Coast, along with IOC members, Reginald Alexander (Kenya), Henry Hsu (Chinese Taiwan), Berthold Beitz (West Germany) and Taek Soo Kim (Korea).

22  Broadcast revenues for the Winter Games rose from $21 million at Lake Placid in 1980 to over $738 million at Salt Lake City in 2002. Similarly, revenues for the Summer Games grew from $101 million in Moscow to over $1,497 million in Athens in 2004. Revenues to NOCs through Olympic Solidarity (the IOC's grant aid organisation to distribute funding to NOCs, especially the Third World) grew from $8 million to over $210 million.

# Chapter 2

# SCORPION WARS

© Getty Images

## Lausanne, January 23rd, 1984

For the first US broadcast negotiations of the Samaranch Presidency, negotiating teams from the three US TV networks, ABC, NBC and CBS, are in their suites at the 120-year old Lausanne Palace Hotel on the shores of Lake Geneva. The prize on offer is the US rights for the 1988 Winter Olympics, in Calgary, Canada.

The process is straightforward: sealed bids are to be submitted by each of the networks to the IOC. It is the first major test of Samaranch's strategy to make the IOC financially independent. He has devoted the previous three years to creating an environment that can produce a deal to launch his vision for a new broadcast-led marketing strategy. The gloom surrounding the broadcast rights after Moscow has dissipated, as changes within the broadcast industry promise more lucrative deals. Broadcasters are just beginning to truly realise the power of sport.

But the IOC is leaving nothing to chance. Samaranch has decided it is time for the IOC to take direct control of the bidding procedure. Dick Pound leads the process. The decision to hold the negotiations in Lausanne is a deliberate attempt to get the networks off their home turf. This, the IOC hopes, will cut the umbilical cord connecting the bidders with their New York head offices. Crucially, the negotiators will be isolated from financial executives in New York who might try to limit an escalation in bidding.

The stakes are so high that the hotel lobby includes network staff charged with spotting and then trailing executives from rival networks to ensure fair play. There is to be no trading of inside messages with the IOC, even if it means following negotiators to the bathroom.

Around the negotiating table are some of the biggest names in American broadcasting. First is the colourful Roone Arledge. Among many other things, he is the creator of the instant replay and is now ABC's Sports and News Network president. Arledge is renowned as one of the sports world's most fearsome negotiators. 'Beneath his Howdy Doody face lurks one of the most ruthless opportunistic guys in the business,' an associate says of him. His competitors say much more.

Arledge's legend precedes him. He has successfully bid for the US rights to virtually every Olympic Games since Mexico in 1968.[1] His tactic of avoiding a formal auction of rights with the organisers has earned ABC the nickname – 'the Olympic network'.

For Arledge and his team there is even more pressure than usual. If ABC loses there could be a knock-on effect on its Sarajevo Winter Games coverage, just over three weeks away. Arledge has grave misgivings about the bidding process, fearing what he calls 'a bid to the death'. ABC's concerns are such that it has already launched a formal protest to the IOC about the sealed bidding procedure.

Representing NBC is the network's sports president, Robert Mulholland. The final member of the negotiating triad is the CBS Sports president, Neal Pilson. Also present are the Calgary Games president Frank King, his legal counsel Bill Warren, and their consultant Barry Frank – the TV rights expert from Mark McCormack's IMG – TWI organisation.

Samaranch and Pound are anxious to ensure that the process is seen to be fair. For years there have been rumours of an ABC mole inside the IOC helping the network win. One of the suspects is the IOC's director, Monique Berlioux who is in the meeting room. Berlioux, a former Olympic swimmer, was first hired at the IOC as a press officer. With a succession of largely absentee presidents, she quickly consolidated her power. Many regarded her as the *de facto* IOC president. In the 1970s, she ran the IOC like the headmistress of a Swiss finishing school. When Samaranch was elected, she observed that Lausanne wasn't big enough for both of them. She was right.

The other networks are, perhaps understandably, wary of ABC's position. Executives at CBS had bid $90 million for the rights to Sarajevo in 1980. Then, in a pre-emptive strike, ABC came in with a winning offer of $91.5 million. On such moves legends are made and doubts raised.

Samaranch is equally determined to get the best financial deal possible for the Olympic Movement. The IOC has already met with the Calgary organisers to discuss the ideal procedure for the negotiations and how to maximise the value of the rights for the TV networks. It has been decided to extend the Games from 14 to 16 days. This provides an extra weekend of coverage and ensures several more hours of valuable prime time advertising.[2] The dates of the Games have also been brought forward a week to coincide with the US television ratings sweeps – the critical reference point that establishes the advertising rate card for the networks for the next few months.[3]

This raises the stakes still higher. The network that wins the Olympic contract is almost guaranteed to win the broadcast ratings battle over the Games period by a large margin. As Arledge later observes: 'There is nothing more anxiety provoking than going into a bidding war feeling you somehow have to win.'

In the morning, each of the networks presents its bid in a sealed envelope to the joint IOC–Calgary negotiating team. This is the signal for the negotiating to begin in earnest. ABC's Roone Arledge likens it to 'placing three scorpions fighting in a bottle, and when it is all over, two will be dead and the winner will be exhausted'.

Scorpions don't give up easily. After five rounds of bidding, it is a two-way fight between ABC and NBC. They have submitted equal bids of $300 million. CBS has dropped out at $195 million. The drama intensifies as Dick Pound summons the two networks to Salon 2 in the Palace Hotel. He tells them that their bids are identical and they, not the committee, will have to break the stalemate.

Without their mole to help, the ABC team seriously consider withdrawing. Jim Spence, a senior vice president at ABC, and right hand to Arledge says that it feels like trying to swim the English Channel and then, a mile or so from Calais, encountering a school of hungry sharks. It seems dangerous to continue, but they are so close that it would be tragic to quit.[4]

## Coining it

Dick Pound candidly informs NBC's Mulholland and ABC's Roone Arledge that: 'The $300 million bid is much more than we expected, more than the Games are probably worth, but one of you is going to have to eliminate the other.'

To the amazement of both TV men, Pound continues: 'We are going to have to toss a coin, and one network is going to make the call. Then whichever of you wins the coin toss can decide whether to bid first or second. Whoever goes first can then make a bid and the other network will have 15 minutes to make its bid. And that bid, gentlemen, must exceed the other by at least one million dollars.'

A flip of a coin? Spence is shocked. He feels that the entire process has become a carnival. The ABC team believe their past successes are now being used against them and that greed has taken over. Amid the frenzy of doubt and suspicion, NBC's Arthur Watson elects to make the call, but he is so nervous that he forgets that he is supposed to call. Dick Pound flips a second time. NBC wins and elects to go first. Its team leave to ponder their bid.

As the minutes tick away, Arledge and Spence retire to their suite upstairs to consult with ABC network president Fred Pierce, back in New York. Barry Frank, the TV rights expert from TWI, speaks to Arledge and Spence. He is met with a barrage of abuse. 'This is crazy, it has to stop,' Spence screams, 'It is sheer insanity.' The ABC team claim that Frank promised them that this sort of thing couldn't possibly happen. Yet, it seems the impossible is now a reality: they are in a wild bidding session in sedate Switzerland.

Minutes later, the NBC delegation comes back and presents its bid: $304 million is now on the table. This means that ABC will have to bid $305 million to win. Roone Arledge is tired of the brinkmanship and decides to send a clear message. ABC is not about to be bluffed in this high stakes poker game. The ABC executives decide on a bid of $309 million.

The NBC negotiating team blinks and withdraws into the night. After more than 11 hours of high drama, ABC has won in the sixth round. There is only one scorpion left. The Olympic TV bidding process will never be the same again.

ABC's offer represents a $217.5 million increase over the sum it is paying for Sarajevo – a 337 per cent hike. It is the most money ever paid for a single event – sports or otherwise – in the history of television. It will be the last of the quantum leaps in sports TV rights fees until Rupert Murdoch's Fox Network strides onto the scene more than a decade later.

Though they have won the day, members of the ABC team are in no mood to celebrate. Spence is embittered, describing the process as 'the most demanding, frustrating, infuriating, nonsensical and historic negotiation in the saga of American television sports.' Roone Arledge is so furious that he refuses to come back down again from his suite to join Samaranch for the celebratory dinner or even to shake hands.

Both IOC and Calgary executives are aware that things have got out of hand. The bidding has clearly gone way beyond expectations. They are worried that it might create problems in the future. Dick Pound is concerned about the huge financial commitment. He believes it is potentially unhealthy for the IOC, as well as for the network, and could negatively impact future deals. Frank King, the president of the Calgary Organising

Committee, worries that ABC will feel it has paid too much and become resentful, leading to operating difficulties down the road.

The long and sometimes fraught relationship between the Olympics and television had taken another turn.

## The TV deal

The evolution of the Olympics and television are closely connected. The Games have given television some of its most thrilling broadcast moments, regularly setting new records for audience numbers. From the tragic to the truly sublime, the Olympics continue to give us outstanding and inspiring images.

Part of the magic is how each country has its own special moment, and each has a different appeal: from gymnasts Olga Korbut in Munich through to Kerri Strug with her broken ankle in Atlanta; from skiers Franz Klammer in Innsbruck to Hermann Maier and his bone-crushing fall, amazing recovery and two gold medals, in Nagano.

These moments translate into huge audience figures – and massive television advertising sales. The Games are regarded by most broadcasters as signature programming, by which all other sports programming is judged.

Over the years, television has been the engine that has powered the growth of the Olympic Movement. It has been an agent of change. Sport and television have been good for each other. Samaranch liked to describe it 'as a match made in heaven'.

Today, it is estimated that close to four billion people watch the Olympic Games. The Games are unique in their ability to deliver a truly global audience, far exceeding anything gained by the soccer World Cup or the Super Bowl.[5] Around 90 per cent of the world's potential TV audience watches some part of the Games. And, normally, they watch a lot, setting their social and work schedules around Olympic programming. In the US, every person watches on average close to 20 hours, rising to nearly 37 hours in Japan. But even that level of saturation viewing is not enough to win the gold medal for Olympic viewing. In Sydney in 2000, the average Australian watched an astonishing 49 hours.

The ability of the Olympic Games to deliver such global audiences and reach gives it immense marketing muscle. It provides a guarantee to effectively control access to a national audience, something that is becoming increasingly difficult in an ever more fragmented media market. At the Salt Lake City Winter Games in 2002, audience shares for broadcasters at times reached over 90 per cent, whether it was for the 12.5km biathlon in Germany or ice hockey in Canada.

Broadcast interest in the Olympics is still growing. At the 2004 Athens Games, NBC broadcast 1,210 hours, nearly triple the coverage of Sydney and more hours than the previous five summer Games put together.

The Olympics is also unique in its ability to pull in female viewers – who advertisers will pay a healthy premium to reach. Robert Apatoff, chief marketing officer of AllState Insurance, captured the prevailing attitude of advertisers when he said that: 'The Olympics gets you an association with the premier event, not just in sports, but in entertainment. It's also a more attractive buy for advertisers looking to target women.'

The global reach of the Games, with their broad demographic appeal and their ability to engage the whole population, makes the Games a uniquely attractive proposition to advertisers. According to David Hill, chairman of the Fox Network: 'Sport is the last frontier of reality on television ... about the only thing that can guarantee an audience, because of its ability to offer viewers around the globe a shared communications experience.'

Television has allowed the Olympic Movement to survive and prosper. Yet, as the events of January 1984 in Lausanne indicate, the relationship has not always been a comfortable one.

## Sting in the tail

The negotiations for the Olympic broadcast rights have long been a cocktail of international intrigue and high stakes poker. Yet, the outcomes have often defined both the future of the Olympic Movement and of the individual broadcasters. The bidding frenzy surrounding Calgary was a critical point for the Olympic Movement. The Calgary rights were the first to be sold during the Samaranch presidency. The first key element in his turnaround strategy was to sort out the IOC's financial situation so that it became self-sufficient. Two sources of income needed to be max-

imised: TV revenues and income from sponsorship. Central to both was
the need for the IOC to take greater control of managing the commercial
affairs of the Olympic Games.

But the IOC's attempts to put pressure on the networks through the
bidding process backfired. From ABC's perspective it was disastrous. The
broadcaster eventually lost around $65 million on the Calgary Olympics
– the first time the network recorded a loss on its Olympic coverage.[6] It took
years for ABC to forgive the IOC for the manner in which the Calgary negotiations had been conducted, and to return to the Olympic rights market
as an active bidder.

The Calgary bid was also a turning point for the IOC. For all Samaranch's intent to take control, the IOC was still not in the driving seat. The
US broadcasters were angry, suspicious and poorer. The result was that
the US TV rights for the Seoul Olympics of 1988 generated less revenue
than Calgary. The lessons learned from the Calgary rights negotiation
and the nadir of Seoul – the first Summer Olympics to generate less revenue than a Winter Olympics – had a major impact on the direction and
manner in which Olympic broadcast rights were sold over the following
two decades. The previously symbiotic and vital relationship between the
Olympic Games and television was put in jeopardy.

To fully understand how the scorpion wars of Calgary came about, you
need to look back over the history of TV negotiations from the previous
50 years.

How the television companies came to pay for rights to the Olympics,
when all other forms of media – including print photographers – continue
to have free access is a story in its own right (recounted in the Appendix).
Throughout the 1950s there were bitter battles between organisers and
broadcasters, both wanting to establish the precedent to pay or not to pay.
In the process, the Olympic Games of Helsinki 1952 and Melbourne 1956
were boycotted by US and other broadcasters. In the end, the sports movement won and the broadcasters began to pay. But it is interesting to ponder
what would have happened to the sports and broadcast movements if the
result had gone the other way.

The IOC itself was far from sure what this new medium might offer.
But Olympic coverage brought a succession of broadcast innovations.
Dick Ebersol, who went on to conceive the groundbreaking comedy show

*Saturday Night Live* in the 1970s, first made his mark on the 1968 Grenoble Winter Games. Aged 19 at the time, Ebersol had taken leave from his studies at Yale to become a researcher for ABC Sports president Roone Arledge.

Ebersol went on to lead NBC's Olympic division and later reflected how, 'Roone had become determined that there had to be somebody whose only job was to know all the stories about the great athletes and the great events ... before they happened. I got to know all the top world class athletes well enough to write mini biographies on each of them, so that when the announcers covered their events, they [the audience] really had a sense of these athletes as people.'

In personalising the athletes, Ebersol helped make the television viewer more of a participant in the events. For the first time, viewers at home were given the human interest stories – the struggle, determination and endeavour – that are the hallmarks of Olympians. They felt a personal connection.

By the 1970s, audiences had grown dramatically. The resulting increase in advertising revenues meant that rights negotiations were becoming a serious business. At times this introduced an element of farce. Set against the Cold War backdrop, for example, bidding for the rights to the 1980 Moscow Games offered all the intrigue of a spy thriller.

Each of the networks embarked on a series of initiatives to win over and impress the Soviet organisers. ABC used its morning programming to court the Moscow leadership with a 10-hour series on life in the Soviet Union. Some of its news team winced as ABC compromised its much vaunted editorial independence and standards in the quest for Olympic rights. One ABC official ruefully concluded that they 'had made Moscow look like Cypress Gardens without the skiers'.

Not to be left out, CBS aired a documentary on Soviet delights, including a TV special on the renowned Bolshoi Ballet, hosted by US TV icon Mary Tyler Moore. According to Arledge, it could easily have been mistaken for a politburo production. NBC concluded an agreement to purchase a series of Soviet films depicting the heroic efforts of farm labourers, new production quotas at lumber mills and the glories of life on the collective farm. These enticing epics cost $1.2 million but were never aired.

The various attempts to curry favour and influence the Soviets had little effect on the overall process. According to one report, the Moscow organisers considered 'the whole episode as a chance to tweak the Americans a bit, watch them squirm and dump on them a bunch of worthless productions gathering dust in some Ministry of Culture Film library.'

Throughout their history, too, Olympic rights negotiations have been fraught with a number of recurring themes. Initially, disputes focused on whether rights fees should be paid at all. More recent times have seen recurring pleas from broadcasters that they are paying too much, and that it is impossible for rights fees to continue to increase. This has been set against the dynamic tension between the IOC and organising committees over control of the negotiation process and the precarious balance between the principle of free-to-air coverage for all, against the commercial dynamic of funding the Games. And never underestimate the Machiavellian games played by bidders to outwit each other.

Since the early negotiations, broadcasters have pleaded abject poverty, arguing that the amount paid for rights cannot continue to rise. In 1980, global broadcast rights for the Winter and Summer Games were worth $121 million. By 2012, the rights for a quadrennial are expected to be in excess of $3.5 billion.

There has been repeated concern over the bidding process, and especially the fight between the US networks. The disparity in rights fees between the US and the rest of the world has proved a lightning rod for a variety of US politicians who have argued that America bears a disproportionate share of the cost. Over the past two decades, the IOC actually succeeded in significantly reducing the gap. The US rights for the Summer Games used to account for over 85 per cent of global broadcast revenue – a figure that for the Summer Games had been reduced to around 50 per cent by 1996.

More often than not, the IOC has not only had to negotiate with the various TV networks, but also with the organising committee for the chosen venue. Often the organising committee challenged the IOC's strategy, questioning why the IOC was so focused on maximising the audience and protecting the free-to-air broadcast principle, rather than maximising revenues. Access for all is at the heart of the Olympic Movement. It would have been a fatal error for the IOC to have ever compromised on this issue.

Over the years, various private networks have made significantly higher offers for the Olympic rights. But they could not guarantee free-to-air coverage and maximum reach, a governing principle of the IOC's broadcast policy. Local politicians and organisers in the host country, faced with their own challenges and caring more about balancing the books than the global promotion of the Olympic Movement, have repeatedly tried to undermine the IOC's efforts and control of the broadcast rights negotiation process.

Samaranch viewed the negotiations with organising committees over the granting of broadcast rights as some of the most challenging and disagreeable of his presidency. The continuing conflicts became one of the key reasons for the IOC adopting a strategy of long-term agreements. Whenever possible, it has tried to award broadcast rights before a city's election and the formation of the organising committee.

## Sucked dry

Before securing the rights to the Calgary Games, ABC paid a then record of $225 million in rights fees for the 1984 Games in Los Angeles (plus a further $75 million for host broadcast costs). Again, it wasn't a smooth ride. By early 1984, ABC's financial leaders were running scared about a potential ratings collapse due to the Soviet-led boycott, and attempted to renegotiate terms.[7] Arledge argued that the Soviets had done them all a favour, as the boycott would only allow Americans to win even more gold medals. 'They would not lose viewers, they would gain them.'

Arledge was right, ABC's coverage of Los Angeles set new ratings records. From Los Angeles in 1984 onwards, the Olympic Games began to have a dramatic effect on the US advertising market. More than half of the advertising available for all sports for all networks for the entire year was spent on the Olympics over two weeks. 'We'd not only captured the market, we'd sucked it dry,' Roone Arledge observed.

After the scorpion war negotiations for Calgary in January 1984, the IOC turned its attention to the Seoul Summer Games in 1988. The IOC again decided to hold the negotiations and bidding in Lausanne, and a large delegation from the Seoul Organising Committee (SLOC) descended on Olympic headquarters. The Koreans hired IMG's Barry Frank as their consultant, in part because he somehow convinced them their US rights could be worth up to $1 billion. This was totally unrealistic.

And Frank's forecast represented a 400 per cent increase over Los Angeles bore no relationship to the potential of the advertising market.

It totally ignored the challenges of an Asian Games, with unfriendly time zones for US prime-time viewing. The Korean organisers were deluded into thinking that there was an unlimited supply of cash on offer from the US networks. This misplaced advice raised expectations way beyond anything that was remotely feasible.

A side effect of this was that it contributed greatly to Samaranch's subsequent refusal to have anything to do with TV agents and consultants. Samaranch believed that agents would stop at nothing to get the contract. To do so they were inclined to misrepresent the value of the market in order to attract the interest of the organising committee. The committee would then refuse to follow the direction of the IOC, mistakenly believing that there was more money to be had. Samaranch also saw no reason why agents should be paid millions of dollars in commission when he and the IOC team were perfectly capable of doing the deals, and were now gaining the experience to run the show themselves.

With their advisors talking up the possibilities, the Koreans entered the negotiating room of the Palace Hotel with high hopes. But when the networks began to submit their offers, the Korean team got a rude awakening. After the Calgary affair, apathy ruled. ABC came in with a token bid of $225 million, the same as it had paid for Los Angeles – and down $84 million on Calgary. CBS offered slightly more. NBC placed the highest bid at $325 million. But even this was a mere third of what the Seoul organisers had been expecting. The Korean delegation was dumbfounded. No one dared take responsibility to call the organising committee president, and future Korean president, General Roh Tae Woo, to give him the news.[8]

Un Yong Kim, a vice president of the organising committee, was probably the only member of the Korean negotiating team with any real experience of the international sports scene.[9] He later recalled how he felt 'caught between Korea's national pride and the cold reality of a maximum market price'.

With General Roh expecting a phone call, the Korean delegation looked on frozen. They were more concerned about public opinion back home and face-saving than the real market situation. As no other network was going in or out of the conference room, the NBC team slowly began to realise that its offer was the only serious one on the table. The Koreans refused to budge. Samaranch and Dick Pound, as chairman of the IOC TV Rights

Negotiating Committee, desperately tried to get the Koreans to accept and even called General Roh directly. Eventually the bidding was brought to a halt with an agreement to meet again a few weeks later in New York.

Things did not get any better when the teams reconvened in the US. NBC, realising that they were the only show in town, dropped their offer by $25 million to $300 million – some $9 million less than ABC had paid for the 1988 Winter Games. It was clear to the IOC that each day the Olympic parties delayed in accepting NBC's offer, there was a very real risk that it would drop even further.

Pound eventually persuaded the Korean negotiating team to accept, but only after NBC had agreed to a face-saving additional formula, which provided for a profit sharing component if advertising revenues suddenly took off. The likelihood of this happening was exceedingly slim, but it allowed the SLOC delegation to finally return home with a proposal that could conceivably bring the rights up to $500 million. In fact ad revenues did not exceed even the preliminary forecasts, and the profit sharing formula was never activated.

*Sports Illustrated* wrote after the conclusion of the bidding process that 'the days of astronomical bidding wars and open cheque books are apparently over.' So it seemed, albeit not for long.

Although the basic financial terms were agreed, the real negotiating work was only just beginning. Over the next six months, legal teams from the IOC, the Seoul organisers and NBC laboriously worked through every issue from TV programming schedules, through to Korea's policy and ban on US meat imports. The latter was a cause of serious concern to the NBC negotiators who did not fancy explaining to their 2,000 strong engineering and production team that they could not have their American hamburgers and might have to eat the local delicacies of dog and snake.[10]

The traditional request for a letter of credit from the government of the host country to cover NBC's advance payments was also seen as an insult in Seoul. It provoked government and popular rage in Korea when news of it leaked. Un Yong Kim wrote in his memoirs on the Seoul Games how senior leaders felt 'that Korea did not need the $300 million and that Korea should make an international signal and broadcast on its own'.

As the negotiation process dragged on, some of the lawyers, even those who billed by the hour, grew tired of the process. Betsy Goff, one of the advisors from IMG's broadcast division, TWI, reflected how she was still 'uncertain of the value of anyone having to spend two days negotiating how many parking places would be allocated to NBC in Seoul'. While the Calgary contract had taken less than six weeks to conclude, the Seoul US rights contract took over six months. Even then many issues were left open and unresolved.

## Lessons learned

The Calgary and Seoul broadcast negotiations taught the IOC many lessons. They underlined the need for the IOC to take more direct management control over the bidding and negotiating processes for television rights.

The IOC decided to hold a special broadcast workshop to take stock of the situation and review its policies. A cross-section of broadcasters from around the world was invited to Lausanne in April 1987 to review the Olympic rights negotiations process and comment on the future outlook. The US networks turned up in force. Each came with a similar message – broadcast rights could not continue to escalate.

Arthur Watson, who had now become NBC's Sport's president, opened the debate recalling that 'the negotiations for the 1988 Summer Olympic Games presaged the most important development in the business of sports television in the US: the end of wildly escalating rights fees for sports events.' 'Rights fees', he said, 'were increasing at a compound rate of 32 per cent.'[11]

The overall outlook was far from promising. The networks' audience share had dropped from around 94 per cent in 1955 to around 50 per cent;[12] cable television was starting to seriously eat into the networks' audience share.

Dick Pound, in his concluding remarks as conference chairman, pointedly told the 1992 Olympic organisers, in an attempt to manage their future expectations, that they should not expect any increase in rights fees for their Games and that the amounts paid for the 1988 Games should be seen as an aberration.

When the 1992 Albertville Winter Games were taken to market, there was, for the first time, a dramatic reduction in rights fees. CBS gained the US rights with a $243 million offer – a reduction of over $66 million from what ABC had paid for Calgary. NBC moguls still nevertheless elected to blast CBS for paying an 'absurdly high sum ...You always want to be a winner. But you do not want to commit suicide at the same time.'

## Barcelona 1992: NBC's triple jump

The negotiations for US rights to the 1992 Barcelona Games fared slightly better. NBC submitted an offer of $401 million, a 33 per cent increase over Seoul. NBC also came up with a novel proposal to create a triple-cast pay-per-view proposal to supplement its network coverage to help finance the increased rights fee.

NBC's Barcelona coverage pulled in 192 million unique viewers and earned a 17.5 average rating according to Neilsen Media Research. NBC defied the experts on New York's Madison Avenue and eventually sold virtually all of the advertising time on its network schedule for the Games. The triple-cast experiment, however, was not so successful and was slammed by critics. Clearly ahead of its time, it was poorly marketed and, with scepticism within NBC's own ranks, it was doomed to failure.

NBC billed the triple-cast as a 'way to stretch the boundaries of sports programming'. In terms of broadcast coverage, it did succeed in dramatically increasing the sports coverage available to the US fan. NBC planned 161 hours of Olympic coverage on its network, with a further 1,080 hours on its three pay-per-view channels. Subscribers were invited to pay $125 to receive commercial-free, round-the-clock coverage on three cable channels.

The actual programming received solid reviews. But, from a commercial perspective, the experiment was a total failure, attracting only 250,000 subscribers against a target of 2.5 million. Total losses were forecast at $150 million, split between NBC and its partner Cablevision, although it is unlikely that anyone will ever know the real figure.

*Business Week* asked: 'How could supposedly media savvy executives be so far off the mark?' In hindsight, the answer is simple. Although awareness of the service was high, NBC soon discovered that there were simply limits to the number of fans with the time and desire to pay significant money to view the Games beyond what is offered for free. The service was just too expensive for all but the most addicted armchair sports fan.[13]

The failure put back the multi-channel approach to Olympic and sports telecasting by several years.

## Europe becomes competitive

Although the IOC's primary focus in broadcast negotiations was towards the US market, the growing gap and disparity in rights fees across the rest of the world began to create problems during the 1980s.

After the success of the negotiations with ABC for the Los Angeles 1984 US rights, Peter Ueberroth turned his attention to Europe. He proposed that the European Broadcasting Union (EBU) pay $1 per TV set. This worked out to the attractively round sum of $100 million. Albert Scharf, the president of the EBU, responded with the low offer of $8.33 million, a 30 per cent increase on the fee for Moscow.

Ueberroth's number did not seem so far fetched when Silvio Berlusconi's private Italian Channel 5 offered $10 million – more than all of Europe combined – just for Italy. There was only one problem: Berlusconi's Channel 5 had only limited reach, and the majority of Italians would not have been able to watch the Games.

Samaranch intervened to protect the basic right of everyone to be able to watch the Olympic Games free of charge. After months of negotiations, the EBU eventually increased its offer to $22 million, less than 10 per cent of what the US was paying, but a three-fold increase over Moscow.[14]

The IOC stepped in many more times over the next twenty years to protect the EBU's position and to drag its rights fee up to a level in keeping with the economic position of the continent. Along the way, the IOC stood accused by US politicians of being protectionist by keeping the rights artificially low. They had a point. The European rights increased by just $1 million to $7 million for the 1988 Calgary Games, whereas the US rights increased by over 300 per cent to $309 million. Europe represented around 2.5 per cent of the US fees for the Winter Games and not that much more for the Summer.

Samaranch realised early on that it was not going to be possible to bring the EBU up to a realistic level through 'normal negotiations'. He began to entertain approaches from non-EBU members, even if this potentially meant a limitation on the overall coverage.

Among the increasingly interested observers was Rupert Murdoch who had spent 35 years amassing a global media empire covering both print (including the *New York Post*, the *London Times*, the *News of the World*, *The Sun*, *The Australian*), television (WNEW-TV, New York; KTTV-TV, Los Angeles; Channel 10, Melbourne), film (20th Century Fox) and, with the launch of Sky TV in 1983, satellite television.

Murdoch made his first approach to the IOC at the end of 1987. He expressed interest in acquiring rights to the 1992 Barcelona Games for a range of territories from the US, through to the UK, across Asia and down to Australia. Within 12 months, a second player expressed interest in European rights: Bertelsmann, Europe's largest media group, threw its hat into the ring for the Barcelona rights.[15]

Leading European broadcast officials started to seriously wonder whether the IOC might switch channels. It dawned on Paul Fox, managing director of BBC Network Television, that it might just be possible for the big satellite broadcasters – Rupert Murdoch, Silvio Berlusconi in Italy and the Bertelsmann Group in West Germany – to get together and eventually outbid the EBU. 'After all,' Fox noted, 'the EBU thought they had European rights to Wimbledon last year, but then they were outbid by Bertelsmann.'

Unlikely as it was that the IOC would ever compromise on its free-to-air principles for the Games, the IOC was not about to correct Paul Fox or anyone else's view that EBU's monopoly was at risk. The EBU and others had to understand that such low levels of rights fees could not continue. The IOC eventually succeeded in persuading the EBU to increase its offer from $30 million for Seoul to $99 million for Barcelona, only after it realised that there were other credible alternative offers.

By early 1992, the European Commission was starting to take a serious look at the EBU's monopoly over exclusive sports rights. It was concerned about the manner in which a network like Eurosport could acquire Olympic rights, while non-EBU members like Screensport were blocked. The EC warned the EBU that it would issue emergency rulings, with the potential of huge fines, if the EBU kept refusing to allow private channels access to coverage of the Barcelona Games. The stage was set for a long and drawn-out battle. More than a decade later and that battle is still being fought, with threats of lawsuits by the European Commission, and appeals and counter appeals as the EBU tries to protect its exclusive rights position and the Commission tries to force the market open.

Bertelsmann kept the pressure on. Bernd Schiphorst, president of Bertelsmann's own agency, UFA, travelled to Lillehammer, site of the 1994 Winter Games, telling the local organisers that he would double whatever the EBU offered for European rights. Samaranch, though, remained nervous at the risk of compromising national coverage. He saw how Wimbledon had lost some of its prestige across Europe without coverage from national broadcasters.

The increased focus, and potential threat from the European Commission, only served to reinforce the EBU's desire to keep the Olympic rights. Bertelsmann increased its offer to a level that it felt would make the IOC think seriously. Schiphorst, along with Manfred Lahnstein, the president of Bertelsmann's Electronic Media Division, and former German Federal Minister, came to Lausanne to table a $300 million offer for the rights to Atlanta in 1996. Their proposed web of networks remained still very much on the drawing board, and they could not guarantee true pan-European in-depth coverage. But their offer was enough to force the EBU to quickly raise its bid to $250 million – a three-fold increase over what it paid for Barcelona – and an 800 per cent increase over the rights for Seoul, eight years earlier. The EBU became the first broadcast group to conclude any rights agreement for the 1996 Centennial Games in Atlanta.

## Taking on the world

Other regions also saw significant increases in TV revenues, albeit again from very, very low thresholds. Japan jumped nearly 500 per cent to $19 million and Australia from $1 million in Moscow to $11 million. Competition within the broadcast community was starting to gain momentum, and the IOC began to take full advantage of the opportunity.

Japan, fearing a competitive bidding war between the different Japanese commercial networks and state broadcaster NHK, decided to form a pool and to keep bidding collectively for the rights. This is what the IOC had always feared the US networks would finally get together and do. The Korean organisers successfully leveraged their position and 'special' history with Japan to force through an important hike in Japanese rights for Seoul. They persuaded the pool (in any other language it would be known as a cartel) to pay $50 million for the 1988 Games. The Japanese paid $62 million for Barcelona – still proportionately well below what the Americans were paying, but they were starting to become an important contributor to the overall budget.

The impact of all this was substantial. The growth in broadcast revenues began to have a dramatic impact on the overall workings of the Olympic Movement.

Until 1992, the IOC allocated the majority, around 70 per cent of the rights fee, to the organising committee as the body with the greatest financial outlay. But with revenues increasing faster than the costs of staging the Games, and each organising committee starting to declare a profit on their hosting of the Games, Samaranch decided that a larger share of the revenues should be allocated to the International Sports Federations and the National Olympic Committees. The idea was to channel more money into supporting athletes 365 days a year, rather than into capital bricks and mortar projects in the host city and profits for the organisers.

The revenue distribution formula was changed to 60 per cent for the organisers, and 40 per cent for the Olympic family.[16] The funds allocated to the local organisers were still more than sufficient to attract a growing list of cities wanting to bid for the Games.[17]

## Split decision

It would be wrong to think that the TV broadcasters were simply one-dimensional providers of money. Relationships between the IOC and the major broadcasters, once rights negotiations had been concluded, were generally not adversarial. On occasions, the networks were important partners with the IOC in supporting the Olympic Movement.

One example of this was the decision in 1987 to split the Winter and Summer Games. This came about after ABC Sports president, Denis Swanson, lunched with Samaranch. Swanson pointed out that for the US networks it was just not possible to finance two Olympics in the same year. The drain that the Olympics placed on the advertising market was too great. He asked Samaranch whether there was any formal reason why both Games had to be held in the same year.

Within a few weeks Samaranch tabled to the IOC Executive Board, and then the IOC Session, to split the Games. He later reflected that 'this was one of the best decisions of my presidency'. The Winter Games had grown dramatically and the IOC was starting to struggle with some of the operational complexities of staging both events so close together. Having two Games in the same year was not easy for some NOCs; finding sponsors for two teams, while negotiating TV rights in the same year was demanding. There was the impression of a Big Games and a Small Games.

In 1994, the Winter Games moved to a new alternate cycle with the Summer Games. But not everyone going to the Winter Games in Lillehammer was convinced that the IOC had made the right decision. Didn't the Winter Games need the kudos of Olympic year to provide them with the promotional platform? Could the Winter Games really stand on their own? The eventual ratings results and the overall success of these Games, silenced the critics. CBS, the US rights holder, produced the two highest sports rated shows in US broadcast history – higher even than the Super Bowl.

One of the key factors was the huge publicity surrounding the attack on American figure skater Nancy Kerrigan before the Games. This was classic sporting soap opera. Kerrigan was clubbed across the knee at a practice session in Detroit. Tonya Harding, Kerrigan's Olympic team mate and rival, was implicated in the plot. It was a tabloid dream: Snow White (Kerrigan) versus the Wicked Witch (Harding).

Harding was allowed to compete in Lillehammer by the United States Olympic Committee, under threat of legal action. She was subsequently sentenced to three years probation for her role in the incident, 500 hours of community service and paid a $100,000 fine, as well as being stripped of her national figure skating title. Kerrigan went on to win the silver medal, and many millions in endorsements.

The joke at the time was just how much CBS promotion executives had paid Jeff Gillooly, Tonya Harding's husband, to do the deed and guarantee their ratings success. There were many other factors ranging from the bad weather keeping people at home, through to the recent dominance of Olympic broadcasting that had finally stopped other networks from counter programming. Advertising giant Saatchi and Saatchi succinctly summed it up, writing in its monthly media bulletin: 'How do you plan a TV programming schedule to compete against the Olympics? The answer is you don't!'

Similar record-breaking TV audiences were gained by other broadcasters around the world. In the UK, the BBC set a new record for Torvill and Dean's ice dancing routine, with the highest single channel television sports audience ever in UK broadcasting history.[18] The Japanese broadcaster NHK regularly enjoyed peak audiences of more than double the average for the soccer World Cup.

## Building a dream

While the Lillehammer Winter Games in 1994 were a huge commercial success, the Atlanta Summer Games of 1996 struggled to put a US broadcast deal in place.

The man under pressure was Billy Payne (no relation), president of the organising committee. Payne was an Atlanta real estate lawyer who woke up one morning, after having completed the latest fund-raising drive for the local church, with the unlikely dream of bringing the Olympics to Atlanta. Against all the odds, he succeeded in convincing the IOC to award Atlanta the right to host the Centennial Games in 1996. By mid-1993 Payne was feeling the heat from banks to lock in the largest single revenue source for the Games. They refused to allow him to proceed with construction of the main stadium unless a deal was in place.

So desperate was the financial situation that the IOC had even suggested to the Atlanta organisers that they scrap plans for a permanent stadium, and explore options for a temporary one. The advertising market and outlook at the time were not strong, and the IOC wanted to wait until market confidence returned.

In the end, the IOC had to agree to proceed with negotiations or risk placing the Centennial Games in jeopardy. The longer term, broader Olympic agenda being compromised by Atlanta's challenging financial plan was a recurring theme. The situation was made worse by the lack of formal government or city support. The IOC and Atlanta negotiating teams convened in New York on 27 July, 1993 to meet with the US networks. It didn't help that the meeting coincided with the very bottom of the US advertising market.

The expectations were that ABC would be the strongest bidder. CBS executives were focused on the Winter Games and NBC was still uneasy after its triple-cast losses in Barcelona. NBC submitted the first offer of $456 million. ABC's offer was sufficiently close for Dick Pound to call a second round of bidding.

NBC's Dick Ebersol, playing high stakes poker, came back with his second offer.[19] Dick Pound opened the envelope as the IOC and the Atlanta Organisers nervously looked on. The single sheet of paper spelt out the same number again – $456 million. NBC had not raised its offer by a single dollar, judging that ABC would not step up to the mark. Ebersol did not blink and locked up the rights to the Centennial Games for a price that was subsequently shown to be an excellent deal.

For ABC the timing of the negotiations could not have been worse. Bob Iger, who had been a member of ABC's production team in Calgary, had just been appointed president of the network.[20] However, on the day of the Olympic negotiations, Capital Cities acquired ABC, and neither the network's new owners, nor its new president were willing to take risks – at least not on the first day in the job. If only Atlanta had been able to wait a few months, ABC would have been a much stronger bidder.

## Implausibly live

Atlanta was the most watched event in US broadcast history, with Ebersol maintaining tight control over the production. Many people in the US later questioned why the rest of the world was so negative in their remarks towards the Olympics in Atlanta, for they had seen a fabulous Games on NBC: they had.

But Ebersol was so dismayed at what the City of Atlanta had done in destroying the image and magic of the Olympics by allowing downtown to be turned into a commercial feeding frenzy, that he minimised the city's exposure. He was reported to have told his producers and cameramen that the first person who produced a shot of downtown Atlanta would be fired, on the spot.

Another controversial element of NBC's coverage was what were labelled 'plausibly live broadcasts'. Perhaps the most conspicuous example of NBC's plausibly live strategy centred on Keri Strug's final vault in the women's gymnastic team competition. The vault actually took place in the late afternoon, but it was not shown on NBC until approaching midnight Eastern time. Endeavouring to capture the emotive narrative offered up by the exploits of the injured Strug, NBC's prime-time programming was used to gradually intensify the drama surrounding the admittedly heroic, triumphant, yet ultimately irrelevant vault (the US had already won the gold medal prior to the vault). The result was NBC's highest, most emotional, most poignant moment which garnered their highest rating of the Games a phenomenal 27.2 Neilsen rating – the highest rating for an event at the Summer Games, since Montreal 1976.

Whether you see this as manipulative jingoism or powerful drama, the simple reality cannot be denied: the Olympics put people in front of their TVs – and keep them there. For the networks, outmanoeuvering their rivals to secure the next Games became a priority. The stakes were about to be raised again.

## NOTES

1 ABC held the rights to the Summer Games in Mexico (1968); Munich (1972); Montreal (1976); and Los Angeles (1984); and to the Winter Games in Innsbruck (1976); Lake Placid (1980); and Sarajevo (1984).

2 The extension ultimately saved the Calgary Games after adverse weather conditions forced the rescheduling of 33 events. Over the Games the temperatures ranged from a low of −28°C to a high of +22°C. To further challenge the organisers, the winds were the strongest seen in Calgary in 25 years, blowing gravel dust onto the bob track and threatening to make the event inoperable. The ever changing nature of Calgary's weather fulfilled the long held local view that if you do not like the weather in Calgary, just wait five minutes.

3 The Games ran from 13–28 February 1988. AC Neilsen samples audience figures from the networks four times a year – February, May, July and November – the sweep weeks. The results are used to set local advertising rates. National advertising rates are based on Neilsen rating figures across the year. Needless to say the networks are keen to pull in the viewers during the sweep weeks.

4 Jim Spence later admitted that ABC did indeed have its own deep throat in prior Olympic rights negotiations and expected its contact to still be active for the Calgary negotiations. The knowledge that it could expect

inside information lessened some of ABC's concerns about the bid process. Spence received a tip-off during the Sarajevo negotiations, allowing ABC to trump the CBS bid.

5 The world's population is estimated at 6.5 billion, of whom around 4 billion have access to a television set – although the number is growing rapidly as audiences in China and India start to dramatically increase. The total host broadcast coverage for the Summer Games is around 3,800 hours, and 800 hours for the Winter Games. Over the years, there has been considerable debate over the scope and size of audiences for major sports events, with reports of 30 billion people watching. The media have dutifully reported these numbers, failing to recognise that there are simply not that many people on the planet. The cumulative audience viewing measurement counts each viewer multiple times. As such, it does not provide any insight into the actual percentage of the population watching, and how much they watch – which is the true benchmark of an event's impact. There was little point in an organiser claiming to be the number one event in the world, if over half of the audience was coming from China, and hardly anyone in North America was watching. In Sydney, the IOC finally succeeded in getting the sports marketing industry to look at a new measurement basis for calculating global viewing audiences. It proposed that a new measurement – television viewing hours – be used, which would detail how much was watched in each market – and what percentage of the overall population was viewing. This allowed for proper comparisons between different events.

6 When network promotion and revenues from owned and operated stations were factored in, along with the benefit of winning the ratings sweeps, the loss was considerably less.

7 At the time the boycott was announced, ABC still owed the Los Angeles organisers and the IOC $90 million in rights fees. The contract included a boycott clause, and Ueberroth was faced with the unpleasant dilemma of potentially having to renegotiate the overall terms of the agreement, placing the financing of the Games back in jeopardy.

8 General Roh Tae Woo went on to become the first democratically elected President of Korea in 1988.

9 Un Yong Kim was president of the General Assembly of International Sports Federations (GAISF) and an experienced international sports official. He was co-opted onto the IOC, and served two subsequent terms as IOC vice president, as well as running for the IOC presidency in 2001. A Korean court later found him guilty of embezzlement – a decision against which he is appealing. In February 2005 the IOC Executive Board recommended that he be expelled.

10 The food entitlements of the production team even prompted the legal teams to come up with new definitions of what might cause a works stoppage – the wrong diet and food being one of them. Twelve years later, it was reported that NBC bought in 7,264 kilograms of Starbucks coffee to the Sydney Games to keep its staff caffeinated in the American style.

11 ABC president, Denis Swanson, continued the theme noting: 'It is apparent that American television business is undergoing unprecedented changes – new ownership, declining market share, fierce competition. These elements must be understood and their impact should not be dismissed lightly.' In case anyone missed the point, Neal Pilson, CBS president hit home with his final remarks: 'We still have a real concern that major sports packages may build their economic model for the future with the expectation that network television will continue to fund the enterprise through the payment of rights fees escalating far beyond audience potential and advertiser growth.'

12 Network audience share in the US dropped even further – down to around 43 per cent by 2003.

13 From a technical standpoint, there were just not enough households which could receive the pay channels – less than 20 million of the 100 million homes in the US market. Management also failed to realise that both network affiliates and cable channels would regard the triple-cast more as a threat than as an opportunity, and therefore set about undermining the new venture by failing to promote it. NBC infuriated its affiliate partners even more when it started to scramble for triple-cast subscribers, adding sports like basketball and gymnastics, which it had previously agreed with affiliates would only be shown on the network; and by dropping the daily subscription rate of $29.95 to $19.95. 'NBC

was attempting to walk a tightrope. They slipped and fell into an alligator pit', said John C Severino, president of Prime Ticket.

14 Considering the 1982 soccer World Cup generated $5.27 million in rights fee from Europe, the Los Angeles result was a major success.

15 Bertelsmann owned 39 per cent of Germany's premier private Channel – RTL – the maximum shareholding permitted at the time under German law. In order to gain access to prime sports programming for RTL, Bertelsmann established its own sports rights agency, UFA, to bid against EBU, who were unwilling at the time to sub-license rights to non-members. UFA quickly shook up the European rights market by acquiring the European rights (excluding the UK) to Wimbledon for four years for DM 60 million, and to the German football league for five years for DM 150 million.

16 The IOC made a further adjustment in the revenue distribution formulas for Athens 2004 onwards, allocating 49 per cent to the Organising Committee and 51 per cent to the Olympic Family. IOC president Jacques Rogge changed the formula again for the 2010 Games onwards, no longer guaranteeing any percentage, just acknowledging that a sum will be allocated to each organising committee, probably in line with the previous Games, index linked, and that any further upside in revenues would no longer automatically be passed through, but be kept for distribution to the NOCs and International Federations. The risk here is that the IOC could revert back to the days of ongoing negotiations and conflict with each organising committee, by not having a clear-cut financial model.

17 No sooner had Samaranch got this rule through than he began lobbying for a further change to 51/49 in favour of the IOC, NOCs and Federations.

18 The BBC rating was 45, a new record for a single channel television sports audience, even topping Britain's most popular programme, *Coronation Street*.

19 Dick Ebersol succeeded Arthur Watson as president of NBC Sports on 1 May 1989.

20 Bob Iger became president of Disney and number two to Michael Eisner when Capital Cities sold ABC to Disney in 1995, and succeeded Eisner in 2005.

# Chapter 3

# SHOCK AND AWE

## Multi-Games strategies

By the mid-1990s, the IOC had had enough of doing battle with organising committees over broadcast strategies. Time and time again the IOC had found itself in conflict with the organisers over the scheduling of negotiations, who would control them and who the rights should be sold to.

The organisers wanted to maximise the revenue, with little attention to ensuring global coverage. The IOC, while needing the revenue to fund the Olympic Movement, had many other factors to consider, including the global and continuing promotion of the Olympic Games. Samaranch decided that the IOC would take total and full control over all future rights negotiations. The seeds for the IOC's strategy of entering into long-term broadcast agreements were sown.

The first broadcaster to come up with a multi-Games offer strategy was not NBC, as is often believed, but Australia's Channel 7. Gary Fenton, Channel 7's sports chief, was struggling to make a realistic offer for Atlanta; one that would meet the expectations of the IOC and the Atlanta Committee for the Olympic Games (ACOG) – the private, non-profit organisation staging the event. In truth, Fenton was far more interested in the Sydney rights, when the Games would be in his own backyard, but knew that the IOC would not start negotiations for those Games until Atlanta was locked up. He knew, too, that if he failed to win Atlanta it would be all the more difficult to get Sydney.

Over a beer at Sportel, the sports industry television conference in Monaco, Fenton explained to me how they were struggling to meet our expectations for Atlanta, and just could not make the numbers work. He asked me if I had any ideas.

'Why not extend the advertising period?' I asked him.

'What do you mean, beyond just one Games?' Fenton looked back bemused.

'Don't know – never been done, but if that's what it will take to make the numbers work, why not look at it?' I said.

Within weeks, Fenton was on a secret mission to Montreal to meet with Dick Pound to present a proposal for a double Games bid. It worked. Channel 7's offer of $75 million for the two Games locked up the rights to Atlanta and Sydney. A new era in broadcast negotiations had begun.

Among those quickly on the phone to Fenton was NBC's Dick Ebersol, asking how he had pulled off the two-Games deal.

Again, circling with interest was Rupert Murdoch. Murdoch's Fox Network had firmly established itself as a major player in the US, successfully bidding for a number of prime sports properties. Murdoch was using sport as 'a battering ram for entry into new markets' throughout the world.[1]

With the Olympics returning to Murdoch's birthplace, Australia, he was even more anxious to lock up the crown jewel for his media empire and set about aggressively pursuing the rights. Murdoch was told that this time he would have a seat at the bidding table alongside the three other networks. He began secretly lobbying the Sydney Organising Committee and its then president Gary Pemberton.[2]

Murdoch was prepared to invest his own time in what he hoped would be a slow process of seduction. On 25 April, 1995, Murdoch came to Lausanne, along with Chase Carey, chairman and CEO of the Fox Network, to press their case with Samaranch and IOC officials. Press reports speculated that Murdoch was considering a global $1 billion plus offer for worldwide rights to the Sydney 2000 Games. Global rights for the 1996 Atlanta Games were worth around $900 million.

Murdoch and Carey spent the day looking around the Olympic Museum, and exploring how it might be possible to expand the coverage of the Olympic Games.[3] Murdoch left Lausanne convinced that he would now be accepted as a serious bidder for future Olympic rights.

## Two's company

Seeing the press reports of Murdoch's visit to the IOC headquarters, the other networks became increasingly concerned. They worried that Murdoch might be unbeatable in a straight rights auction. CBS decided that its Olympic future best lay in cultivating its long-running Winter Games franchise. This left ABC and NBC to decide how they could take on Murdoch. For a while the two networks felt that their best chance might be to form a joint venture to acquire and share the Olympic rights. But when the Walt Disney Company announced its acquisition of ABC from Capital Cities on July 30, 1995, NBC began to rethink the proposal fearing that Disney might suddenly want to make its own expensive Olympic TV statement.

Dick Ebersol and NBC president Randy Falco were also struggling with the potential impact of the time difference between the US and Sydney, and its likely impact on advertising sales. But, with the Winter Games now confirmed for Salt Lake City in 2002, they figured that if there was a way to amortise the advertising revenue, the host country advantage might even out any shortfalls from the Summer Games.

It suddenly struck the NBC leadership that the best way to deal with the advertising risk, and to beat Murdoch, was to bid for two Games – Sydney and Salt Lake. They would mount their own multi-Games bid. Bob Wright, NBC's chairman, called Jack Welch, the celebrated chairman and CEO of General Electric, NBC's parent company, and outlined the proposal. Within twenty minutes Welch agreed they should go for both.

Once the decision was made, speed and total secrecy were essential. Ebersol and Falco were told by Welch to take GE's private jet to Europe to find Samaranch, who was in Gothenburg at the 1995 World Athletics Championships. Waiting for them was NBC's senior vice president, Alex Gilady. When Ebersol and Falco arrived, they were so scared they might be seen entering the hotel that they took the staff elevator up to Samaranch's room. Ebersol made a short, fifteen minute presentation to Samaranch. Samaranch listened carefully. He told Ebersol how impressed he was, but explained that he could not accept without first hearing Dick Pound's view, and that of his executive board.

Ebersol, recalling how Arledge, his mentor, would close rights deals by giving a tight deadline to accept or reject, told Samaranch that the IOC had just thirty six hours until Friday night to agree. Samaranch said, 'So go and speak to Pound.' Ebersol, expecting to find Pound in Gothenburg, was dismayed to find that he had stayed at home in Canada. Within a few hours, the NBC delegation was back on the jet crossing the Atlantic to Montreal.

Ebersol and Falco met Pound in his offices in downtown Montreal. They made the same presentation for the double Games proposal. Within minutes, Pound pulled out his laptop, and began bashing out the basics of the deal in a three-page memorandum. NBC had pulled off a unique coup – a $1.25 billion offer was agreed for the Sydney and Salt Lake City Games.

## The pre-emptive strike

On 7 August, the deal was announced to an astonished world. [4]

So high was the price – a 56 per cent increase over Atlanta – that Bob Wright, NBC's chairman, joked at the press conference that 'as part of the arrangement, we are also selling NBC to the IOC'. At short notice, Gary Pemberton, the president of the Sydney Organising Committee, was summoned from Australia to New York for the press conference. He didn't have time to pull together any commemorative souvenirs for the signing ceremony so he grabbed some Sydney Olympic caps and T-shirts from a souvenir shop in Manley on the way to the airport. It was only as he handed them out that he realised they were all counterfeit.

CBS, meanwhile, looked on aghast as its Winter Olympic franchise of three successive Games was brought to a grinding halt. One of the most difficult lunch meetings of my entire career was the regular Olympic review with CBS bosses to see how Nagano advertising sales were progressing. The lunch, with CBS sales president Joe Abbruzze and Olympic sales boss JoAnne Ross, took place just three hours after the press announcement of NBC's new deal, in a New York Italian restaurant straight out of an episode of *The Sopranos*. I sat with my back against the wall, grilled by Abbruzze and his colleagues about how the IOC could sell out the Winter Games without even giving them a chance. It was not fair, he said, but we all knew that if they had come up with the idea of a double Games bid first, they would have done exactly the same as Ebersol.

NBC's new long-term broadcast agreement changed the dynamics of the relationship between the IOC and the broadcasters from a traditional 16-day event into an ongoing strategic partnership. TV networks recognised that in a soon-to-be 500 channel television universe, they could stand out only if they could pull in the big events. It was the only way to guarantee the mega advertising audience. That guarantee would help build relationships and loyalty with their affiliate stations – at a time when affiliate switching was becoming commonplace – and would help them solidify partnerships with leading advertisers.

On 26 September, the NBC team was back in Lausanne for the formal contract signing. Samaranch recognised the extent of NBC's commitment to the Olympics; he also understood the benefit to the IOC of locking up long-term revenue and broadcast agreements before the organising committee became involved. He told Dick Pound to sound Ebersol and Falco out to see if they wanted to keep going and strike a further deal for another term beyond 2008.

After the celebratory dinner at the Palace Hotel, Pound retired to the bar with Ebersol and Falco for post-negotiation cigars. By the end of the evening, the IOC and NBC were on the way to pulling off an even more remarkable deal. Under discussion was a further three Games agreement for 2004, 2006 and 2008 – three Games where host cities had not even been appointed. Within a couple of months, a new secret agreement was hammered out. The deal was codenamed 'Sunset', as both Pound and Ebersol reckoned that this deal went so far into the future that it would be the last of their Olympic careers.

On 12 December, 1995, the biggest broadcast deal in sports history (at the time) was announced with NBC paying a further $2.3 billion for the next three Games. In less than five months, NBC had committed over $3.5 billion in Olympic rights fees. The face of the Olympic TV market had been changed for ever. The other networks were left speechless.

## Out-foxed

Rupert Murdoch, however, was not yet ready to throw in the towel. Seeing that the IOC was willing to take its rights out long term, he promptly proposed a $2 billion offer for European rights through 2008. This time the EBU responded by bringing its offer up to $1.4 billion and a 50 per cent share in any profits. Samaranch defended the deal stating that 'the reason we accepted a smaller sum from EBU than from News Corporation is that we reach a far larger audience with terrestrial channels, especially young people. That has always been our priority, rather than simply to accept the highest bidder.'

The sale of the Olympic rights was a rare piece of good news for the EBU and its public sector members. The rise of the cash-rich satellite broadcasters was threatening their major sports monopoly.[5]

Despite the criticism of the IOC and Samaranch for commercialising the Olympic Movement and chasing the dollar, an important principle had been upheld. The IOC had accepted an offer of $600 million less to protect the basic concept of free-to-air coverage for the Olympic Games. Samaranch's critics in the media were strangely silent.

Murdoch responded to the snub of losing – perhaps the first time that he had not been able to buy his way in with his cheque book – with dignity. The politicians in the New South Wales Government were less sanguine. They immediately called a press conference and complained that 'their Games were being robbed of almost $200 million in extra revenue'. This made headlines in the Australian media. The same media and politicians would no doubt have been equally outraged if four years earlier, the IOC had accepted a pay-per-view offer from Australian media groups, thereby denying the Australian public free access to watch the Olympics. It's a good example of the IOC, and Samaranch in particular, being on a hiding to nothing.

The multi-Games genie was well and truly out of the bottle. The rest of the world soon followed suit. Long-term agreements through 2008 were agreed with the other broadcast unions in South America and Asia, along with Canada and Japan.

Broadcasters could now invest in premium Olympic coverage, secure in the knowledge that they were not supplying just a one-off event. The longer contracts provided a vested interest in building the Olympic brand, concentrating on the overall production without having to worry about bidding every two years. The Olympics had always attracted the best production talent and the networks could now engage the very best sports production talent on long-term contracts. Ebersol joked that the reason he made his first double bid was that he needed some incentive for his engineers to leave Sydney after the Games and the opportunity of Salt Lake City was the only way to drag everyone back home.

## Channel hopping

By the new millennium, the broadcasting environment was hugely different to that of 1980 when Samaranch became president. In 1980, the average American home had around nine TV channels. By 2002 this had risen to an average of 75; by 2012, 500 channels are predicted. The growth in consumer choice led to a dramatic reduction in prime-time ratings for the networks from an average of 16.9 in 1980 to less than 7.5 by 2002. The networks' overall share of the broadcast market crashed even more dramatically.

Industry experts forecast that the advertising market would remain depressed.[6] The investment bank Morgan Stanley anticipated write-downs by the networks on their sports properties of over $900 million in 2001 rising to over $1.1 billion in 2006. The unstable global situation with terrorism was eroding confidence in the markets, curtailing enthusiasm for risky agreements that looked out into an uncertain future. New tech-nology was continuing to threaten to eat away at the networks' already diminishing audiences. TiVo, a system which allows viewers to skip TV commercials, was widely regarded as having the potential to undermine the business model on which the networks and other advertiser supported television channels were founded.

Recognising the importance of the issue, the changing environment and the sheer number of variables, Jacques Rogge (who succeeded Samaranch in July 2001 as IOC president) decided to form a special TV Rights Com-mission – the only commission that he would personally chair.[7] During the summer of 2002, we embarked on an intensive fact-finding exercise to review the true state of the market and the options. Experts from around the world were called in to talk about how they saw the broadcasting and advertising industries evolving over the course of the next decade.[8]

Next, we called in the networks and media groups to find out how they saw things. The goal was as much to do with creating a climate of confidence and openness in the process, as it was to do with picking up information. As well as finding out what their issues were, it was also clear that we needed to get all the US networks back to the negotiating table and create real competition.

Some fences needed to be mended. ABC was still smarting from past Olympic bidding experiences. The Calgary bidding process, nearly two decades before, had left it feeling betrayed. A decade later with Sydney, it thought it had a joint bid with NBC, only to see its 'partner' bail out to make its own unilateral bid at the last minute.

CBS remained enraged over NBC's pre-emptive strike for Salt Lake City, breaking its long-standing Winter Olympics franchise, for which it had invested close to a $1 billion in rights fees in the past decade. And, after its own unsuccessful attempts to gain the Sydney rights, Fox also needed to be convinced that it would be an open and fair process.

To show that the IOC was also willing to think about fresh options, we invited executives from AOL Time Warner to come along and present their perspective. Several networks asked what AOL Time Warner was doing at the table. As a major media group, we thought it could bring new thinking about how the Olympics might be presented. The networks were not pleased to see a fifth player joining the table to bid for rights.

In truth, none of the players were now simply broadcast networks, as they had been the last time they had met the IOC across the bidding table. ABC had been purchased by the Disney Group; CBS had been acquired by Viacom; Rupert Murdoch's Fox media empire had continued to grow; and NBC's parent GE was slowly expanding its broadcasting portfolio with the addition of Telemundo, the US Spanish broadcasting network, and various other cable channels.

## Levelling the playing field

Much of the strategy for any successful broadcast rights negotiation is the creation of competition – or at least the perception of competition. Having all the networks and their respective sports division presidents turn up in Lausanne was a first critical step to achieving that objective. To ensure that the networks understood that it would be a level playing field, the IOC made it clear that no pre-emptive bidding would be allowed and that there would be no preferred position for the incumbent partner. Of course, there were attempts in the ensuing months at a pre-emptive bid, but to his great credit Rogge held firm.

After listening to the industry experts and the networks, the negotiating strategy began to take shape. Rogge turned to a member of the TV Rights Commission, Richard Carrion, IOC member for Puerto Rico and a highly respected international banker, to chair a small working group to lead the US rights negotiations.

It was also decided that with five potential bidders, we needed the support of a US-based consultant who could help the IOC to truly understand what the other side was thinking; Neal Pilson was brought in. Pilson, a former president of CBS Sports, had participated in eight Olympic bids, winning three of them and establishing CBS's winter strategy for Albertville through Nagano. A US law firm, O'Melveney and Myers, was also hired to complete the roster of American advisors.

Pilson was much more upbeat about the US market than the media and other industry experts. Pilson argued that although prime-time ratings had declined year on year over the past two decades, the actual premium the Olympics gained in ratings, over normal prime-time programming, had risen dramatically from a 7 per cent bump in Sarajevo to a 118 per cent bump in Salt Lake City.

Carrion's group decided that all rights should be bundled together, with a single gatekeeper controlling the distribution throughout the territory. The revenue potential of the so-called 'new media rights' (the internet, broadband and telecoms), the group felt, did not justify splitting them off. It would have only led to different media outlets competing against each other for the same eyeballs and advertising dollars, without creating any new revenue.

If possible, the negotiations and bidding would take place before the decision on the host city for the 2010 Olympic Winter Games in July 2005. This meant the broadcasters would be bidding blind, not even knowing on which continent the Games would be held.

But there was one important and ultimately critical caveat to the success of the final bid. The IOC could elect to freeze negotiations indefinitely if the bidding did not meet expectations. This was vital in sending the necessary signal to all bidders: that this time the IOC would dictate the timing and that we did not have a gun to our heads dictating when we had to strike a deal. The IOC could afford to wait until the deal was right. If one network wanted to lock up the rights now, then there was a minimum expected price that would have to be achieved. It was the equivalent of having a reserve price on a lot at auction.

Networks would be challenged to look at all of their media and promotional assets, and explore how they might be used to build the Olympic brand. The final decision would not just be based on the financial rights fee on offer, but how a true promotional partnership could be formed.

## Signed and sealed

Another critical, and very ambitious, goal was established. In order to bid, all networks had to sign the definitive and binding broadcast agreement – not a simple outline version as in the past, but the full hundred page master contract. The IOC goal was to leave nothing to chance. We wanted to make sure that after accepting a bid, we didn't spend the next twenty four months, as had often been the case, negotiating the small print of the deal and having to make concession after concession.

There were obstacles to overcome. Two of the potential bidders – Fox and AOL – had never seen a full Olympic broadcast agreement. The terms had also evolved substantially since ABC and CBS had last bid. Some people argued that we would never be able to get the five media groups to sign the same contract – and then, having signed it, get their boards to approve it. To make it even harder, the plan was to do all this before bidding started – in less than six weeks. This was going to test the US legal system and the lawyers to the limit. All that would remain to be done, once the sealed bids were opened, was to fill in the blanks for the rights fee and the promotional commitments.

In addition to getting the media groups signed off on the draft, the IOC team needed the approval of the United States Olympic Committee, which traditionally also granted critical marketing rights that helped to build the overall value of the bid.

Rogge and Carrion were adamant that all the agreements had to be drafted and signed before bidding could begin. This was easier said than done. Teams of lawyers pored over the drafts. Getting everyone to agree, especially with each group having different views and comments, was no small feat.

The networks were briefed and the date set for the two-day bidding process on June 5, 2003 in Lausanne. We focused on delivering a single, simple message: it would be an open, transparent bidding process. After meetings and calls with the leadership of the various networks, Rupert Murdoch at Fox, Mel Karmazin at Viacom, Richard Parsons at AOL and Bob Iger at ABC, along with Bob Wright and Ebersol at NBC, confidence was slowly built in the market place. Everyone accepted that this time it would be a level playing field for all.

But as the clock began to tick down, some of the CEOs and their respective boards started to get cold feet at the potential size of the commitment required to win. AOL withdrew, after deciding it was perhaps premature to take on the overall Olympic portfolio on its own. Everyone had been expecting AOL to team up with one of the other networks, as Turner Sports had done to bid for the Albertville and Lillehammer Games. But this time all the networks had their own set of media and cable partners within their holding companies.

Then, with less than a week to go, CBS suddenly pulled out of the race, reducing the number of potential bidders to three. CBS decided that the risk of not knowing on which continent the 2010 Winter Games would be held was just too great. If Korea was elected, advertising revenues could be seriously reduced due to the impact of time zones on live coverage. Sean McManus, CBS Sports president, called me late one weekend to say that he would not be making the trip to Lausanne. My initial reaction was one of great surprise. A couple of months earlier, McManus had announced to the astonishment of the assembled media at the *Sports Business Journal* World Conference in New York, 'that the Olympics were the one property immune from a push back on rights fees'. But McManus told me he could no longer make the numbers work for the Viacom board.

When the ABC team called a few days later, saying that it wanted to explore a revenue-sharing formula as part of their proposal, and should it still make the trip to Lausanne, some of the team started to get nervous. If ABC backed out, the number of bidders would be reduced to two. This, we knew, could have a very damaging impact on the dynamics of the bidding process.

Barry Frank, TWI's senior TV agent, had been advising the USOC through the process. Seeing that Disney might also now be getting cold feet, Frank suggested to the USOC that it consider lobbying the IOC to postpone the bidding. The stakes were mounting. Carrion and I called round to say we were not postponing. The media sensed the tension escalating. *Sports Business Journal* described the process for the networks 'as sort of like going into battle with kamikaze fighters, while trying to resist your own suicidal tendencies'.

Rupert Murdoch was sending very mixed messages. In a series of press statements in the lead up to the bid, Murdoch talked of how 'you could bid a figure today and you might go broke, or you could have big inflation and end up with a bargain.' David Hill, Fox Network president, talked of the new media potential and how 'that's the catch-22. It's do you feel lucky today?' Rumours started to circulate in the press that Murdoch might even turn up himself in Lausanne to make the final pitch for Fox.

## Lausanne, June 2003

Continuing the pattern set with the rights negotiations for the 2004 and 2008 Games, we were, once again, selling the US broadcasting rights to the 2010 Olympic Winter Games and the 2012 Games before the host cities had even been established. In June 2003, the announcement of the venue for the 2010 Winter Games was still a month away (at the IOC Session in Prague).[9] And the 2012 venue was to be chosen in the summer of 2005. By 2003, however, there were already nine candidates, including some of the greatest and most famous cities in the world – Istanbul, Havana, Leipzig, London, Madrid, Moscow, New York, Paris, and Rio de Janeiro. Contrast this heavyweight list with the days when the IOC had to plead with cities to bid – and then to do so on their terms.

We were calling the shots more than ever before. But, given the anxious build-up, it was with a considerable sigh of relief when we saw the three remaining networks arrive in Lausanne, with no further defections. The scene was set for what proved to be the biggest TV rights negotiation in Olympic history.

The negotiations took place in the IOC's main conference room, the de Coubertin Room. With stunning views over Lake Geneva, across to Evian and the French Alps, and a state-of-the-art multi-media suite, the room is impressive.

The IOC negotiating team was made up of IOC president Jacques Rogge; chairman of the IOC Finance Commission and chair of the US TV working group, Richard Carrion; Francois Carrard, the IOC director general; myself; and the American consultant Neal Pilson as well as a team of lawyers. Each network was given 90 minutes to present their case. The running order had already been drawn by a secretary at O'Melveney's offices in New York during one of our lengthy legal drafting sessions.

ABC kicked off with a strong presentation on what the Disney Group could bring to the table, especially in the area of youth promotion. The Disney team was led by ABC president Alex Wallau. Also present were ESPN and ABC Sports president George Bodenheimer, Olympic Project managing director Dick Glover, and ABC sports commentator, and Tokyo 1964 swimming gold medallist, Donna De Varona.

Rupert Murdoch's Fox Network followed. Its chairman, David Hill, provided a hilarious commentary on the US sports scene. This caused repeated outbursts of loud laughter from the IOC team. NBC executives, waiting for their turn to present in an office beneath the IOC conference room, and who heard the noises emanating from the room, were perplexed about what Hill was up to.

Finally Dick Ebersol and Randy Falco led the large NBC team into the room for what was described as its 'shock and awe' presentation.[10] Ebersol took the IOC team through the 11 Olympic Games to which NBC had the rights, starting with Tokyo in 1964. He moved on to talk about their expanded programming commitments for Athens and Beijing.[11] Ebersol and John Miller, president of the NBC Agency, NBC's in-house promotions unit, then outlined a new proposal for the promotion of the Olympic brand – an estimated $600 million commitment over and above any rights fee.

Ebersol closed with a video message from General Electric chairman and CEO Jeff Immelt, the man who had succeeded Jack Welch. Immelt talked of an even larger and more focused commitment to the Games, bringing the full resources of one of the world's largest and most successful companies to bear in support of the Olympic Movement.[12] At this stage, it began to dawn on me that Ebersol was going to pre-empt any competitive bid by taking NBC's offer to a new level that competitors would be unable to match. Ebersol was looking to expand NBC's partnership by bringing GE into the Olympic corporate sponsorship programme.

Once all the presentations were complete, Jacques Rogge called the three networks back to put the details of their bids in a sealed envelope. Each was placed in a transparent voting box symbolically guarded by a uniformed security guard.

Before opening the bids, Rogge offered a lunchtime cocktail to the delegates of the three networks and the IOC team, along with representatives of the United States Olympic Committee. No-one was in the mood to drink or eat. At 15.35, the IOC team went back into the boardroom to open the envelopes.

The network presidents and their delegations withdrew to their hotels. The Disney delegation headed back to the Palace Hotel. Dick Ebersol, NBC Olympic chief, and Randy Falco, president of the network, led their team back to the Beau Rivage Hotel to anxiously await our deliberations. Fox's David Hill, along with network president Ed Goren and chief operating officer Larry Jones, decided they wanted to scout out the local casinos – as if there hadn't been enough gambling over the previous few days.

Rogge opened the voting box and handed the sealed bids to Richard Carrion. Carrion calmly opened each offer in turn and read out the terms. ABC proposed profit sharing with no fixed guaranteed income; and Fox came in with $1.3 billion. When he opened NBC's offer it became clear that we had succeeded in taking Olympic rights to a whole new level.

Aside from a $2.001 billion offer for the US TV rights, NBC proposed a dramatic increase in coverage of the Games – potentially, to 3,000 hours in multiple languages. This was a massive rise on the 120 hours that NBC forecast for Moscow in 1980, and the 172 hours it actually provided for Atlanta in 1996. In addition, NBC proposed a multi-year, multi-hundred million dollar promotional commitment to the Olympic brand – as well as a $10 million interactive library system to support the Olympic Television Archive Bureau.

Lest there be any doubt about NBC's commitment to keep the Olympic franchise it had carefully nurtured since Seoul 1988, the network topped its offer with a unique $200 million proposal from its parent company General Electric, to become a sponsorship partner through 2012. General Electric had never before sponsored anything on an international basis in its corporate history.

NBC had pulled out all the stops. Not knowing where Murdoch and Fox might come in, it had decided that it had to find a proposal that would take its bid beyond the traditional rights fee-advertising calculation, to be certain of locking up the rights.

Although GE's offer was clearly the magical element over and above their basic rights offer, there were a series of complex issues that had to be worked through before the IOC could accept. General Electric has one of the broadest business portfolios of any major corporation, and was submitting a shopping list of categories and businesses that it wanted to see included in its Olympic sponsorship. Many of the business areas were likely to have an important operational impact on the Games. Issues of value in kind support – partial or full payment of the sponsorship fee with the sponsor's goods or services – would have to be resolved. Finalising such issues would normally take months of detailed discussions with an army of lawyers.

Rogge turned to me and asked what we could do. I told him that we needed to get together with NBC and work through the basics of the general business arrangement. Given a few hours, I said, we just might be able to pull something together, at least to a level that would allow the IOC to take a decision on the overall deal, and whether to proceed with NBC's sponsorship proposal.

My feeling at that time was one of relief that we had broken through our key reserve number. While I was impressed by Ebersol's creative approach, it was clear that getting the GE details agreed and the USOC on board would make it a long night.

We needed to get the NBC executives back in the building without the press seeing them. Journalists were hanging around at the IOC entrance trying to spot the comings and goings of any executive. It was decided that I should go and pick Ebersol and Falco up from their hotel, and bring them back in through the IOC's underground car park, and up the service lift away from the prying eyes. Picking the NBC team up, they knew that they were still in play. As I drove them back to the IOC, I was grilled over whether it was the GE aspect of the deal that we wanted to talk about. I told Ebersol that there were a number of issues on a number of fronts, and that it might be a very long night.

Back in the IOC board room, Carrion advised NBC that there were several aspects we needed to discuss, but the GE proposal was the main one. I outlined the issues, and what we would need to clarify before the IOC could evaluate the overall offer. The key issues for us were exactly which product categories would make up GE's exclusive sponsorship. After all, its activities stretched from engines to finance to medical systems. How could we work through all the conflicts with other sponsors? How would we deal with the issue of value in kind – services for the organising committee, and how would these be priced?

NBC, anticipating this discussion, had smuggled into the country its own 'stealth consultant' to assist it in understanding the whole sponsorship process. Ebersol's team had been working on the proposal secretly for a couple of months. But it had been hard for anyone to get a full picture since they could not speak to any of the other sponsors for fear of showing their hand. Recognising the problem, it had brought in the former Salt Lake City marketing chief, Mark Lewis, as its advisor.

Lewis and I had worked closely together for nearly seven years. He joined the IOC's US-based marketing operation in 1996 as one of the deal lawyers helping to draft sponsorship contracts. After a couple of years, he left to join the Salt Lake team. Lewis and I knew each other well and immediately understood what it would take to hammer out the sponsorship side of the deal.

## Tempered tantrums

While the NBC team believed it could probably work through the issues with the IOC, it had forgotten about the United States Olympic Committee, which would also need to sign off on any sponsorship aspect of the agreement. The USOC had come to Lausanne with a high-level delegation led by Jim Sherr, the acting executive director, to try and muscle in on the negotiations. But it had no one on its team in Lausanne to deal with sponsorship issues. USOC legal counsel, Jeff Benz, promptly told the IOC that it would be impossible to conclude anything in Lausanne. It would need to take this proposal back home to think about it.

Benz was bluntly told that this was not an option. The USOC is entitled to receive 12.5 per cent of the US broadcast rights. The deal on the table from NBC would give it over $250 million, around 70 per cent of their current quadrennial operating budget. The USOC, not for the first time, was in danger of losing sight of the bigger picture – by becoming tangled in petty category and territorial issues.

The USOC team started to tell me and Lewis the various reasons why it could not close on the GE deal. The clock slowly counted down to midnight. By now, the IOC team had been sequestered away for over seven hours. We would soon have to tell the other bidders and the media what was going on.

The USOC group was told that we were closing the deal – unless it wanted to join the IOC at a press conference to explain why the negotiations had collapsed. Still Benz did not want to move. I stormed out of the negotiating room, past a pale faced and nervous Rogge, shouting that I had had it with the USOC and that it was incapable of closing anything.

After a few more theatrical tantrums, the USOC representatives were finally bought to the table. At 1.30 am the IOC and NBC leadership reconvened for a global teleconference to announce that NBC had won the rights to be the US broadcaster for the 2010 and 2012 Olympic Games – achieving an uninterrupted 24 year run at the Summer Games.

At 2.30 am, exhausted but very happy, the IOC and NBC teams joined for a celebratory dinner at the Beau Rivage Hotel. The strategy outlined to Rogge a year earlier had paid off. It was not just the huge amounts of money involved that was satisfying. We had persuaded NBC to engage with the IOC brand strategy – creating a unique new partnership for the future, and a whole increased level of benefit. We knew we had established a new benchmark for the industry. The media were unanimous in their praise for how NBC had set out to keep its Olympic franchise intact, comparing Ebersol's strategy to the recent US invasion of Iraq.

ABC and Fox left Lausanne quietly. While disappointed that they had not been successful in their bids, they were nevertheless encouraged that the IOC had stuck to its promise of ensuring an open and transparent bidding procedure. The era of pre-emptive bids was over. All of the networks were pleased with the new process. The IOC had achieved one of its key objectives of getting all the networks back to the bidding table, safe in the knowledge that the next time the Olympic rights were put out to bid the media groups would be back. The rest of the world's broadcasters looked on dismayed at what this deal might do to future negotiations in their market.

## American pie

The hard negotiating we had to go through with the United States Olympic Committee in 2003 was not unusual. Indeed, a recurring theme over the past two decades has been the ongoing attempts by the USOC to lay claim to an ever larger share of the US broadcast rights fees. Since the 1980 Winter Games in Lake Placid, the USOC has argued that it should be entitled to a direct share of the US fees, first trying to persuade the IOC of the legitimacy of its case and, whenever that failed, endeavouring to persuade the US Congress to consider special legislation to take control of the broadcast rights away from the IOC.

There was no question that the US market was paying a disproportionate share of the global broadcast rights. In reality, however, it was less that the US was paying too much, since the local market forces dictated the amount, and rather more that the rest of the world, without any true competition in the broadcast market, wasn't paying its fair share. When Samaranch took over the IOC presidency in 1980, US rights fees accounted for around 85 per cent of global rights fees and 80 per cent of all revenue; now the US broadcasters account for around 50 per cent of the Summer Games rights fee, and around 30 per cent of total revenue.

Some of the USOC's arguments for a share of the revenues were, perhaps, legitimate. But it was the manner in which it pressed its claim that alienated most international observers.

The first serious attempt was made in 1985. The USOC waited until the Calgary and Seoul broadcast agreements were concluded before pressing their case. The USOC's then executive director, General George Miller, presented the IOC with a multi-million dollar claim for the use of the Olympic marks in the US, basing his argument on a technical interpretation of the US Amateur Sports Act. The USOC deliberately waited until after the rights negotiations had been concluded, believing that they could force the IOC into a corner – which they did.

The IOC was faced with the dilemma of challenging the claim, and risk watching over $700 million of US broadcast agreements unravel, or trying to find a settlement. As it was unlikely that similar rights fees could be negotiated if the IOC was forced back to the market, especially with respect to Calgary, the IOC reluctantly began negotiating a compromise with the USOC, finally offering $5 million for the 1988 Games, and a 10 per cent cut of all future US broadcast revenues.

As was often the case in any dealings with the USOC, as soon as one agreement was reached, USOC officials saw it as time to start pressing for a new and even better deal. Soon after the 1988 Games, they were back pushing for a dramatic increase in their share.

In Autumn 1989, the Brookings Institution, a US think tank, published an article that inflamed the debate.[13] The article, entitled 'Fools gold: How America pays to lose in the Olympics', began by reporting that 'America is bankrolling the Olympics' and then asking the question, 'What is the reward? ... Worse coverage. The huge price tag might be justified if Americans received superior coverage. But broadcasters from all nations get access to precisely the same feed ... In sum, the funding set up for the Olympics is a travesty. Americans get bilked in three ways: we pay more than our fair share for the Games; we have to put up with an excessive number of commercials to see them; and our athletes receive little of the money they pay.'

The tone of the article was designed to get the attention of congressmen. It conveniently overlooked what had happened a few years earlier. When Los Angeles was faced with the Soviet-led boycott of their Games, which had played havoc with the overall sporting schedule and put the Games financing at risk, many nations stepped up at significant cost to send additional athletes. When the Los Angeles organisers then declared a $240 million surplus, Samaranch proposed that a few million dollars be set aside to repay those NOCs for the additional costs. Although Peter Ueberroth, the Los Angeles organiser, lobbied hard in support of the deal, the USOC vetoed it, electing to keep the surplus for its own sporting programmes.

The Brookings article did acknowledge that, 'As the world's richest economy, the US should remain the largest contributor to the Games', but that the US should run all future US broadcast bids, submitting a number to the IOC for the rights based on what other nations paid, that for a transitional period would equate to half of what the rest of the world paid, and that the balance would be spent on US athlete support. The *Brookings Review* article also proposed that the US Congress consider granting the US networks an anti-trust waiver for future Olympic bids.

The USOC denied that it had anything to do with the article and was, it said, as shocked as the IOC about any suggestion of removing the IOC's authority over broadcast rights. As the IOC session to elect the host city for the Centennial Games was less than six months away, and with Atlanta as a candidate, albeit still an outsider, the USOC and the US authorities wisely decided not to press the matter any further at this time. If the text of the Brookings article had ever been circulated among IOC members at the IOC Session in Tokyo, it is questionable whether Atlanta could ever have been elected.

Fortunately, few people were ever aware of the academic article and Atlanta went on to be elected host city of the Centennial Games. The USOC was forced to place any ideas for an increase in broadcast revenues on the back burner, until its Games were over – or nearly over.

As soon as the Atlanta Opening Ceremony was under way, expecting that the IOC would be totally focused on Games operations and management, the USOC moved to quietly slip new legislation through the US Congress. Again it addressed the issue of US broadcast rights, and sought to place the USOC in the driving seat for all future negotiations by giving it a veto right over the terms of future deals. If it was not for an alert lobbyist, the IOC would probably not have been aware of the move until it was too late.

Armed with the tip-off from Washington, Dick Pound immediately sought out USOC executive director Dick Schultz at the opening ceremony, asking him what he knew about the proposed legislation. Unfortunately for Shultz, Pound had in his back pocket a copy of Schultz's briefing instructions to his Washington lobbyists on the finer points of the legislation. Pound showed Shultz the letter. It is not known if Dick Shultz ever had time to actually enjoy watching the opening ceremony, but the legislation was quietly and quickly withdrawn.

After the Games, the IOC met with the USOC to negotiate a new agreement without having the pressure of the legislative gun of the US Congress to its head. The USOC was offered an increase in its share from 10 to 12.5 per cent against its demand for 20 per cent.[14]

The battle over revenues continued to sour relationships between the IOC and the USOC, undermining any attempt at a collaborative effort to develop programmes for the broader good of the Olympic Movement. For the USOC, it was a matter of who really controlled the Olympic Movement. Its view was that it should be run from its Colorado Springs headquarters and not from Lausanne.

But, by 2000 the USOC was facing its own series of internal management problems, having gone through five presidents, six executive directors and five marketing directors in less than four years.[15] As such, the USOC didn't have time to lobby Congress to force the IOC to increase its share. The USOC was too busy lobbying Congress fighting for its own constitutional survival. The revenue disparity between the US and the rest of the world, at least for the Summer Games, was now a lot more equitable. And with a new IOC president, Jacques Rogge, suggesting that perhaps the basis for any future negotiations between the IOC and the USOC be a reduction in its share, the USOC elected not to test the point further, and accepted the current formula.

## The tail wagging the scorpion

The story of the relationship between the Olympic Movement and broadcasters over the last two decades is one of power shifting. From being a peripheral complication, broadcasting rights have become crucial to the success of the Olympic Movement. But it should not be forgotten that it is a mutually beneficial arrangement.

The shared realisation is that the Olympic Games now have a huge impact on the advertising industry. The 2003 annual *Media Week* conference saw the industry's leading forecasters predicting that the 2004 Summer Olympics and the US presidential campaign would end the ad-spending recession, adding about $1 billion each to the world's total ad-spending growth. In fact, the Games added far more.

But with rights fees continuing to escalate, broadcasters and sponsors are faced with a growing dilemma: it is simply not possible to allocate such a large portion of your annual advertising budget to the 17-day Olympic period. The challenge for broadcasters going forward will be how to create an Olympic offering that allows advertisers to extend their budgets over a much longer time frame.

Bell Globe Media–CTV understood this concept when it bid for the Canadian TV rights for the Vancouver 2010 Olympic Winter Games in February 2005. The previous year, Richard Carrion and I had met with the CTV bosses, and challenged them to explore a multi-year programme counting down to the Games. By the time they came to submit their bid, they were able to offer a massive 200 per cent increase over the rights paid by CBC for the 2006 Winter Games in Torino.

Similarly, as broadcasters have defined the Olympic image for many people, how they continue to cover the Olympic Games will further define the Olympic brand. Every Olympic telecast should become a living advertisement for the Olympic brand. Not so long ago, this would have been seen by the TV producers, as 'bolshevism' and the IOC interfering in the editorial content of the broadcast. Today, there is much greater understanding of the potential of the partnership, and the need for the two sides to work much more closely together. For its part, the IOC has learned how scorpions behave.

With the success of its broadcast rights strategy, the IOC delivered on the first part of the financial plan inspired by Samaranch. But it was not out of the woods. If anything, the second part of the two-legged plan, securing ongoing corporate sponsorship, was to prove even more challenging. It brought the IOC within a whisker of failure.

## NOTES

1 As Peter Chernin, News Corporation's president and chief operating officer, outlined: 'This company is so defined by sports right now because what we have found in building our worldwide TV ventures, is that the two things that drive them are movies and sport. And sport is the more important.'

2 Murdoch expressed interest in bidding for the US rights to the 1998 Winter Games in Nagano, but was dissuaded by the IOC because the network did not have any sports broadcasting experience in the US. Fox subsequently acquired the rights to American football, and overnight built a premier sports broadcasting division.

3 Francois Carrard was appointed director general of the IOC in 1989, having served as the IOC's senior outside legal counsel for the previous decade. Carrard was a brilliant political strategist, and a popular communicator with the world's media – always bringing colour and a sharp tongue to Olympic press conferences. In 2003 Carrard stepped down as IOC director general and returned to his law practice, retaining his position as senior IOC legal adviser.

4 'In the past, when networks paid steep prices for sports, howls of over-
   bidding could be heard from competitors – this time hardly a murmur
   was heard, just secret admiration,' reported *USA Today*; 'Dick had
   understood where the market is going out front and adjusted to it,'
   commented Jim Host, chairman of Host Communications. 'I think the
   way in which he got the Olympic rights and the way he went at it was
   absolutely one of the most genius things I have seen done'; US sports
   agent Bob Rosen noted that 'Ebersol made a brilliant move and the
   other networks have to be mad'; *The New York Times* talked of NBC
   firing a 'remarkable pre-emptive strike at networks – executing a triple
   gambit – shutting Rupert Murdoch's News Corporation from acquiring the Olympics in his homeland; preventing Disney/ABC from
   making a quick splash in sports TV and ending CBS's run with the
   Winter Olympics.'

5 In a BBC press release, Jonathan Martin, BBC Television's head of
   sport paid tribute 'to the visionary leadership of Samaranch ... who
   was no doubt placed under pressure by more lucrative alternative
   offers, but he stuck resolutely to the view, enshrined in the IOC's
   Charter, that the Olympics should continue to be seen by the largest
   possible number of viewers worldwide.'

6 *Broadcaster and Cable Magazine* reported: 'Cable operators are ganging
   up on sports rights fees', describing how cable systems throughout the
   US were determined to resist paying increased sports rights fees. And
   to cap off the grim outlook, *Advertising Age* reported that 'not since the
   last recession year of 1991, has negative ad growth been recorded.'

7 In addition to IOC president Rogge as chairman of the Commission,
   other senior IOC members on the commission were: Thomas Bach
   (Germany), chairman of the IOC Juridical Commission and Olympic
   gold medalist; Gerhard Heiberg (Norway), chairman of the Marketing Commission, and former president of the Lillehammer Organising
   Committee; Richard Carrion (Puerto Rico), chairman of the Finance
   Commission; Un Yong Kim (Korea) and chairman of the TV Commission, and former chief organiser of the Seoul Games, and Ottavio
   Cinquanta (president of the International Skating Union) along with
   the IOC director general, Francois Carrard, IOC legal director Howard
   Stupp and IOC marketing director, Michael Payne.

8 Experts attending the IOC TV Workshop in Summer 2002 included Sir Martin Sorrell, chairman of advertising communications company, WPP; Bill Cella, CEO of media buying conglomerate, Magna; Octagon's CEO, Rick Dudley; IMG's Eric Drossard and Bill Sinrich and Mark Dowley, president of Interpublic's entertainment division. Sponsors, led by Coca-Cola Media boss, Chuck Fruit, presented their viewpoint. New media experts from Kudelski Group, the digital communications company, gave their perspective on the role the internet and telephony would have in the new media portfolio.

9 The 2010 Olympic Winter Games had three candidates: the eventual victor, Vancouver; Pyongyang and Salzburg.

10 NBC turned up in Lausanne with the largest team of any of the bidding networks, led by Dick Ebersol, chairman of NBC Sports/Olympics, and Randy Falco, NBC president; in addition were Gary Zenkel, executive vice president business affairs; senior Olympics producer, David Neal; Olympic programming senior vice president, Peter Diamond; and John Miller, head of NBC's promotions agency.

11 NBC increased its programming commitment for every Games since Atlanta, when it provided 171 hours of network coverage. In Sydney, NBC increased this to over 400 hours across three channels, and by Athens, over 1,000 hours across six channels including, for the first time, a dedicated Spanish language channel, Telemundo. By 2012 NBC is talking of over 3,000 hours of coverage with the inclusion of video-on-demand and other additional pay services.

12 Jeff Immelt, chairman and CEO of General Electric pointed out during his video presentation to the IOC that in April 1892, the same month that Baron Pierre de Coubertin moved to form the IOC, a young engineer in America, Thomas Edison, inventor of the phonograph and the light bulb, merged his fledgling company with a competitor to create General Electric.

13 The Brookings Institution is a private not-for-profit organisation devoted to research, education and publication on US domestic and foreign policy. The paper by Robert Lawrence, and Jeffrey Pellegrom came out in the Fall 1989 issue of *The Brookings Review*.

14 The increase for the USOC was the same proportionate amount as the IOC was providing to the Olympic Family as a result of the over-

all change in broadcast revenue allocations to OCOGs being adjusted from 60 to 49 per cent.

15 USOC presidents: Bill Hybl, LeRoy Walker, Sandy Baldwin, Marty Mankamyer and Peter Ueberroth. Executive directors: Harvey Schiller, Dick Schultz, Norman Blake, Scott Blackmun and Jim Scherr. Marketing directors: John Krimsky, Dave Ogren, Matt Mannelly, Toby Wong and Jim Grice.

# Chapter 4

# THE SHOEMAKER'S VISION

## Dazzling

The Olympic turnaround was based on the development of two financial strategies. The first and most important was income from broadcasting rights. The second was the exploitation of the Olympic brand through sponsorship. This is where the debate about the involvement of commerce in the Olympics was, and remains, at its most fierce.

When Samaranch took over the IOC, its commercial operations were a mess. To sort it out, he enlisted the help of Horst Dassler. Dassler's link to the Olympics began in 1956 when, as a twenty-year old, he was sent to Australia by his mother, Kathe Dassler, to distribute shoes made by the family sports shoe company Adidas to athletes at the Melbourne Olympics. This was a novel tactic at the time. Horst Dassler later recalled how 'athletes were surprised when I came up, as a young chap and offered them a pair of shoes. It was very easy'. Horst's father, Adi Dassler, founded Adidas in 1948 following an argument with his brother, Rudolf, while both were managing their father's shoe company. Rudolf set up camp on one side of the Aurach River in Bavaria, founding the sports shoe company Puma. Adolf set up Adidas on the other side. For a time, the remote German town of Herzogenaurach (population 18,125) became the capital of the world sports goods industry.

Thanks to Horst Dassler's Australian visit, four years later at the Rome Summer Olympics, 75 per cent of all track and field athletes were wearing Adidas shoes.

Over the years, Dassler built up close relationships with the leaders of the International Sports Federations. He helped them understand the potential of partnering with the business community, and companies like Coca-Cola, to help promote and fund their sport around the world. First, with the UK-based sports marketing agency West Nally in the 1970s, and then with Swiss-based ISL in the 1980s, Dassler showed unparalleled vision and focus.

Dassler was one of the most important sports leaders of the twentieth century. He created many of the foundations of event marketing, and pioneered the partnership between commerce and sporting federations. As a person, he was discreet, quiet even, preferring back room discussions to the main stage. He courted world leaders, and was probably better known in Moscow and the Kremlin than many heads of state. As a result, the whole Soviet team, as well as nations like East Germany, wore Adidas. Dassler maintained a dedicated intelligence office at Adidas headquarters to track sports leaders and political elections. For those seeking success in any sports industry election – whether for the presidency of FIFA or the selection of an Olympic host city – his support was critical.

Dassler submitted his ideas on the development of an Olympic marketing programme with a short video to the 86th IOC Session in New Delhi in 1983. The presentation delivered a stark message to the 78 IOC members in attendance. 'You, the International Olympic Committee, own the most valuable and sought after property in the world. Yet the Olympic rings are the most unexploited trademark in existence. No major corporation in the world would tolerate such a situation.'

When the quiet Dassler spoke, the industry listened. His long-standing sporting links meant he was well placed to play a part in exploiting the Olympic brand. In May 1985 he came to Lausanne to sign a mould-breaking marketing agreement with Samaranch.

For an event that would revolutionise the fortunes of the Olympic Movement, there was remarkably little ceremony. Howard Stupp, the IOC's director of legal affairs, pulled together the contracts which Samaranch and Dassler signed. There were no speeches. No champagne celebration. And no media representatives, except a solitary photographer.

Monique Berlioux, the IOC's long-standing director, looked on in dismay. She had done everything possible to delay the signature of the contract. Berlioux believed that the IOC was giving up far too much control to outside commercial interests and, perhaps more to the point, that this would weaken her own position. The differences between Berlioux and Samaranch were becoming a serious obstacle to change. On the occasion of the 90th IOC Session in Berlin, Berlioux was removed from office.[1] Samaranch rightly saw her as a block to his vision of modernising and reforming the IOC. But Berlioux was not the only person in the Olympic Movement to resist the changes. The debate about the commercialisation of the rings was becoming louder.

## 24 carat rings

Many inside and outside the Olympic family were concerned that using the Olympic franchise to generate revenue was a dangerous road. My own view is, and always has been, that we had to professionalise the Olympics or lose it, but there were many who disagreed with Dassler's vision of an Olympic franchise. The Corinthians saw it as a slippery slope, with potentially disastrous consequences.

Horst Dassler's ideas were not exactly embraced by the IOC Session. But enough members understood that there was a clear need to build some form of marketing platform. The marketing efforts of the Los Angeles Organising Committee had shown that there was strong potential interest from the business community to support the Olympic Games, but the Movement's structure made it increasingly difficult, if not outright impossible.

Would-be sponsors or commercial supporters of the Olympics faced a complex labyrinth of vested interests. Although the organising committee could grant marketing rights to the Games, these rights could not be used outside of the host country, without the express approval of each national Olympic committee. The NOCs controlled all Olympic marketing rights for their territory, and could effectively veto any programme by a Games sponsor. Gaining access to a territory quickly evolved from a simple request for approval, to a long drawn-out and expensive negotiation, with the Games sponsor being forced to also become a sponsor of the National Olympic Team. This effectively meant that any company wanting to develop a global programme had to enter into 160 plus separate agreements with the NOCs. All too often, the organising committee would conveniently forget to tell the potential sponsor during the course of the negotiations that the rights did not extend beyond the host country. Games sponsors would begin negotiations with an NOC, only to find that their competitors had pre-empted them with a direct team sponsorship, effectively blocking them from the market.

The true complexity of the challenge facing would-be sponsors is hard to overstate. It involved persuading over 160 countries to sign up for a single marketing strategy. In many ways, it was like the political challenge of unifying the members of the United Nations or the European Community around a single policy. Sponsors found this highly complicated structure time consuming, frustrating and unworkable, aside from feeling misled. It was an unwieldy and inefficient way to run a major brand. Gary Hite, Coke's sports marketing chief at the time, explained to Samaranch that, although Coke believed in the Olympic Movement and its marketing potential, the IOC had to find an easier way for companies to get involved.

My own involvement in trying to cut through the complexity began in 1983 when I joined ISL from West Nally, as Olympic project manager. My mandate was to help Dassler and ISL deputy CEO Juergen Lenz, create a global marketing programme for the Olympics. After the 1984 Los Angeles Games, it was decided that the best place from which to develop and manage the project, would be from the host country of the next Olympic city. So I moved to Seoul, Korea, and embarked on the long road of creating sponsorship income.

## Solving the puzzle

The basic marketing concept generated by Horst Dassler, Juergen Lenz, and myself was remarkably simple – on paper at least. It was to bundle all the rights together – the IOC, the Winter Olympic Games, the Summer Olympic Games and over 160 National Olympic Committees – into a single four-year exclusive marketing package, offering companies one-stop shopping for their global Olympic involvement. The programme operated under the secret code name 'TOP'. This initially stood for absolutely nothing. Later, the sheer complexity of pulling all the different elements together meant that TOP stood for 'The Olympic Puzzle' – in the minds of those involved at least. Only after the project was fully established, did the TOP code name stick, as 'The Olympic Programme'. Later we officially re-christened it as 'The Olympic Partners' to reinforce the partnership element. Within the marketing industry TOP became a brand name in its own right.

There was just one problem with TOP: neither the Olympic organising committees nor the National Olympic Committees wanted to sign up. Nor was there a long queue of companies wanting to exploit the potential of a global Olympic association.

Dick Pound kept telling Samaranch that the concept would never work. So, Samaranch turned to him and responded, 'Right, you're responsible for making it work.' This was not what Pound had in mind. 'The difficulties of persuading the organising committees and the NOCs were such that I believed the programme would never get off the ground, least of all in time for the 1988 Games,, Pound later observed. Even after a couple of years of development, Pound was still far from sure that TOP would ever make it. 'This is a trial,' he told journalists. 'If it works, great. If not, we'll go back to the old way.'

The first challenge was to get the NOCs to sign up for a centrally co-ordinated marketing programme – and give up all their marketing rights in select potential sponsorship areas. Although few NOCs had a really developed marketing programme, this proposal was seen as a threat to their control. It meant ceding authority back to the IOC, and worse, working with an untried marketing agency.

Few NOCs were happy. It was like being back at the UN or EC negotiating tables, but this time we were pushing not just for a one-off agreement but for a whole new constitution. The NOCs that were generating any revenue from sponsors were deeply suspicious of the true motives of the TOP programme, expressing reservations about any initiative that would potentially 'milk the countries with the most potential'.

Strangely, there was also a sizeable group of NOCs who did not want to see a sudden increase in their financial support. A significant number received substantial funding from their governments. It was not in their interests to see the funding gap between government-funded comparatively wealthy NOCs and the competition closed. It would mean having to petition their governments to increase their own funding to stay ahead of the game.

The biggest battle of all was with the United States Olympic Committee (USOC), which jealously guarded its control over the Olympic trade marks in the US territory. Participation of the USOC in the TOP programme was absolutely critical – as many of the prospective sponsors were US-based.

Over three years, monthly meetings were held with the USOC. This was still the Cold War era. The USOC Executive Committee members wanted to know on what basis Olympic organisations in communist countries would receive sponsorship revenues from TOP. To American sports leaders the idea that funds from US corporations might be used to help fund communist sports training (as one member of the US Olympic Committee put it to me) was wholly inappropriate. The fact that many of their corporations were already trading in several of these countries, and sending their profits back to their US head offices that indirectly helped fund US athletes, was seen as totally irrelevant.

Slowly, very, very slowly, the NOCs were brought on board. All were offered a modest $10,000 payment spread over three to four years, and an additional $300 for every athlete they sent to the 1988 Games. About 20 NOCs who had some form of established marketing programme were offered financial guarantees by ISL to buy out their rights. Some of these guarantees ran into millions of dollars.

Some NOCs signed up with little comprehension of what the TOP programme was all about. Other NOCs took upwards of 50 individual rounds of negotiations, with long drawn-out arguments about the real economic value of their territory. Juergen Lenz, at ISL, was responsible for the overall Olympic project. If it were not for his permanently optimistic, but nevertheless stubborn Germanic approach, we may never have succeeded in getting all of the countries on board. In the end, the vast majority of NOCs signed up, 154 out of 167 signed. Only 13 NOCs refused – most, like Afghanistan, North Korea and Cuba, for political reasons.

## Seoul searching

Aside from a big question mark over whether we would succeed in bringing all the major NOCs on board, there was also considerable doubt about whether the 1988 Seoul Olympic Games would even take place.

The country was still technically at war with its neighbour. For the first few years following Seoul's election, the Soviet media questioned the decision and challenged the IOC to move the Games.[2] Although Soviet propaganda against Seoul eventually subsided, local student unrest in South Korea did not. Nightly news bulletins in the US showed violent student demonstrations. By 1987, these had reached hysteria level. Howard Cosell wrote in the New York *Daily News*: 'You read it here first. You read it this time last year. William Simon, former head of the United States Olympic Committee, told you. Peter Ueberroth, former head of the Los Angeles Olympic Games, told you. This reporter told you, too. We all told you that the 1988 Summer Olympics would never be held in Seoul, South Korea.

Not for the citizens of the US at least ... What does it take for the IOC to respond to the safety of its athletes?'[3]

Clearly, this was not an inspiring backdrop to convince companies to invest in the Olympic Movement and to use the Seoul Games as the focal point for their corporate hospitality programmes. Taking customers into a potential war zone lacks obvious commercial appeal. One TOP partner went so far as to send over body bags as part of its hospitality operations plan for the Seoul Games, just in case anyone needed to come back as cargo.

Even so, we carried on developing the programme. We drew up a list of more than 44 potential product categories to sell exclusive sponsorship rights to. The corporate sponsors had to be given clear instructions about which products and services they were the official sponsors for. The list had little to do with any true market evaluation and more to do with what each of the Olympic parties did not want to or could not sell. Hence categories like pretzels joined the list, alongside the more traditional areas of soft drinks (covered by Coca-Cola) and film (Kodak).

The financial modelling for the first TOP programme was even more arbitrary. There was no analysis of what the actual market place might be worth. Dassler decided that the programme could generate $300 million – the only thing he forgot to say was when. We sat around the conference table at Adidas' headquarters in Landersheim, France, with a mandate to make the numbers add up to $300 million. 'But what happens if they don't?' I asked. 'It doesn't matter, they will one day,' came the reply.

The individual pricing of the categories was even more haphazard. Members of an IOC committee set up to co-ordinate the TOP programme were asked by Dick Pound how much income they expected from any given category.[4] Each party gave its number, and we then added up the total. That was the pricing model and the full extent of the market research for what ultimately became the largest and most prestigious global marketing programme in the world.

## Spinning TOP

Predictably, the media's attitude towards TOP was decidedly mixed. It was seen as yet more commercialisation.[5] There was still a lingering nostalgia for the traditional values, the Corinthian spirit, no matter how unrealistic.

The critics were premature. We first had to sell the programme to corporations. If we couldn't persuade the business world to sign up there would be no TOP programme. This was a harder sell than anyone could have foreseen. Yet it began well.

Coca-Cola committed itself to Samaranch from the outset and joined the programme. However, it kept all its options open by making unilateral deals directly with each of the organising committees, and then sitting back and waiting for ISL to bring all the NOCs on board. Kodak and FedEx also signed fairly quickly but the sales momentum did not last very long. Months passed and nothing happened.[6] Every single sales approach was rejected, and doors slammed in our faces.

The Los Angeles Games were viewed by the public as a great success, but the feedback from within the business community was less positive. Some of the Los Angeles sponsors had been frustrated by their Olympic experience and the problems of activating their rights. Some, like Levi Strauss, simply decided to get out of the Olympic business all together.

The surprise $225 million profit declared by Los Angeles Committee president, Peter Ueberroth, after the Games did not help build business confidence in the Olympics. Several companies felt that they had been unduly squeezed to prevent the Committee from going bankrupt and embarrassing the US. Ueberroth even admitted how 'time and again we went back to them and asked for more. They always gave. We had them. They knew it.'

Other companies, like American Express, refused to believe we would ever get all the NOCs on board. They were sure we would have to break up the rights in the end, and that they would then be able to cherry-pick the key territories.

Samaranch appealed directly to Amex chairman James Robinson without success. Amex was certain it had no competitors who could step up to the programme. Rival firm Visa, an association of over 20,000 member banks, was seen as having too complex an organisational structure to make any global marketing decision.

I tried to sell Swiss Timing – Swatch – on the benefits of a global deal with the IOC, by implying that its competitor Seiko was ready to jump in. Manfred Laumann, president of Swiss Timing, called my bluff. He told me bluntly that I misunderstood the dynamics of the whole operation. 'You pay us to time the Olympics, we do not pay you!' As it turned out he was right. Seiko felt the Olympics was too big an undertaking and didn't return my calls. Swiss Timing was paid to time the Seoul Games.

At one stage, we got so desperate to create the necessary critical mass to kick-start the programme that we even offered certain TOP marketing rights free of charge to companies. IBM had already committed at a local level to the Calgary and Seoul Committees to provide basic technology support. We suggested that if IBM head office would support an approach to its individual local operating units to present the Olympic marketing opportunity, we would automatically make IBM a TOP partner, and give it the rights to the Olympic symbol for free. IBM sent us packing, saying that it was not interested in putting the Olympic symbol on computers.

Elsewhere, none of the big Korean companies – Samsung, Hyundai, Daewoo or GoldStar – came forward. They decided that, in 1986, they were not yet ready to take advantage of the global opportunities that TOP presented. Dentsu, the Japanese advertising giant and ISL's partner, was also not having much luck in persuading any Japanese companies to sign up.

## Visa accepted here

By late 1985, with just over two years to go until the Seoul Games, we were desperate. We only had three partners on board. After nearly three years of effort, Dassler and ISL had guaranteed millions of dollars to NOCs for their rights and yet companies were just not buying. Internally at ISL, it was recognised that if we didn't sign up at least two more partners by the following summer, the TOP programme would probably have to fold – and with it the IOC's attempt to create a marketing strategy.

Rob Prazmark was ISL's senior sales executive in the US. He was one of the best and most determined salesmen in the business. Prazmark never, ever gave up. He kept calling every company he could think of, trying to get his foot in the door to make the Olympic sales pitch.

One of Prazmark's calls was to Jan Soderstrom, Visa's vice president of marketing. Soderstrom had only recently joined Visa from computer games maker Atari. As a sponsor of the Los Angeles Games, Atari's experience had been disappointing. Not surprisingly Soderstrom was less than enthusiastic.

But the timing of Prazmark's call in late 1985 was perfect. The new management team at Visa was exploring how to move Visa upmarket. It was looking at ways to enhance its image in the upscale travel and entertainment markets – a consumer franchise long dominated by arch-rival American Express. Despite being accepted in three times as many locations around the world than Amex, Visa did not have the cachet of Amex. It wanted to become the corporate card for high-spending business expense accounts and reinforce its image of international acceptability. To do so, Visa wanted to create a unified international programme that all of its 20,000 member banks across 150 countries could use.

BBDO, Visa's ad agency, immediately saw the potential of an Olympic partnership. They relished the idea of an advertising campaign showing Olympic venues and athletes, ending with the tag line, 'and bring your Visa card, because the Olympics don't take American Express'. The challenge now was how to sell such an aggressive tag line to the Olympic parties, a habitually conservative group, many of whom were still cautious about TOP and the Movement's entry into sponsorship.

Despite her initial misgivings, Soderstrom quickly realised that 'the Olympics could be the ultimate merchant that takes Visa and not Amex'. We had Visa hooked. But landing a catch takes time and the Visa board was still struggling with the decision due to what they saw as sticker shock. While American Express paid $4 million for its Los Angeles sponsorship; Visa was being asked to pay $14.5 million for TOP. Even though it was a global programme including the Winter as well as the Summer Games, the price stuck in their throats. The Visa board needed persuading. Senior vice president for marketing John Bennett told his board that Visa was 'going to stick the blade into the ribs of American Express'. This was brutal, but persuasive. The board agreed, and instructed Bennett and Soderstrom to begin negotiations.

In early 1986, the Olympic parties and ISL met in New York for a regular TOP programme review meeting. Prazmark introduced the Visa team. John Bennett and Jan Soderstrom then proceeded to sell the IOC and the Olympic parties on why we should accept Visa as an Olympic partner. We were totally confused. We thought that we were the ones having to sell and yet here was a major blue chip international brand trying to sell us on why we should select them.

Visa joined the TOP programme. The decision paid off. John Bennett later reflected that 'the 1988 Olympic Games put us on the world stage and gave us tons of credibility. We were players. American Express gave up the ball.'[7]

## The end of the beginning

Rob Prazmark wasn't finished. He also organised a second surprise presentation at the New York meeting. This time it came from 3M, the sprawling conglomerate making more than 50,000 different products with a portfolio ranging from magnetic media to thermal insulation, from industrial reflective materials through to office supply products. Charles Eldridge, 3M's vice president of marketing, was also looking for a programme to unite its disparate workforce of 85,000 employees and 50 divisions. With such diversity and an appetite for change and innovation, 3M faced very specific communications challenges. It was better known for its individual brands (such as Post-It Notes) than as a dynamic global corporation. 3M had never been involved in any major sports sponsorship programme, for the simple reason that no programme had ever offered the necessary scope.

Eldridge understood that TOP and the Olympics could potentially provide 3M with the umbrella theme needed to build corporate awareness and unite all the divisions. 3M could adopt the Olympic ideals and merge them with its own success and commitment to innovation. 3M quickly became the fifth corporation to sign on.

Suddenly the TOP programme looked like it had turned the corner. The announcement by two major global companies – companies that had no track record of sports marketing – grabbed the market's attention and provided the IOC with the necessary critical mass to drive the programme forward. Four more companies joined TOP in the coming months: Dutch electronics giant, Philips; US publishing titan, Time-Sports Illustrated; along with Matsushita-Panasonic and Brother Industries from Japan.

In total, the first TOP programme attracted nine leading multinationals and generated around $95 million. But, perhaps the greatest success of the first programme was persuading virtually all of the NOCs to sign up to a centralised marketing programme and establishing the structures for a global marketing plan. Out of the 167 recognised NOCs at the time, 154 signed up. Only Greece, among the major developed markets, refused to participate. It opposed the commercialisation of the Olympic ideal as a matter of principle – somewhat hypocritical considering the profusion of Olympic trinkets and trash sold at the souvenir stalls around Olympia.[8]

There is no question that if Samaranch and the IOC, with Dassler's help, had not launched the plan when they did, it would have been virtually impossible to get all the countries together. Even partners like Coke and Kodak were sceptical about whether the IOC could really pull it off. 'It's been a major accomplishment for something that was deemed impossible,' Kodak's then marketing boss, John Barr told the media on the conclusion of TOP I.

Sadly, Horst Dassler died suddenly in April 1987 at the age of 51. He never saw his original vision for the future of Olympic marketing fully realised. However, he helped to establish the foundations of a programme that revolutionised the IOC's financial fortunes and changed the basis of sponsorship for the whole sports marketing industry.

## Membership is a privilege

Traditionally, sports sponsorship is based on advertising inside the venues and on the athlete's bib, with the goal of providing maximum brand recognition through the television broadcast. The Olympics is different. It is free of advertising. No commercial signs. No large brand logos. No hoardings or banners. This challenges marketing executives to approach the Olympics with a totally different mind set. It forces them to devise innovative and creative programmes.

Companies relying only on venue signage had become lazy, treating their sponsorship deal as a straight media buy and not trying to understand the true power and potential of the partnership.

Visa and 3M joined TOP with no pre-conceived ideas on sports sponsorship. They proceeded to re-write the sports marketing rule book, teaching many of the long-standing traditional sponsors how it should be done. They made the Olympics the core of their marketing strategies. They integrated it into their advertising, their public relations, their internal communications and on through to their product development.

In the credit card world, American Express dominated Asia. Carl Pascarella, CEO of Visa Asia Pacific, was anxious to change things. He had ambitious plans to open up China, Japan and Korea, and the 1988 Games in Seoul offered the perfect platform to improve Visa's image and market share. The Olympics provided Visa with the opportunity to develop its first co-ordinated advertising campaign across the region – and tackle Amex head on. In 1987, when Visa launched its Olympic marketing campaign, it was the number three card in Asia. Within three years, it overtook Amex to become the market leader.

Visa launched its first Olympic advertising campaign in Calgary with a series of hard-hitting advertisements that said that if you were going to the Games, 'bring your camera and your Visa card, because the Olympics don't take place all the time, and this time they don't take American Express'. Another ad noted: 'At the 1988 Winter Olympics, they will honour speed stamina and skill – but not American Express.'

On seeing the ads, American Express went ballistic, claiming that the adverts were misleading. As soon as Visa saw American Express' reaction, it knew that it was on to a winner. 'This is a clear signal that we're having an impact,' said John Bennett, Visa's marketing boss, 'It's a marketing war, and that's new to American Express.'

For Visa the pay-off was dramatic. Global sales volume for the first three years of its Olympic partnership increased 18 per cent against its own forecast of 12 per cent. Results from direct response campaigns and other promotions were 17 per cent higher when Olympic imagery was used. Card volume increased by 21 per cent during periods of Olympic promotion. Consumers who were aware of Visa's Olympic sponsorship had dramatically better views of Visa, doubling their perception of Visa as a good corporate citizen; a 50 per cent increase in attitudes of overall best card and use for international travel was also recorded.

The Olympics provided Visa with an overall marketing focus that it had never had before. Visa developed one of the most comprehensive marketing programmes centred on a sports sponsorship yet seen. The results had a major impact on Visa's bottom line.[9]

Since 1992, Visa's own market research has shown that the percentage of consumers calling Visa the best charge card has ballooned from 40 per cent to 63 per cent. That increase has helped pull Visa's market share from 40 per cent to 53 per cent.

It goes without saying that American Express rued the day it passed on the TOP programme. In 1996, I had dinner with James Robinson, who by now had retired as chairman and CEO of American Express. He admitted that losing the Olympics was one of the worst, if not the worst, mistake that he made at Amex. The media concurred, calling it 'the greatest marketing blunder in its history'.[10]

The TOP programme also paid off for 3M.[11] It used the awareness of the Olympic rings to break down the anonymity of its brand, which had been particularly acute in Europe. The Olympics gave 3M instant brand recognition with the consumer. It provided a platform to unite all its employees, across the many diverse divisions and product areas, creating for the first time an environment and culture to talk across business areas. 'Sponsoring the Olympics allows us to integrate our worldwide marketing programmes to support selling efforts in highly competitive markets and increase our visibility where we are less well known,' announced Don Osmon, vice-president of marketing and public affairs, when 3M joined.

## Twin peaks

The commercial success of the Seoul sponsorship deals gave real momentum to the second TOP programme for the 1992 Albertville and Barcelona Games.[12] TOP II nearly doubled its revenue base to $175 million and all but a handful of NOCs signed up.

The sales effort continued to present unique challenges. In his enthusiasm to close the sale, Rob Prazmark occasionally drifted from the set script with creative ideas as to how a partner might activate their Olympic involvement and get the full return on their investment.

Bausch & Lomb chairman Dan Gill was sold on an Olympic partnership on the basis of his personal involvement in the medal awards ceremony. Prazmark suggested to Bausch & Lomb that they produce a special set of commemorative Ray-Ban sun glasses in gold, silver and bronze, for the medal winners at each Games. Seeing that Bausch & Lomb was interested in the concept, Prazmark went for closure.

He suggested that the glasses could be presented as part of the official medals award ceremony. The IOC has over time developed a very strict set of protocols for the award of medals. No deviation from the carefully choreographed ceremony is permitted. An IOC member leads a small, formal delegation out to the centre of the stadium to award the Olympic medals. The IOC member is accompanied by a single representative of the International Federation who presents flowers to each athlete, after the IOC member hangs the medal around their neck. Prazmark decided that it was now time to embellish the protocol by proposing that next, Dan Gill, chairman of Bausch & Lomb, should step forward, in front of the world's television viewing public, and place the gold, silver and bronze glasses on the athletes' noses. Not surprisingly Gill and Bausch & Lomb jumped at the idea; the IOC did not.

Prazmark called me with the good news. 'We have a new partner on board,' he said before explaining about a 'minor' rights detail that might need to be sorted out. I am not sure how we explained the dilemma to Dick Pound. He was tasked with going to visit Dan Gill in Rochester, New York, Bausch & Lomb's headquarters, to welcome the company into the TOP programme. At the same time, Pound diplomatically told Gill that he was not going to be part of the medals awards ceremony and not stand in front of the world's TV audience. Pound, as usual, delivered and Bausch & Lomb still signed up.[13]

## That dog won't hunt

The TOP III Programme paired the Winter Games in Lillehammer with the Summer Games in Atlanta. Total revenues grew to $376 million.

When Billy Payne, president of the Atlanta Olympic Bid Committee, began to conceive the idea of trying to bring the Centennial Games to Atlanta, not surprisingly one of the first companies he turned to was Coca-Cola. Atlanta was defined worldwide as the headquarters of the world's largest soft drinks company, and Coca-Cola was the biggest and one of the most active sponsors of the Olympic Movement. Coca-Cola could trace its involvement with the Games back to 1928, when it sent over 1,000 cases of Coke to Amsterdam with the US Olympic team.[14] Former Coke president and CEO, Paul Austin, even competed at the 1936 Berlin Olympic Games as a member of the US rowing team.

Coca-Cola, though, was well aware of the dangers of being seen to support one particular Olympic bid over any other city. It was especially wary of any attempt to involve it in a bid with its own headquarters city. It was, after all, a global company. In the early 1970s Atlanta had considered bidding for the Games and bid leaders had approached Paul Austin. Austin rejected the idea out of hand, throwing the bid team out of his office. He did not want to risk alienating Coke customers around the world.

Coke chairman Roberto Goizueta took much the same approach when Billy Payne tried to pin him and Coca-Cola down for their support for the Atlanta bid. When Atlanta finally did beat Athens by 51 to 35 votes, at the IOC Session in Tokyo, Gary Hite, Coke's sports marketing boss, summed up the situation: 'Everyone is going to be thinking that Coke bought the Olympics for Atlanta. If anything we did not want it in Atlanta. We wanted it somewhere else.'

Several months before the IOC Session, I suggested to Gary Hite the idea of producing a special commemorative set of pins. Olympic pins had become the most popular Olympic souvenir – practically a currency in their own right. Creating a special pin commemorating the winning city would become a special and valuable Olympic collector's item. Immediately following the announcement, the plan was to have Coke hostesses hand out the pin of the winning city to the 2,000 guests in the hall of the Takanawa Prince Hotel, where the IOC Session was taking place.

Hite liked the idea. It was a simple public relations stunt that would get Coke some publicity and reinforce the company's long-standing Olympic role and international perspective. Coke produced six pins, one for each of the bidding cities: Athens, Atlanta, Belgrade, Manchester, Melbourne and Toronto. Each Coke hostess was given a bag of 2,000 pins of each city, with the instruction to just hand out the pin of the winning city, straight after the announcement. We had thought through all the scenarios – except one, Atlanta winning!

Atlanta entered the IOC Session as a dark horse and not many people gave the city a chance. Nobody thought through what in hindsight was the glaringly obvious: the immediate reaction of the guests, especially the Greeks, on being given a Coke Atlanta 1996 Games pin. Their reaction, understandable in the circumstances, on leaving the ceremony was, 'How could Coke have produced them so quickly? Coca-Cola must have known. There must have been a fix!' What a blunder.

Within seconds of the announcement that Atlanta had beaten Athens for the right to host the symbolic Centennial Games, the Greeks looked for their scapegoat.[15] Coke quickly became the culprit. Coke had stolen their right to the Games. The media jumped at the story. It was fuelled by statements from Greek delegates like Melina Mercouri, the Oscar winning movie star, and then Greece's Culture Minister, such as 'Coca-Cola has won over the Parthenon' and 'this will be the Coca-Cola Olympics'.

Coke's Gary Hite and I immediately tried to grab a few complete sets of pins of all the cities and thrust them into the hands of the communications team. We wanted to show the media that no matter which city won, Coke had prepared a commemorative pin. But it was too late. The damage had been done. The headlines the following day were negative: 'Money and power triumph over sentiment ... And a Coke bottle belching sacred Olympic flames.'

Coke bottles were cracked open in the streets of Athens and poured into the sewers. Coke's market share in Greece took a dive, taking years to recover. The IOC, the Atlanta organisers and Coke spent the next seven years trying to dispel the perception that Coke had bought the Games. Andy Young, the chairman of the Atlanta Organising Committee and former US ambassador to the United Nations, repeatedly denied the accusation, using the old-fashioned southern-Georgia expression of, 'that dog won't hunt'. Doug Ivester, who succeeded Goizueta as Coke chairman, told journalists time and time again that Coke 'did not need the Olympics in Atlanta – it could be anywhere.'

## Blink and you might lose

Over the years, Olympic negotiations were littered with casualties – companies who blinked, and let their competition step in to take over the rights. As with the Games, there are losers as well as winners.

In 1982, Peter Ueberroth had been trying for over a year to close a $4 million sponsorship deal with Kodak. Someone in Kodak's finance department worked out that for each week they delayed signing the contract, they were saving the company several thousand dollars in interest charges. Ueberroth's patience eventually ran out, and he turned to a senior executive at the Japanese advertising agency, Dentsu, for help. Reiji Hattori had begun to understand the power of sports as a tool to build brand recognition for his clients around the world (and is credited by many as the founding father of Japanese sports marketing). Ueberroth proposed to Hattori that he pitch the Olympic sponsorship to Fuji Film. He gave him a week to succeed.

Hattori knew that it was impossible for Fuji to take a decision that quickly. Hattori also knew that the Olympics could be the key vehicle to open up the US market for Fuji, so he told Ueberroth that Dentsu would take the sponsorship and they would work out later how to deal with the issue with their client.[16] In the interim, Hattori, with the help of a young executive at Dentsu, Haroshi Takahashi, set about explaining to his own board just exactly what they had gone and done.[17] Hattori stayed in Los Angeles for two weeks, long after the deal had been signed with Ueberroth, and did not dare return home to Tokyo until he was sure that Takahashi had settled everything with the Dentsu board.

Kodak executives were apoplectic with rage when they learnt that the company had lost the Olympic rights in its own home market. Kodak embarked on an aggressive public relations campaign against Ueberroth and the Los Angeles organisers. The thrust of the press campaign was that Eastman Kodak, a great American company, had expressed its willingness and interest in sponsoring the Olympics, but the grubby guys from LA only wanted to talk money.

Ueberroth responded in a press release explaining how sponsors were selected – and, to ensure no one missed the point, headlined the press release, 'How Kodak lost the Olympics'. The Kodak executive who had decided to delay signing the contract lost his job, and went on to try and sue, unsuccessfully, the Organising Committee for his plight.

Fuji went on to build its market share in the US from three per cent to nine per cent in a couple of years on the back of its Olympic sponsorship, despite vociferous competition from Kodak.[18] When the Olympic rights came up for renewal a few years later, Kodak made sure it did not blink a second time.

Other companies have paid the price of not hanging onto Olympic rights. American Express, years after it had lost the rights to Visa, is still licking its wounds and will be doing so for a while longer, as Visa has extended its Olympic partnership out through 2012.

Another company which eventually jumped at the Olympic opportunity when given the chance was Korean electronics giant Samsung. Motorola was a long-standing local Olympic partner and, after the 1996 Olympic Games, decided that the time had come to upgrade to a full global TOP partnership.

Negotiations dragged on for months, but eventually an agreement was reached. Then, a couple of weeks before the deal was scheduled to be formally signed, the senior vice president of Motorola's mobile division called me at home, late on a Friday evening. There was 'a small problem, with the deal,' he said. They had looked through all the numbers, they wanted to proceed, but could only now offer half the agreed sum – a reduction of tens of millions of dollars.

Motorola's real motives were far from clear. The company knew that we could not deliver global Olympic marketing rights at this level. After expressing surprise at its negotiation tactics, I responded that the IOC would think about Motorola's proposal and, if there was any interest, we would call them back. Motorola fully expected that we would call back the following week and hold further negotiations leading to a substantial reduction over the original agreed sum.

The IOC never called Motorola back. Instead, we immediately let Samsung know that an opportunity had opened up and it had three days to get to Lausanne. If the Korean company could conclude a deal on the spot, then it could join the TOP programme.

Samsung dispatched a senior team of negotiators to Switzerland. Three days of round-the-clock negotiations led to an agreement. A few weeks later, Samaranch and I flew to Seoul to formally sign the agreement and announce the partnership to the world. The first Motorola knew that it had lost the Olympic rights was when it read in the press that Samsung was the newest Olympic sponsor. At the time, though, even the Korean media were astonished that the IOC had chosen Samsung to be the Olympic wireless communications partner. In 1997, Samsung had only a limited presence in international markets in mobile phones. Six years later Samsung unseated Motorola for the number two slot in the mobile communications market.[19] At the time Samsung joined TOP, Interbrand ranked the company 96th in its global brand survey; by 2004 it was 21st. Today, it is a premium brand with technology leadership and one of the biggest net incomes in the world.

## Connecting with customers

With all the inherent complications and challenges, it's important to remember why companies spend tens of millions of dollars sponsoring the Olympics. The bottom-line is that they do so because they hope it will make them more money. Whether as a consumer or a key business client, whether you are in central China or downtown Manhattan, nothing has provided sponsors with a stronger or more powerful unified global platform to connect with their customers than the Olympics.[20]

Market research continually underlines this point. One study by US broadcaster NBC found that 85 per cent of viewers saw Olympic sponsors as leaders, with 80 per cent of them seen as committed to excellence and quality.

Part of the power of the appeal of the Olympics is passion. 'People are passionate about the Games,' is how Coke sports marketing boss Scott McCune begins to rationalise the basis for his company's Olympic involvement. 'It is a great vehicle for us to develop a relationship with the consumers.'

In a blunt appraisal of Coca-Cola's marketing strategy, senior Coke executive Stu Cross explains that: 'We have to constantly market our beverage in a way that creates the impression that there's more than just the liquid in the package, something refreshing the spirit. The Olympics do that for us. All that fun and excitement, and global nature accrues to an image that, at a given point in time, makes people pick our product up, versus a lot of other choices that they have out there.'

Over the years, Coke has developed a series of on-site promotional, experiential marketing activities. These range from Olympic pin collecting, which in Salt Lake City alone attracted 460,000 visitors, to themed sporting attractions that give families the chance to try out different Olympic sports – from push starting an Olympic bobsleigh to curling. The goal is not to sell more Coke the following day necessarily. Instead the strategy is about providing memorable experiences for consumers, restaurant executives, retailers and bottlers, that pay off over the long term in increased brand loyalty.

The TOP programme, with its sponsorship of each national Olympic team, presented the opportunity for companies to embrace a truly local image, shedding the perception of always being the big US multinational. 'The Olympics enhance Kodak's image as a world leader in the photographic industry, but at the same time enhance its image as a local company, be it in Germany, Australia, the UK, Canada or wherever we have operations,' notes John Barr, the Kodak marketing executive who led its negotiations to get back into the Olympics, and one of the first to see the true potential of the local partnership. When the Olympics returned to Japan in 1998, for the Nagano Winter Games, Kodak set about avenging its loss, 14 years earlier in Los Angeles.[21]

Sometimes the Olympic connection is a little too successful, as McDonald's discovered with one of its 1984 Los Angeles Olympic promotions. A scratch card promotion, with the name of an Olympic event, ran throughout the US, with the customer winning a prize every time a US athlete won a medal. The promotion was obviously designed before the Soviets decided to boycott the Games. Unfortunately, no one bothered to recalculate the potential medal haul of the US team.

Within a few days, stores were running out of prizes, as the US team results outpaced supply. 'This is the most successful Games, but it is also the most costly,' McDonald's executives reflected once the Olympics were over.

Nearly twenty years later in Sydney, McDonald's made the same mistake. This time the company underestimated the potential success of the Australian team. McDonald's ran another scratch card competition, offering free burgers for sports depicted on the cards that match Australian gold medal winning events. When Simon Fairweather won a surprise gold for Australia in the men's archery event, McDonald's faced a claim for an additional 140,000 free hamburgers at a cost of over $200,000.

## The world's largest stage

With the whole world watching, the Olympic Games have become a unique platform for companies to launch new technologies, new ideas, new thinking, and to prove that they can perform and deliver under the most difficult and testing of environments.

Kodak used the Olympics as its main vehicle to remind the world of the power and potential of imaging – from the amateur photographer through to professional diagnostic imaging expert. In Sydney, Kodak established a state-of-the-art health imaging centre in the athletes village, allowing athletes not only to receive the latest diagnosis on the spot, but also remote intercontinental consultation between the team doctor at the Games and any specialist back in the athlete's home country. Kodak conducted 1,948 diagnostic exams for 1,410 athletes over three weeks. With the world media looking on, the Games provided Kodak with a rare opportunity to talk about and present the future of medical diagnostics to a global audience.

3M used its TOP sponsorship to launch a new global marketing campaign designed to reinforce the image of the company as an innovator of new ideas, new products and new thinking. 3M focused on athletes who had smashed barriers in their sport with a totally new approach – such as Dick Fosbury's revolutionary new approach to high jumping, first seen at the Mexico Games in 1968. The campaign proved an excellent example of how a sponsor could highlight its corporate philosophy by a direct association with the Olympic values.

Both Coke and Visa used the Atlanta Games to test new smart cards – Coke with vending and wireless inventory monitoring, and Visa with their new stored value cards – prompting the *Wall Street Journal* to note that 'To corporations, the Olympics represents a mini test market'.

Value in kind services and support from sponsors now account for over 50 per cent of any organising committee's sponsorship budget. What started out as companies donating free product has been transformed into a kind of exhibition for new products and brands. The 1964 Tokyo organisers turned to Japanese industry to donate products for the Games and more than one hundred companies answered the call, providing the committee with everything from 9,200 rolls of Daishowa toilet paper to Sanyo hair driers.

By the 1980 Lake Placid Winter Olympic Games, more than 200 companies were involved. The Organising Committee found itself with a lifetime's supply of chapstick and yoghurt, but only $25 million in sponsorship revenue to run the Games.

Over the years, sponsors have been quick to respond to opportunities to gain global media coverage by taking advantage of sudden last-minute requests. McDonald's launched its Olympic involvement when an executive watching ABC's telecast from the 1968 Olympic Winter Games in Grenoble learned that the one thing the US athletes wanted was a burger and fries. A large shipment was immediately airlifted to the US team.

Another US company which undertook an airlift to those in desperate need was Hanes, the US clothing company. Its president, Jim DeRose, watched CBS's Olympic telecast from Lillehammer and learned of the thousands of visitors who were unable to get their underwear washed because of a shortage of public laundries. DeRose promptly dispatched 47 cases of underwear to Norway.

At the 2000 Olympic Games in Sydney, Ansell delivered what it thought would be a sufficient quantity of condoms to the athletes' village. The batch of 100,000 ran out after just a few days and urgent orders for a further 400,000 were made. Somehow, each athlete used 50 condoms.

## Jockeying for position

The Games have become not only a platform for launching new products and new systems, but have also helped companies launch whole new corporate position statements. With increasing sensitivity to environmental issues, the Games have become a showcase for sponsors to show their commitment towards environmental issues and the efforts that they are taking to change their way of doing business.[22]

For the same reason that sponsors are attracted to the Games, so are specialist interest groups. Various groups have used the Games to get their message across, singling out Olympic sponsors to get everyone's attention to the issue at hand. In Atlanta, the gay rights movement descended on Coke and other sponsors, demanding a nationwide boycott of their products if the issue of the location of one of the sports venues was not resolved within a week. Human rights groups and others are carefully watching China's Olympic journey towards 2008 and how critical social issues are dealt with.

Environmental groups like Greenpeace have used the Games to encourage multinationals to speed up adoption of better environmental practices.

Campaigner Michael Bland admitted that, 'the sponsors have a special set of obligations that are not necessarily taken on by anyone else.'[23]

Three months before the Sydney Games, on 1st June, Greenpeace launched a global internet campaign against Coca-Cola for undermining the environmental guidelines of the Sydney 2000 Games and for its worldwide use of HFC gases, with the headline-grabbing and aggressive slogan – 'Green Olympics, Dirty Sponsors'.[24] The campaign featured polar bears, one of Coke's icon symbols, struggling to find a block of ice in the Arctic, due to global climate change.

After four weeks of protests by Greenpeace outside Coke's offices in Australia, and a global campaign against the company, Coca-Cola announced that it would phase out potent greenhouse gasses from all of its refrigeration systems worldwide by the Athens Games in 2004. Within a matter of weeks, Coca-Cola went from being Greenpeace's public enemy number one to being lauded as a role model for the rest of the industry.[25]

## Invitation of a lifetime

For corporate sponsors the message isn't simply an external one. They also use their Olympic involvement internally. The insurance company John Hancock pioneered Olympic hospitality as an internal marketing tool for its sales force. In Lillehammer 1994, John Hancock saw the number of salesman qualifying for its sales incentive, once a trip to the Olympic Games was identified as the prize, increase by 47 per cent generating an additional $60 million in revenues.

Rewarding employees with Olympic trips is the glamorous tip of the iceberg. Communicating Olympic involvement internally can radically improve employee perceptions. The boost to employee morale from UPS's first Olympic experience was so strong that, by the Sydney Games, the company devoted more than 50 per cent of its Olympic marketing budget to employee communications.

UPS also became one of the first sponsors to realise the value of having Olympic hopefuls in its workforce. Soon after it signed up as an Olympic sponsor, it discovered that there were 24 potential Olympians on its staff worldwide. The idea came about after a Houston-based marathon coach, Al Lawrence, who was training Melissa Hurt, a UPS driver based in Angleton, Texas, wrote to her employer asking for help. 'I wanted to train for the Olympics and keep my job', Melissa recalled, 'and my coach saw I was killing myself trying to do both.' UPS developed a programme called Olympic Hopefuls. It provided its athletes with flexible working arrangements, including time off to train for the Olympics, and sports equipment. Nine UPS employees went to the Games as members of their various national Olympic teams.

A number of partners have found the Olympics a useful recruitment vehicle. For example, IBM realised that when it started talking to students about what it was doing to develop the technology systems for the Olympic Games in the mid-1990s, it was viewed as a younger, more dynamic and innovative company. The Olympic association helped it shed its image of a stiff organisation, with starched white shirts and blue suits.

## The results

One of the best testaments to the success of TOP is the programme's 90 per cent plus rate of renewal – virtually unheard of within the industry. With corporate expenditures coming under ever increasing scrutiny, the fact that the partners have repeatedly committed hundreds of millions of dollars, and a sizeable proportion of their global marketing budget, to the programme speaks for itself. It says that TOP has been delivering the necessary results to the corporate bottom line.

Initially many media and industry commentators judged sponsorship success on the basis of name recall – whether the consumer could name the sponsor of an event. After the Games, various research agencies would rush out a quick recall study. These had more to do with getting the agency's name in the press than any serious academic analysis. The studies missed the point about why a company sponsored the Olympics and the broader strategies that were involved with each programme. It was like asking TV viewers if they could remember which companies advertised on television the previous night, and then judging the success of the commercials on whether the viewers could recall the advertisers.

'Recall might be good for the consumer-based products, but the important thing for us it to raise awareness in the business-to-business market,' was Rosemary Windsor Williams, UPS Olympic director's reaction to the various recall studies. Even consumer marketers like Visa questioned the value of sponsor recognition as a criterion for success. 'We monitor our brand globally and, frankly, the key determinants of our success are card preference and usage, and incremental volume as a result of our sponsorship activities – not awareness.'

A research study carried out during the Atlanta Games to see how sponsors evaluated the success of their Olympic programmes identified the four most important aspects as: first, hospitality opportunities; second, sales; third, media coverage; and fourth, image and public perception. The absence of sponsorship awareness from the list was not lost on the researchers who noted that: 'Surprisingly, sponsorship awareness ranks the lowest among all evaluation criteria.'

Name recall research gave a false picture of the value of sponsorship. The bottom line is that sponsors do not go into the Olympics for recall. Who cares about recall when your market share goes up five per cent directly as a result of the Olympics? Several Olympic partners, particularly those who made the Olympics the core of their marketing strategies, have been able to show strong results and prove the power of the Olympics as a marketing tool.

When Visa began its Olympic adventure, it trailed Amex as the true card for international travel in terms of brand image and perception. Although Visa enjoyed a 42.7 per cent market share in terms of the number of cards issued, against Amex with 21.9 per cent, Visa was just not pulling its weight in the high-spending expense account and travel revenue. Within a few years, Visa had overtaken Amex as the global travel card. The industry grew at an annual compound growth rate of 16 per cent, but Visa's brand perception grew at over 50 per cent after 1986, the year Visa joined the TOP programme.

UPS reported how the power of the Olympic rings and related imagery delivered compelling business results, with 'direct mail promotions before the Atlanta Games (using the Olympics as a promotional platform) bringing in results three to four times higher than any previous campaign.' Bausch & Lomb reported similar results of how an Olympic-themed promotion would always outperform any other promotion that the company ran.

Sponsors saw particularly dramatic results in host countries, even where they already enjoyed a dominant position. Coke, for example, announced an increase of 20 per cent in Norway after the Lillehammer Games; equal to $170 million per month. Visa reported a 42 per cent increase in card holder usage in Australia in the lead up to and through the Sydney Games.[26]

John Hancock saw equally strong results from its Olympic promotions. The insurer enjoyed a 12 per cent increase in purchase consideration after its first Olympic involvement with the Lillehammer Games. It also saw significant increases in company's corporate brand equity – as a successful and energetic company, dedicated to excellence, highly reputable and an industry leader.[27] A classic example of how Olympic brand values could be transferred to support the sponsoring brand.

## Ensuring success

The TOP programme became the most successful global marketing programme in the world, establishing itself as the benchmark for the sponsorship industry. It revolutionised the IOC's financial fortunes, bringing in the financial and promotional muscle of some of the world's greatest corporations. Yet, at the outset, no-one believed in the programme and it very nearly did not happen.

Experience suggests that successful sponsors share a number of characteristics. First, they have clear objectives and then build a programme to help achieve those objectives. They then regularly track progress and are not fearful of making mid-stream adjustments if things aren't going to plan. The sponsorship is integrated into their overall business objectives and way of doing business. It is fully supported from the top down. And, they understand the Olympic brand and what it stands for.

It was this final point which increasingly became the centre of the IOC's focus. Through necessity, we had created the two commercial pillars on which we could build. Next, we needed to really understand what we were selling: which parts of the Olympic brand were sacred and could not on any account be damaged by misplaced commercial programmes.

The IOC was the steward of the Olympic flame. To protect it, we had to truly understand what made the Olympics special. We had to be clear about what the rings really stood for. It was only in this way that we could preserve them for future generations. Getting it wrong would be fatal.

## NOTES

1 This was Samaranch's second attempt to remove Berlioux. In 1981, he obtained the IOC Board's approval to dismiss her before one senior member got cold feet. Berlioux went on to become sports advisor to the then Mayor of Paris, Jacques Chirac.

2 In November 1984, *Sovietsky Sport* wrote: 'It is really not too late to correct the blunder [the selection of Seoul] made three years ago. Is it not better to decide now once and for all in advance not to go as far as a new Los Angeles nightmare?' *Izvestia* stated that the IOC should not delay in transferring the Games from Seoul.

3 The *New York Post* went even further: 'There is blood on the streets of Korea these days, but apparently even in 1987 word is sent by sea. Nobody at the IOC in landlocked Switzerland has blinked an amateur eyelid.'

4 The committee was the MCM which stood for Marketing Co-Ordination Meeting. It became the effective oversight management board for the TOP Programme until the IOC took over total control of the programme for TOP IV.

5 In the UK, the *Guardian* newspaper wrote of the 'once lordly IOC climbing down into the marketplace'. The *Financial Times* said that 'the modern benefactors of the Olympics are the TOP partners'. The *International Herald Tribune*, though, began to examine and explore the true power of what TOP could offer, writing, 'If the battle of Waterloo was won on the playing fields of Eton, it may be that the international trade wars of the 1990s and beyond will be decided at the 1988 Olympic Games in Seoul and Calgary ... an ambitious programme, in which companies are seeking a marketing edge by securing exclusive rights to the Olympic rings.' Elsewhere the *Berner Zeitung* and the *Zurich Tages Anzeiger* expressed concerns about allowing commerce to compromise ideals. 'The Olympic Games must take a step back or else money and commerce will stamp out the Olympic ideal once and for all,' wrote the former, while the latter newspaper headlined

its editorial: 'Money Games – Big money made the Olympics artificial and sterile.' Meanwhile, the *Daily Telegraph* observed: 'The soul of the Olympic Movement is being devoured by avarice and the IOC would do well to remember the effect that had on the ancient Games.'

6　Kodak traces its Olympic involvement back to 1896 when it helped fund the official results books with a page of advertising. But the company was still smarting from losing the Los Angeles sponsorship to Fuji and seeing its US market share slip under a barrage of Olympic marketing initiatives from its Japanese competitor. Kay Whitmore, chairman of Kodak, made it clear that: 'We are not going to take the kind of beating the auto companies have.' He was anxious to get back into the Olympics. The sponsorship deal with Kodak was one of the fastest Olympic rights negotiations on record. It involved a few calls in the middle of the night during the Los Angeles Games from ISL and Kodak was back on board. Fuji baulked at the asking price for TOP and lost its place.

7　Rick Bush, Visa's Asia ad manager talked of how 'the Olympics were an amazing tool. They gave us instant credibility across Asia. We were playing with the big boys, Coke, Kodak and the rest.'

8　13 NOCs chose not to participate in TOP 1: Greece, Afghanistan, Albania, Burma, Cuba, Iraq, Kuwait, Libya, Mongolia, North Korea, Qatar, Yemen Arab Republic and Venezuela.

9　For Malcolm Williamson, president and CEO of Visa International, 'the Olympic Games truly are a global event that transcends sport. No other sponsorship opportunity compares with them in offering a combination of international exposure, broad-based audience and a wide range of events with global appeal.'

10　Other competitors looked enviously on. Norman J. Tice, chairman emeritus of MasterCard International, observed: 'Visa has very appropriately capitalised on the rings and absolutely used them as an important part of its global campaign to develop new market share at the expense of American Express.'

11　Don Linehan, a senior marketing executive at 3M, oversaw their Olympic marketing effort, and commented: 'If they could get into the Olympics or the World Cup, we could achieve impact on the consumer market. Our turnover (prior to the Olympic sponsorship) was $10 billion ... now, perhaps partly as a consequence (of our sponsorship), our turnover has risen (in four years) to $13.5 billion.'

12  TOP II attracted 12 partners. Federal Express bowed out, having never really successfully integrated the Olympics into its global marketing strategy. FedEx handed much of the implementation over to a collection of public relations agencies. They were too concerned about getting FedEx to develop numerous side programmes at great expense, instead of focusing on what they had already acquired. FedEx was replaced by the US Postal Service, which set out with a vision to use the TOP programme to try to unite the world's postal systems with a new courier/express package service to challenge DHL and FedEx. Three other partners joined – Mars, in the confectionary category; Ricoh from Japan, which went on to help the IOC establish the first ever global fax network; and Bausch & Lomb, the US optical and dental conglomerate, best known for its Ray-Ban brand of sunglasses.

13  Among other things, Bausch & Lomb set up eye and dental care clinics in each of the athlete villages at the Olympic Games. Bausch & Lomb found that an amazing 50 per cent of all athletes had never received a ' complete visual examination, and established a series of tests to help athletes according to their specific sport. Ice hockey players were found to have an eye–hand co-ordination speed on average 10 per cent faster than all other Winter Olympians.

14  In 1929, Robert Woodruff, president of Coca-Cola, published a special edition of the company's newsletter, 'The Red Barrel', citing Coke's growing presence throughout the world, 'few Americans realise that Coca-Cola is now found within the bull fight arenas of sunny Spain and Mexico, at the Olympic Games stadium below the dykes of Holland, atop the Eiffel Tower above 'Gay Paree', on the holy pagoda in distant Burma, and beside the Colosseum of historic Rome'. Coca-Cola's product support grew from the 1,000 cases in Amsterdam to over 10 million drinks in Sydney, 72 years later – enough, according to the PR executives, to fill the 50 metre Olympic Pool at the Olympic Park complex in Homebush, one and a half times.

15  The Greeks later acknowledged that they had run a poor bid campaign for the 1996 Games, assuming that hosting the Centennial Games was their birthright and that the IOC had to give them the Games. Although

there was tremendous sympathy within the IOC membership towards awarding the Games to Greece, there was also a realisation that Greece was just not ready for the challenge, with non-stop political infighting and a city lacking much of the basic capital infrastructure to stage the Games. By the time Greece bid again, in 1997 for the 2004 Games, some of that basic infrastructure such as the new airport had been built and there was an appreciation that staging the Games requires a united national effort.

16  This decision by Dentsu, and the process to take on the sponsorship of the Olympics for their client, provides a fascinating insight into the unique workings of the relationship leading Japanese ad agencies enjoyed with their clients – with the agency often becoming the de facto marketing department of the company.

17  Hayashi Takashi became overall director of Dentsu's sports division and perhaps the most influential marketing executive in Japan in sports and event related matters.

18  Fuji president, Minoru Ohnishi talked of how the Olympics was a 'cheap advertising expense for the worldwide publicity it entitled us to'.

19  By late 2004, Samsung had overtaken Motorola in terms of both global revenue and market share, and set its sights on unseating market leader Nokia. It recorded profits of $2.7 billion on revenue of $12 billion for first quarter 2004. Il Hyung Chang, Samsung's senior vice president and head of their Olympic project, talked of how their Olympic partnership 'has proved a powerful marketing tool ... Through our programmes, we demonstrated our leadership in wireless communications technology globally and leveraged our key business strategies for the twenty-first century. We had a second-tier brand awareness, which is why we utilised the Olympics to make people more aware of us. Being a sponsor means we're world class.' Chang recognised that Samsung had entered the wireless game as a latecomer. 'We are a little late in the telecommunications industry compared to Ericsson, Nokia and Motorola and we have to catch up the gap through Olympic sponsorship.'

20  David D'Alessandro, chairman and CEO of insurance giant, John Hancock summed up the sponsorship proposition in his book *Brand*

*Warfare*: 'However crucial advertising is, it has one severe limitation as a brand-building tool. You are asking something of consumers – that they pay attention to your message and buy your products – without giving them very much in return. Sponsorships, on the other hand, offer consumers a much more even exchange ... By contributing to something that the consumers value, you may win their interest and respect, perhaps even their gratitude. Ideally they see the glamour, the excitement and emotion of the event or person you are sponsoring as attributes of your brand as well. Well chosen and well managed sponsorship can move your brand forward more dramatically than almost any other marketing activity. And the Olympics are absolutely unique – the only sponsorship that delivers a mass audience and at the same time qualifies as a good cause in consumer's eyes.'

21 'We've always seen an up-tick in revenues in brand awareness after the Olympics,' Carl Gustin, Kodak's chief marketing officer claimed, 'and what could be better than making a splash in Fuji territory?'

22 UPS used the Games to test and present its first hundred vehicles to be powered by clean-burning compressed natural gas and launched new package envelopes with Olympic imagery, as the first example of colour printing on recycled board. Considering that UPS have a global vehicle fleet of over 85,000 vehicles, and consumes 100 million express envelopes annually, these were small, but not insignificant long-term contributions to the environment.

23 On occasions environmental groups singled out marketing activity just because the company was an Olympic sponsor. In Sydney, local banking sponsor Westpac was taken to task by Greenpeace over an Olympic toy mascot box promotion. Westpac ended up having to withdraw 150,000 premium toy boxes bearing the Olympic marks, because the product breached PVC guidelines by containing phthalates which could potentially be harmful to children. The fact that the premiums had been developed, based on advice from the Australian Toy Association, and were widely used by other companies, did not matter.

24 HFCs are chemicals invented as a substitute for CFCs and HCFCs – ozone destroying gases that are being phased out worldwide. HFCs are mainly used in the refrigeration and air conditioning industries.

On average, over 20 years one tonne of HFC has 3,300 times more global warming potential than one tonne of carbon dioxide.

25  In Sydney, Coke dispensed all drinks in 100 per cent biodegradeable cups for the first time.

26  Local sponsors also benefitted. Southcorp Wine recorded 32% growth and AMP saw sales in certain sectors increase by 40% on the back of Olympic sponsorship.

27  John Hancock's research results: successful 71%; vital and energetic 60%; dedicated to excellence 36%; industry leader 27%; highly reputable 27%.

**Plate 1**  Olympic marketing always provided great inspiration for the world's cartoonists. (© Raymond Burki.)

**Plate 2**  Cathy Freeman, Sydney 2000, anxiously waiting for the technicians to unblock the Olympic cauldron. (© Getty Images.)

**Plate 3**    Samaranch and Horst Dassler sign the initial agreement creating TOP. (© Olympic Museum.)

**Plate 4**    The NBC Olympic team: David Neal, executive vice president; Dick Ebersol, chairman; and Bob Costas, prime time show host. (© Getty Images.)

**Plate 5**  Marc Hodler (centre) fields questions during the Salt Lake crisis, watched by an anxious Mitt Romney, leader of the Salt Lake Committee, and Gilbert Felli, IOC executive director. (© Getty Images.)

**Plate 6**  For those who suggest that recent commercialisation corrupted the Olympic ideal: the official Olympic cigarette from 1968. (© Olympic Museum.)

**Plate 7** The Olympic flame arrives in Greece escorted by COO of ATHOC Marton Simitsek, the Greek President Gianna Angelopolous and her husband Theodore. (© Getty Images.)

**Plate 8** Roone Arledge (left) and Bob Iger, who rose from ABC programming manager at the Calgary Olympics to become CEO of Disney. (© Getty Images.)

**Plate 9**    The previous management team: IOC president, Avery Brundage, flanked by his successor, Lord Killanin and IOC director, Monique Berlioux. (© Getty Images.)

**Plate 10**    The founders of the Olympic Television Archive Bureau: Eric Drossart, Michael Payne, Stewart Binns, and Mark McCormack. (© Olympic Museum.)

**Plate 11**  Payne, Carrard and Samaranch enjoy a joke. (© Olympic Museum.)

**Plate 12**  Dick Pound. (© Getty Images.)

**Plate 13**   Peter Ueberroth feted by *Time* magazine. (© Time Life Pictures/Getty Images.)

**Plate 14**   Samaranch meeting with Robert Goizueta, chairman and CEO of Coca-Cola and his successor, Doug Ivester. Left to right: Michael Payne; Francoise Zweifel, IOC secretary general; Goizueta; Samaranch; Ivester; Francois Carrard, IOC director general; Stu Cross, head of Coke sports maketing. (© Olympic Museum.)

**Plate 15**  Pele is overcome with emotion as he holds the Olympic torch. (© Getty Images.)

**Plate 16**  The launch of the Beijing Olympic Emblem, with Chinese dignataries including martial arts legend and film star, Jackie Chan; Beijing Organising Committee executive vice president, Jiang Xiaoyu (centre); four time Olympic table tennis gold medallist, Deng Yaping; IOC design consultant, Brad Copeland; and Karen Webb (far right), from IOC marketing communciations. (© Michael Payne.)

**Plate 17**  The late Christopher Reeve epitomises the bravery and fortitude of many who hold the torch. (© Getty Images.)

**Plate 18**  Samaranch and his successor, Jacques Rogge. (© Getty Images.)

**Plate 19**   Samaranch, Bill Clinton and Billy Payne at the opening of the Centennial Games in Atlanta. (© Getty Images.)

**Plate 20** The McDonald's sign that mysteriously appeared at the Atlanta opening ceremony. (© Getty Images.)

**Plate 21** Eight living legends lead the Olympic flag into Salt Lake City. (© Getty Images.)

**Plate 22** Sir Steve Redgrave carries the Olympic torch in front of Buckingham Palace as part of the Athens Global Relay. (© Reuters.)

**Plate 23** The class of 2000: the IOC Executive Board and directors in front of IOC headquarters, Lausanne. (© Olympic Museum.)

# Chapter 5

# BEYOND A BRAND

## Lillehammer, Norway, February 9th, 1994

Preparing for the Lillehammer Winter Games in 1994, the news was dominated by coverage of the destruction of Sarajevo. Some of the venues which had played host to the Winter Games ten years before were now cemeteries.

Approaching the opening ceremony, Samaranch had a formal prepared speech. As usual, it had been worked on repeatedly to strike the right chord, acknowledge the right people and send the right message. There was nothing radical in it; nothing that could be construed as political.

Truth be told, the set piece was awful. I was supposed to rehearse Samaranch for the English part. I went to his office and read through the prepared text, but had to tell him that there was no way he could read it in front of a worldwide TV audience. He was not amused by this piece of advice and responded that it was simply too late to change. I persisted, so he told me to go and find someone to write a new speech and be back within a couple of hours. There was not enough time to find and brief speechwriters. So, I found the IOC director general, Francois Carrard, and the two of us set about preparing a new speech. When it was finished, I went back to Samaranch, told him the new draft was a bit stronger and far more direct than he was used to. I fully expected him to throw it out. I handed it over, watched and waited. Samaranch frowned as he read through it – and then said: 'It is different, it is very good.'

The news from Sarajevo struck a chord with Samaranch – as it did with all of us who'd enjoyed and participated in the Sarajevo Games. For this reason Samaranch was happy to make a bold statement during his Opening Ceremony address – happier than the arch diplomat normally would have been. Francois Carrard and I were sworn to secrecy about the change from the official text, but I agreed with Samaranch that we would brief CBS, the network which had the US broadcast rights to the Games.

When the time came, Samaranch invited all 40,000 spectators in the stadium to stand up in a moment of silence and respect. He then invited everyone around the world, even those in their own homes watching the Games on television, to stand up in memory of Sarajevo. 'Please stop the fighting. Stop the killing. Drop your guns,' he implored.

The CBS executives immediately saw the potential symbolism of the moment. When Samaranch delivered his speech, CBS cut to a living room in Sarajevo where a Bosnian family was watching the Games. As the camera panned around the living room, you could see the bullet holes that had broken the windows and the confusion on the faces of the children who had never known peace. The imagery was compounded by the family looking at the TV set as Samaranch invited everyone watching to stand up. The parents looked at their children, wondering what to do.[1]

Samaranch's speech at Lillehammer was an attempt to reintroduce the tradition of the Olympic truce. The literal meaning of the Greek word for truce is *ékécheiria* – the laying down of arms – based on an ancient Greek tradition dating back to the ninth century BC.[2] The truce began seven days before the opening ceremony of the Games and ended seven days after the closing, so that the athletes, relatives and spectators could travel to and from Olympia safely. This became a tradition and, in over 1,000 years of ancient Olympic competition, the sacred truce was never violated – making it perhaps the longest peace treaty in history. Olympia was the only Greek city never to build walls to defend itself.

## The ring ritual

Sport is often said to be a metaphor for war. But, really, it's a catalyst for peace. The Olympic brand is where the world of sport and the yearning for peace meet. No other brand has such power.[3]

Harnessing and better understanding the power of the Olympic brand became an increasing focus for the IOC in the mid-1990s. The revenue foundations from broadcasting and sponsorship were basically sound. It was time to look ahead and see what structure the IOC wanted for its future marketing programmes. Concern was already mounting that the desperate search for revenues by the Atlanta Organising Committee risked compromising the Olympic brand. The IOC needed to exercise greater oversight and control, taking a far more active and direct role in building value in the Olympic brand.

Over the previous 100 years the Olympic brand had evolved organically, with little if any direct structured or formal management. This had to change. For years, Dick Pound and I had advocated that, to protect its brand, the IOC could not afford to delegate the management of marketing-related issues to an organising committee. More often than not, the organising committee had a very short term focus – namely how to get through to the closing ceremony without facing bankruptcy. We needed continuity. We needed to give our marketing and broadcast partners far greater insight into what the Olympic brand really represented. They had to understand what made the Games so unique and special. They needed stability and, more than anything, a clear long-term vision.

What we now call 'branding' was actually at the heart of the Olympic Movement from the very start. Think of the defining brand vision *Citius, Altius, Fortius* – 'Swifter, Higher, Stronger' – adopted by de Coubertin as the IOC's motto after he heard the Principal of Arcueil College, Father Dideon of the Dominican Order, address his students.

The Olympic Games was always based on symbolism, powerful images and rituals. These have been key in building Olympic brand equity over the past century. In 1910, de Coubertin observed that 'without rituals, the Games would become merely large multi-sport world championships'. He later presented the Olympic flag and emblem to represent the 1914 World Congress. In so doing, de Coubertin created one of the most recognisable emblems of our time.

De Coubertin wrote in the *Olympic Review*, in 1913, how 'the five rings represent the five parts of the world, now won over to Olympism, ready to accept its fruitful rivalries. In addition the six colours, combined in this way, reproduce the colours of every country [flag] without exception'.

Alternatively, it has been suggested that de Coubertin got the inspiration for the Olympic symbol from an advertisement for Dunlop tyres. The ad showed angels holding interlaced bicycle tyres, with the inscription 'Africa, America, Asia and Europe', representing the four continents, and no reference to the fifth continent, Australasia.

To some, the Olympics were much more than a brand. After all, they had a 3,000 year history and encompassed a global movement long before globalisation was even talked about. Yet, it was also clear that there was much for the IOC to learn from the corporate world in how to manage and cultivate its image.

## Yin and yang

By the 1990s, with growing pressures from an array of stakeholders – host cities, broadcasters, sponsors and numerous other bodies – the time had come to develop a much stronger vision for the future presentation of the Olympic brand. 'So where is the plan, we need a plan,' Samaranch declared at the end of the traditional marketing report to the IOC Executive Board in 1995.

Numerous market research studies have identified the Olympic symbol as the most recognised trademark in the world. No other symbol is identified across so many cultures and continents.[4] A much broader question remained: what did the Olympic symbol really stand for? It was all very well, sitting at the IOC headquarters in Lausanne, with our own views of what the rings meant, but what did they really stand for in China, in the sub-Sahara and in Peru?

So after the Winter Olympic Games in Nagano, the IOC embarked on the broadest market research programme ever undertaken by a sports organisation. The aim was to better understand the consumer's true perception of the Olympic brand.

The brand analysts, Edgar Dunn, along with Terence Burns from the IOC's marketing agency, Meridian, undertook a comprehensive study across 11 countries with interviews and focus groups with over 5,500 consumers, and a further series of 250 in-depth interviews among key media, broadcaster, Olympic family and sponsor opinion leaders.

The results were remarkably consistent. Not surprisingly, the Greeks were often the most passionate about the Olympic brand. To the Greeks, every time the Games travels away from Greek shores, its values are placed in jeopardy. One of the focus groups in Greece wondered whether 'the competition had gotten out of hand, and the Olympics were no longer pure. The Olympics were like a Greek virgin, who is raped every time she leaves Greece'.

Greek patriotism aside, the research confirmed that the Olympic brand differs from other brands because it straddles two distinctive universes. It is not strictly humanitarian, like the Red Cross, nor is it strictly commercial like Disney or other entertainment or sporting brands. The Olympic brand's sports association gives it more dynamism and modernity than other non-commercial organisations, yet its spirit and heritage give it more morality and depth than often found in commercial brands.

After Samaranch's Lillehammer plea, Kofi Annan, the UN Secretary General, called for the Olympic Truce for the 1998 Nagano Games. 'At a time when crises are multiplying, when conflicts are emerging within the very heart of nations, truce provides a gleam of light in a world beset by hate and destruction. Olympism is a school for democracy. There is a natural link between the ethics of the Olympic Games and the fundamental principles of the UN,' he said. The Olympic Truce was adopted unanimously by the 48th Session of the United Nations.

The research identified four key propositions for the Olympic brand:

- *Hope.* The Olympic Games offer hope for a better world, using sport competition for all and without discrimination as an example and a lesson.
- *Dreams and inspiration.* The Olympic Games provide inspiration to achieve personal dreams through the lessons of the athlete's striving, sacrifice and determination. This intrinsic brand message conveys the enduring power of the Olympic Games to inspire humanity to achieve.
- *Friendship and fair play.* The Olympic Games provide tangible examples of how humanity can overcome political, economic, religious and racial prejudices through the values inherent in sport.
- *Joy in effort.* The Olympic Games celebrate the universal joy in doing one's best, regardless of the outcome. Through their honour and dignity in competition, Olympic athletes teach lessons to us all.

There was a paradox here. It became clear that non-commercial values provided the Olympic brand with its true commercial value to the marketing partners.

## Sceptical sponsors

Initially, broadcasters and sponsors were very sceptical about the IOC's plans for a global brand audit. They were convinced that the IOC would try to use the results to dictate the terms of their programming and advertising, and use it as a check on the approval process for their Olympic marketing campaigns. In some ways the sponsors were absolutely correct. We did want to provide a clearer road map. We wanted to illustrate what the Olympics really stood for. It was a way to develop more integrated marketing programmes – while still protecting the Olympic values.

The sheer weight of sponsor advertising and promotions in the market place was starting to define the public's view of the Olympics. The sponsors were the heaviest users of the Olympic brand equity and for that reason the IOC had to engage all the partners. It was essential that they became true champions and promoters of the Olympic brand values through their marketing programmes.

Sponsor advertising was often a hit-and-miss exercise. More often than not, the commercials were in line with the Olympic values. But every now and then, a campaign would come along that risked trivialising the Olympic brand. The IOC needed to find a way to manage the process. It had to ensure there was an effective review process that did more than just check that the colours of the Olympic rings were accurately reproduced.

Initially, the IOC proceeded discreetly, slowly winning over the hearts and minds of the marketing executives of each partner. When a campaign was proposed that was not in line with the Olympic brand, we gently debated the issue, asking the executive to put him or herself in our shoes. Usually we won the day, although occasionally a promotion slipped through that made us cringe and provided fuel to the critics who lamented the negative consequences of Olympic marketing.[5]

An important part of the IOC's strategy was selecting the right companies to be Olympic sponsors, in the right categories. Historically, the Olympic marketing rules were far from rigid. Those who criticised the commercialisation of the Olympics in the 1980s might not have been so vocal if they had considered what went before. The tension between the Olympic values and commercial interests is long standing. One of the most successful licensed Olympic products ever produced, for example, was 'Olympias', a brand of cigarette. Produced from a mixture of Turkish and Greek tobacco, it was designed to generate funds to support the organisation of the 1964 Olympic Games in Tokyo. Olympias generated over $1 million in revenues for the Organising Committee.

The marriage between cigarettes and the Olympics was a promotional theme at the 1964 Games. A popular Japanese cigarette brand, 'Peace', ran a promotion where each packet was sold with a numbered premium ticket. This entitled anyone drawing a winning ticket to claim a prize of a further 365 packs. Even back in the 1960s, marketers realised that the Olympic rings could draw consumers' attention to a product. Every packet of 'Peace' cigarettes, carried the Olympic emblem.

Four years later, at the 1968 Winter Games in Grenoble, the organisers again licensed two brands of cigarettes to use the Olympic marks. This prompted the then IOC president, Avery Brundage, to write to IOC members complaining about rampant commercialism. The media also remarked on what was seen as the rapid growth of commercialism. *Skiing Magazine* mourned: 'The Olympic ideal died somewhere in Grenoble.'

Even long after the IOC had banned any association with cigarettes, organisers or government authorities still launched special tobacco packaging commemorating the Games. The Korean tobacco body, for instance, launched a series to commemorate the 1988 Seoul Games. This was later withdrawn after formal IOC protests. There are reports that the Chinese tobacco body has signed up an Athens gold medal winner to endorse cigarettes; even today, the problem hasn't yet fully gone away.

The challenge has always been to manage two issues. On the one hand, there is the organising committee's focus on generating enough revenue to avoid bankruptcy and balance the books. On the other, there is the IOC's need to ensure that the Games are successfully staged, and that the scramble for revenue does not undermine the overall Olympic ideal.

As the IOC succeeded in building the revenue base from broadcast rights and the TOP programme provided an ever greater share of the organising committee's budget, the IOC introduced tougher guidelines. These included protocols on which product categories and which official supplier designations were truly suitable for an Olympic association, and would not undermine the Olympic image.

The majority of the official sponsor relationships for the Centennial Games in Atlanta were excellent examples of the partnership between the business community and the Olympics. But as the organisers became ever more desperate in their final search for revenue, they were forced into last-minute supplier arrangements that clearly undermined the Olympic image and their own efforts. The media jumped on these inappropriate categories and used them as examples of crass commercialisation. They pointed to 'Jeopardy – the official Olympic Game Show', the official Vidalia onion sauce or the official toilet seat cover, as illustrations of how the Olympic commercial agenda was out of control. And when Billy Payne announced that ACOG planned to grant a license to the 'official feminine hygiene products' of the Olympics, and started to present the proposed advertising treatment, the IOC felt that enough was enough.

It did not matter if 39 out of 40 partners proved a perfect match with the Olympic brand. If just one partner was counter to the Olympic brand, or stretched the public's credibility about the supplier designation granted, it could undermine the value for all official partners and diminish the long term value of the Olympic brand. Rob Prazmark, who had now moved on from ISL to become president of IMG's Olympic marketing division, accused the ACOG of 'damaging the Olympics, almost beyond repair, by undermining the value of sponsorship, and inking too many deals and slicing product categories and letting in lower tier sponsors at bargain rates'.

## Celebrate humanity

One of the first concrete steps that the IOC took as part of its broader brand-building strategy was to create a series of public service TV announcements, promoting the Olympic values. The timing of the IOC's decisions could not have come at a more difficult moment – the middle of the Salt Lake City crisis (see Chapter 9).

Six leading advertising agencies were invited to pitch for the IOC's account. The account, in itself, would not be worth much financially to the winning agency as all of the media would be bartered through existing IOC broadcast and media agreements. But winning the account offered considerable prestige.

The agency review narrowed the field down to two players – Young & Rubicam and TBWA, Chiat Day. Lee Clow, chairman and worldwide creative director for Chiat, led their pitch. Clow is one of the most creative minds in the industry, responsible for many great advertising campaigns over the years, including the famous Big Brother commercial that launched the Apple Macintosh in 1984, and Apple's 'Think Different' slogan.

Clow and his visionary creative director, Rob Siltanen, presented a series of creative spots that immediately captured the essence of what the Olympics stood for. Their tag line was 'Go Humans'. All of my colleagues from the IOC and our marketing agency Meridian loved the tag line. I hated it and knew that it would be impossible to sell to the IOC board. It seemed to me to be overly American and that it wouldn't be easy to sell – or translate – internationally. It sounded gimmicky, and the slogan in itself did nothing for the brand. I had my hands full convincing the IOC about the principle of the campaign to begin with and I did not need to add to the risk. Everyone across all 200 countries had to immediately say when they saw the campaign that it was what the Olympics are about.

Chiat Day clearly had nailed the right creative direction for the IOC's first campaign. All that was left to do was find the right tag line. It was amazing how many months and meetings it took for the team to come up with the eventual tag line 'Celebrate Humanity'. The words *celebrate* and *humanity*, along with 50 other words, were up there on the white board, but it took forever for the simple idea of putting the two words together to materialise. This is no doubt true for many great ad campaigns.

The next challenge was to find the voice for the campaign. Numerous names were proposed, but we all agreed that the actor Robin Williams would be the best. We also all knew that Robin Williams had never done a single voice-over for an advertisement in his career. But Chiat knew someone, who knew someone, who might be able to approach Williams's agent – his wife. We did not have particularly high hopes that he would accept, and continued to explore alternative solutions, but kept coming back to the power and diversity of Williams's voice.

Out of the blue, a call came through from Marsha Garces Williams, saying that, if the agency team could get themselves to the recording studios, Robin was on board. Williams captured the true magic of each Olympic moment. 'Many of my favourite Olympic memories were not gold medal situations,' Williams recalled, 'they were inspiring moments of humanity that transcended borders, obstacles and languages – and unified people around the world.'

The first Celebrate Humanity campaign was launched in New York in January 2000 to a highly sceptical audience. Twelve months previously, the IOC had been in front of the same audience defending the organisation's very existence as a result of the Salt Lake City bribery scandal. The press were convinced that the campaign was part of a broader strategy to advertise our way out of our Salt Lake difficulties and rehabilitate the IOC's image. The media only began to accept that the campaign had little to do with the crisis when they realised that none of the spots even mentioned the IOC.[6]

Six broadcast spots, eight radio spots and a series of print ads were produced. The visual imagery, recalling some of the most magical and special Olympic moments, combined with the tight scriptwriting of an advertising agency, who had to get their message across in under 30 seconds, proved a powerful combination.

One spot showed the British athlete Derek Redmond struggling around the track at the 1992 Barcelona Games after he pulled his hamstring in the back straight of the 400 metres, only to collapse in the arms of his father, who had jumped the barriers to evade the security guards and help his son over the line. The voice-over pronounced: 'Strength is measured in pounds, speed is measured in seconds. Courage? You can't measure courage.'

Another captured the sheer delight of the Nigerian 400 metre relay team, thinking that they had finished in fourth place and then seeing on the scoreboard that they had won a bronze Olympic medal.

Radio spots told other inspiring stories, like that of Karoly Takacs. Takacs, who was a member of Hungary's Olympic Team, and one of the finest rapid-fire pistol shooters in the world, was expected to win a medal at the 1940 Games until they were cancelled due to the Second World War.

During the war, a grenade exploded in Takacs' right hand, blowing it off. Undaunted, Takacs vowed to learn to shoot with his left hand. For the next few years he practised in solitude. Most of his friends thought he had died during the war, and were surprised to see him turn up at the 1948 Olympic Games in London, where, left-handed, he won the gold medal beating the world record in the process.

Or the story of Bill Havens, who was favourite to win gold medals in the rowing events at the 1924 Olympic Games in Paris. Shortly before the American team were due to leave for Paris, however, a trip that would take several months, Havens learned that his wife was expected to give birth to their first child at approximately the same time as the Games.

After much contemplation, Bill Havens decided he would give up his Olympic dream to remain with his wife. Four days after the Games were over, on 1 August 1924, his son Frank was born. For 28 years, Bill Havens secretly wondered whether he had made the right decision. Then, in 1952, he received a telegram from Helsinki, the site of the 1952 Olympic Games. The telegram read, 'Dear Dad, thanks for waiting around for me to get born in 1924. I'm coming home with the gold medal you should have won'. Frank Havens had just won the gold medal in the 10,000 metre canoeing.

Many of the spots were inspired by one of the greatest Olympic story-tellers of all time, the legendary and award winning film maker Bud Greenspan, who has chronicled the Olympics since 1948.[7] Greenspan had the uncanny eye to catch the magical moment that best captured the Olympic spirit – not only telling stories about the winners, but often of the athlete who came last. One of his most moving films told the story of John Stephen Akhwari, the Tanzanian marathon runner who competed in the 1968 Mexico Olympic Games. The race had been won. The medals awarded. Night had fallen and most of the spectators had left. Into the stadium, came the lonely, limping figure of Akhwari, an hour after the rest of the field, his leg bandaged after a bad fall and obviously in considerable pain. Despite this, he struggled around the track to finish. When a journalist asked Akhwari why he kept on to the very end, Akhwari replied: 'My country did not send me 7,000 miles away to start the race. They sent me 7,000 miles to finish.'

Even the most cynical commentators were moved.[8] Media companies around the world embraced the campaign, all running the advertisements for free as public service announcements. CNN ran the campaign 30 times a day for the eight months leading up to the Games; 30 airlines showed it as part of their in-flight programming; over 200 radio stations in the US aired the campaign; and Val Morgan Cinema advertising took it to the big screen across three continents. Print publications ranging from *Time* to *USA Today*, from *National Geographic* through to *Rolling Stone* ran spreads. By the time the Sydney Games were over, it was estimated that the Celebrate Humanity campaign had received over $120 million in free advertising.

It was not a difficult decision to continue the Celebrate Humanity campaign through to Salt Lake City. The brief to Chiat was simple – don't touch anything, just winterise the message! Chiat came back with the spots adapted to the Winter Games, plus an additional series of youth spots set to the music of Daft Punk and Radiohead.

The decision to engage the MTV generation was critical in ensuring that the IOC and the broadcasters broke through all the clutter and noise in the market place, to keep the world's youth engaged with the Olympic values. Research showed that the Olympic message still resonated as strongly as it ever had with youth groups. But there was so much going on in their world that they needed to be reminded of why the Olympics were special and different, and to take the time out to stop and watch.

One of the most dramatic spots was the image of the Austrian, Hermann Maier, in slow motion crashing in the men's downhill at over 130 km an hour, with the sound of his bones cracking against the ice as he flew through the safety netting. It was one of the most frightening crashes ever seen on the ski circuit. The voice-over talked of how 'Falling is easy, Getting back up, that's the hard part', noting that a few days later Maier went on to win two gold medals.

The Winter Celebrate Humanity campaign was scheduled to be launched in mid-September 2001, providing for a six-month count down to the Salt Lake City Games. All the broadcasters had received the spots and were preparing their schedules when September 11 happened. As we thought of postponing the launch of the Celebrate Humanity campaign, CNN decided that it would be appropriate to start running the IOC spots straight away. All other advertising was on hold and the message was timely:

*You are my adversary, but you are not my enemy*
*For your resistance gives me strength*
*Your will gives me courage*
*Your spirit enobles me*
*And though I aim to defeat you, should I succeed, I will not humiliate you.*
*Instead I will honour you,*
*For without you, I am a lesser man.*

Within days other broadcasters were calling the IOC, asking for copies of the spot, and how much they had to pay the IOC, to air the campaign.

What did we learn from all this? In the old days, a brand signified ownership. Later, a brand came to mean a promise of quality. But some represent much more than that. The Olympic brand is about athletic prowess and fair play, but it is also about trust in the Olympic ideals – fraternity, friendship, peace and universal understanding.

## Bringing the heritage home

A key element of the Olympic brand is its heritage, the powerful visual images that helped define the twentieth century. There was just one small problem. The IOC did not have the rights to use many of these images.

Over the years, the IOC, like all sports organisations, had paid little attention to the question of copyright ownership to the official films and broadcast coverage of the Games. Right up until the early 1980s, IOC lawyers still allowed US networks to acquire broadcast rights exclusively, and in perpetuity. That meant that not even the IOC could use footage of Carl Lewis winning his four gold medals in Los Angeles, or Franz Klammer's bone-breaking downhill descent on the Patscherkofel to win gold at the 1976 Innsbruck Games, without paying substantial fees to ABC.

The IOC could talk about Olympic history, show still pictures of the great moments, but was effectively blocked from creating any documentary or film that would tell the story of the past 100 years. Broadcasters found it too difficult to gain access to historical footage and sponsors were prevented from developing strong visual programmes that captured one of the most important elements of the Olympic brand – its great heritage.

By the mid-1980s, media barons around world were beginning to realise the potential value of film and sports libraries, to support their new television channels. They weren't alone. The boxing promoter Bill Cayton amassed an Olympic and boxing archive which he eventually sold to ABC for over $70 million.[9]

It was increasingly apparent that if the IOC did not make its own move to acquire back the rights to past Olympic films and news archives soon, others would do it ahead of us and access to the Olympic heritage might be lost forever.

Samaranch and Pound recognised the importance of the IOC getting back control and ownership of its visual heritage, and a secret budget of $5 million was established to quietly start acquiring back the rights. It was critically important that the process be conducted discreetly for fear of waking up the commercial market as to exactly what the IOC was up to and thereby driving the price through the roof. It was clear that the IOC could never compete against the major media groups should the rights end up in a bidding war.

It was also apparent that the IOC did not have the internal expertise or resources to start trawling through the world's film libraries and searching out long-lost Olympic footage. I turned to Eric Drossart president of Trans World Sport, the broadcast arm of Mark McCormack's IMG group, to see if they would be interested in helping out. At the time, no sports organisation had, with the possible exception of the National Football League in the US, built any form of historical sports archive.

Drossart liked the idea and together we came up with a plan and created the Olympic Television Archive Bureau (OTAB), which set about acquiring whatever past Olympic film and television footage that could be found, restoring it, and then making it available to the Olympic broadcast and sponsor partners, and other television producers.[10] A small team was established at OTAB led by Stewart Binns, an award winning Olympic and historical documentary film maker, along with a specialist film archivist and historian Adrian Wood.

Ten years later, the acquisition programme was close to completion, with the IOC having brought back the rights to virtually every known piece of Olympic film and broadcast material, creating what is now viewed as one of the world's largest sports libraries – a library that exceeds over

50,000 hours of Olympic footage, dating right back to the 1900 Olympic Games in Paris.[11]

The story of how the IOC acquired back all the rights is, at times, a story of intrigue and secret undercover missions that would do justice to any spy novel: dedicated painstaking research from the depths of the former Soviet state archives through to lock-up garages in Mexico; last minute court injunctions and quiet long drawn out diplomacy; of negotiations that would lead to the highest office of the land, with the direct intervention of the head of state.

In many cases the IOC found films rotting away in archives and at grave risk unless immediately restored of being lost forever. On other occasions the IOC was in a race against time with lawyers to reassert the IOC's ownership over a particular film.

The acquisition programme was finally completed in December 2003 when, after five years of negotiation with the German government and Leni Riefenstahl, the IOC was able to acquire the copyright to the classic 1936 official Olympic film, *Olympia*. In 1936, Riefenstahl was commissioned by Goebbels to produce the film of the Berlin Games. Riefenstahl invented or enhanced many of the sports photography techniques that we now take for granted: slow motion; underwater diving shots; to magnify the height of the pole vault, she would dig camera pits next to the jump, so that the cameras could film from ground level; and the installation of tracking systems for following fast action.[12]

The acquisition of all the films of the Olympic Games right up until 1984 was of particular importance. The film record was of dramatically better quality than any broadcast coverage. And some of the greatest film producers of the twentieth century had made Olympic films. Kon Ichikawa's film of the 1964 Tokyo Games, for example, became as much a document of the event as of a time, a place and a culture, as Japan reconnected with the global community.[13] David Wolper's *Vision of Eight in Munich* brought together a cross-section of legendary producers from around the world including the British John Schlesinger and Milos Forman from Czechoslovakia. It was only in the late 1980s that broadcast equipment and technology began to compete with the quality and intimacy that celluloid film could offer.

The IOC was now able to finally totally control who could use Olympic imagery, ensuring that all actions were in support of the Olympic brand.

# The fire of the gods

At the heart of Olympic symbolism is the Olympic torch. Throughout history, fire has been a powerful and sacred symbol. Greek mythology tells of how fire was stolen from the gods and given to man by Prometheus, its power revered by all. Ever since Prometheus brought the spark of heavenly fire to earth for man, it has been a purifying symbol in most cultures. In some cultures, a torch was held beside a new-born child. At marriages the mothers of the bridal pair carried torches. At funerals, as they took place before sun-rise, torches lit the way of the procession, as well as purifying the air and, where appropriate, lighting the funeral pyre. And fire has long been a symbol of sacrifice.

The lighting of the torch in the olive groves of Olympia provided a direct symbolic link between the modern and ancient Games, adding to the power and legitimacy of the Olympic ideal. It was an ancient myth brought back to life. The former president of the Hellenic Committee, Antonios Tzikas, noted that each time the world gathered 'on the same spot in Olympia, among the ruins of the Temple of Hera, we again rekindle the Olympic spirit as the flame bursts to life'.

From the start, Baron de Coubertin wanted the modern Games to reflect the rituals of the ancient Games. The Olympic flame was introduced at the Amsterdam Olympics in 1928. Without formal ceremony, it burned for the duration of the Games above the entrance to the Olympic stadium. But it wasn't until the 1936 Berlin Games that the president of the organising committee, Carl Diem, reintroduced the tradition of the Olympic torch relay. In honour of various Greek gods, runners at the ancient games ran from one altar to another, with the winner lighting the sacrificial flame with the fire from his own torch and then carrying out the sacrifice.[14] Unfortunately, Diem's concept of a peaceful relay was hi-jacked by the Nazi propaganda machine, which immediately understood its power and symbolism.

Over the years, the lighting of the flame has provided some of the most symbolic moments in Olympic history. At the 1964 Tokyo Games, the final torch-bearer was Yoshinori Sakai, who had been born in Hiroshima, Japan, on 6 August 1945, at the exact hour the atom bomb was dropped.

Four years later, the torch was lit by the first woman, Enriqueta Basilio de Sotelo, after the relay followed the route Christopher Columbus took to discover the New World. In Seoul, Sohn Kee Chung, the 1936 Berlin Olympic marathon gold medallist, carried the final torch into the Olympic stadium as a Korean; unlike fifty-two years earlier, when Sohn had to register under a different name Kitei Son, and compete under the flag of occupation, Japan.

The Olympic torch has become a magic wand for the Games. The torch carrier is transformed into the bearer of the Olympic message as the flame makes its great journey from Olympia, Greece, to the site of the Games.

## Something unusual and unplanned

It was Peter Ueberroth who took the torch relay to a whole new level. Ueberroth understood the potential of the torch to spark national interest and pride, uniting people behind the Olympic Games. The rest of his management team at the Los Angeles Organising Committee did not have the same vision. They outvoted him seven to one. Ueberroth nevertheless stuck to his instincts and overruled his executives, unleashing the torch's true potential by creating a community approach to the relay, where each runner's life story fuelled the spirit of the Olympic flame.

Ueberroth turned to US telecommunications giant AT&T to sponsor the flame's epic journey. AT&T needed to reconstruct its national image after a federal judge had ruled that it should be broken up. The relay was an ideal platform to reconnect with communities across the country. It was decided to use it to raise money for a cross-section of American charities. Each relay slot was sold for $3,000, eventually generating close to $11 million for the charities.

The Greek Olympic Committee was not amused and saw the selling of relay slots as a sacrilege against the Olympic ideal. The fact that in ancient times the relay was sponsored – to provide the runners with food and lodgings, pay for the torches and decorate the route – was conveniently forgotten. That you could also walk into any souvenir shop in the village of Olympia and buy a cheap plastic Olympic torch – far tackier than anything offered up by the Los Angeles licensing programme – was also overlooked. The Greeks made it known that they would not allow Peter Ueberroth and the Los Angeles organisers to come and light the flame at Olympia.

Ueberroth was at a loss. The failure to light the flame in Olympia called into question the very legitimacy of the Games and was certain to be exploited by

the boycotting nations. After weeks of negotiations with the Greek committee had failed, Samaranch concocted a simple plan. Two Swiss students were
sent to Olympia to light the flame, photographing and filming the whole
exercise to verify the authenticity of the process. The students brought the
flame back to Lausanne in a miner's lamp. Samaranch then presented the
Greek Committee with a simple choice. The Greeks were told to either allow
Ueberroth to come to Olympia and light the flame in the traditional manner,
or the IOC would dispatch the flame from the IOC headquarters in Lausanne.
The Greek Committee accepted Samaranch's proposal.

Samaranch advised Ueberroth that his 'little problem' had been solved.
The Olympic torch relay began its 84-day journey through America. It
quickly turned into a feel-good patriotic celebration. The relay helped lift
the country out of the lingering malaise of the hostage crisis in Iran and
the deadly terrorist bombing on the marine barracks in Beirut, Lebanon.[15]
At the Republican party convention a few months after the Los Angeles
Olympic Games, US President Ronald Reagan talked in his main address
of the impact of the Olympic torch relay on America.

Four years later, the Calgary organisers again saw the potential for the
torch relay to create a community spirit across the country and embarked
on a programme to invite the whole population to nominate people to run
in the relay. More than 17 million nomination forms were issued to every
household across Canada – one of the largest Canadian mailings ever.

A total of 6,624,582 nominations were sent back for the 6,525 slots
to run the relay. The relay was sponsored by Petro Canada and went on to
become one of the most successful sponsorship marketing programmes
ever. As a result of the National Energy Programme – a Federal Government policy that Albertans believed had caused economic devastation
throughout the region – Petro Canada was regarded by many as public
enemy number one. The company's involvement with the torch relay was
a turning point. It banked immeasurable goodwill as it made its way across
Canada and sold 55 million commemorative Olympic torch relay glasses,
using the profits to establish a scholarship fund that is still in existence.

The Atlanta Organising Committee decided to build upon the community spirit programme developed by Calgary. With the support of
Coca-Cola, it saw a relay embark on a 15,000 mile journey, with more
than 12,467 runners carrying the flame across 42 states over 84 days.

The community hero programme developed by the Atlanta organisers and Coca-Cola added a new dimension to the relay. The stories it produced were some of the most powerful and emotional symbols of the Olympic ideal. In Milwaukee, a torch-bearer, Barbara LeClair, who had received a bone marrow transplant took the flame from a stranger, Suzy Wells, the anonymous marrow donor who had saved her life. In Yuma, Arizona, Mark Haugo, a wheelchair-bound torch carrier, secretly underwent exhaustive physical therapy so he could climb out of his chair, strap the torch to his walking frame and thrill his community with his bravery, bringing the relay team to tears.

When the relay passed through small communities, it placed them in the spotlight like no other previous event. *Business Week* profiled the impact of the Atlanta relay visiting Scottsburg, Indiana, a dot on the map of less than 5,000 people. 'Nothing had come close to the impact [of the torch] – except if you go back to 1812, the year of the Pigeon Roost massacre, when Indians slaughtered 22 townsfolk. The Olympic relay gave the town a sense of importance that finally eclipsed the Pigeon Roost tragedy.' The whole town turned out, from schools with their home-made flags, to nursing home residents wheeled into the street. 'For Scottsburg, the torch symbolises a renaissance; like many small rural towns, it took the 1980s on the chin – with unemployment climbing to 20 per cent. In places like Scottsburg, optimism and idealism are more than just words. They are a way of life that does honour to the Olympic torch as it passes through the town.'

There are a host of moving stories about torch carriers. Travis Roy from Kittery, Maine, and a quadriplegic, ran with the torch during the Centennial Games. Travis won a hockey scholarship to Boston University but, during his first 10 seconds on the ice, was slammed into the boards and broke his neck. Nine months later, Travis was selected as a torch-bearer, carrying the flame in his wheelchair with the torch mounted on the side. He controlled his wheelchair by blowing through a straw. On arriving at the torch collection point, he asked the relay team 'Before I start, do you mind putting the torch on top of my head, so that I can feel how heavy it is?' The torch relay manager placed the torch on top of his head. As Travis felt the weight of the torch, he broke out in a big smile, and said, 'OK, now I am ready'.

Another torch-bearer, Jeff Kalail, was dying from soft tissue sarcoma at the age of 42. After a sixteen year battle against the illness, he had discontinued all forms of treatment. Jeff and his father Ed were chosen as an inspirational pair of runners. But on the day that Jeff was due to run, he was not sure he would make it through the day. Ed prayed with Jeff that his son would be able to make his last walk with his father. Ed was at peace with his son's dying, but he wanted to spend the last day with him. Jeff was able to make his last walk, with his proud father at his side.

The *International Herald Tribune* reported that the relay had become an advertisers' dream, 'a continuous 84-day commercial affecting people on an emotional level that companies hope will cement a lifetime bond.'

## The greatest

The identity of the final torch-bearer has become one of the most eagerly awaited moments of the Opening Ceremony, and one of the Games' most closely guarded secrets. A few months before the Atlanta Ceremony, I questioned Billy Payne, the Organising Committee President as to who he had in mind. Billy had not decided and asked what did I think?

'Well,' I said, 'with this being the Centennial Games, to my mind it should be the greatest living US Olympian, but in the eyes of the rest of the world.'

'Well, who do you think that is?', Billy enquired.

'I have no idea – let me think. ... It has to be Muhammad Ali.'[16]

Four months later Evander Holyfield, one of Atlanta's favourite sons, ran around the track sharing the torch with Greek hurdler Voula Patoulidou, a gold medallist from Barcelona. The torch then passed to swimming legend Janet Evans. She in turn handed it onto Ali who emerged from beneath the tower of the cauldron and grasped the torch with both hands. The stadium erupted in a roar at the sight of one of the greatest athletes in the world, as he struggled to light the taper to ignite the cauldron, both hands shaking, uncontrollably – a sad reminder of the effects of Parkinson's Disease.

Two years later there was a similarly emotional moment when Chris Moon, the anti-personnel mine campaigner, who lost part of his right leg and right arm while attempting to defuse mines in a remote village in

Mozambique, ran into the stadium holding the torch high above a crowd of children. Moon handed over to Midori Ito, the silver medal figure skater from Albertville, who was wearing a traditional kimono dress.

When the Olympic flame travelled down under to Australia, it became a symbol of hope and national reconciliation, and healing for the Aborigines. A barefoot Nova Peris-Kneebone, one of 11 Aborigine members of the Australian Olympic team and a hockey gold medallist from Atlanta, became one of 11,000 Australians to carry the torch over the next 100 days. The relay had a dramatic finale when fellow Aboriginal athlete Cathy Freeman stood in a circular pond of water that then turned into a circle of fire, as the blazing cauldron arose around her.[17] More than 500,000 people turned out on the streets of Sydney for the final day of the relay.

Around 100,000 people have had the honour of carrying the Olympic flame over the years. Their memories of their special moment carrying the flame from Olympia to the host city of the Games have provided some of the most poignant and inspirational commentaries of the Olympic ideal. Occasionally, when you become ever so slightly jaundiced reading through the barrage of cynical media commentaries suggesting the Olympic Movement has lost its direction, it is good to read through the runner's log from the torch relay bus. You are reminded of the true meaning of the Olympic spirit and its potential to inspire.

The Sydney organisers added an extra piece of symbolism. At the closing ceremony, a Royal Australian Air-Force F111 jet streamed over the Olympic stadium at the moment that the Olympic flame was extinguished. As the jet passed just 160 metres above the dying cauldron, a plume of flame spurted out from its afterburners lighting up the night sky. It was as if the sacred Olympic flame was being taken back to the heavens – returning to the Greek gods from whom it came, for safe keeping.[18]

## The Olympic DNA

The power of the Olympic torch's symbolism was brought home to me in October 2001, when I was with Jacques Rogge as he completed his first tour of the US as IOC president. Francois Carrard, the IOC director general and I accompanied him as he met the CEOs of the TOP partners, along with the editors of America's leading media.

We arrived in New York late Thursday evening October 10, after three days of non-stop travel, six cities and interminable meetings. New York was the last port of call. We were scheduled to be up early the next morning at the NBC studios, where Rogge was to be a guest on the *Today* show to talk about preparations for the Salt Lake City Games.

Sitting in NBC's hospitality suite waiting for Rogge's interview to begin, firefighter Kevin Hannison walked into the room. He was in his uniform with his fire-station dog. A month on from September 11, Hannison poignantly explained that he had found his younger brother, also a fireman, in the rubble of the twin towers and had been able to give him a proper burial. I made a note of Hannison's address and later contacted him to ask if he would like to run in the Salt Lake City Olympic Torch Relay in memory of his brother. The theme of the relay was an inspiration, to light the fire within. Local communities were challenged to nominate their heroes to run in the relay.

The Salt Lake City torch relay became a symbol of hope after the trauma of September 11.

And so, we had finally come to understand what the Olympic brand really meant – its special place in the world. We had identified the Olympic DNA. We had taken those findings and cultivated, reinforced and enshrined them in Celebrate Humanity campaigns. We had reached out and touched people by distilling the essence of what the Olympic Games are.

The decision to embark on a brand management programme in the mid-1990s – the first by an international sports organisation – dramatically increased the value of the Olympic franchise and, we hoped, put the Olympic Movement on a firm financial footing. But understanding what is unique about the Olympic brand was not enough. We had to be prepared to go to the barricades to protect it. Over the years, the IOC has been sorely tested. Some of those who have pushed their luck the hardest are household names.

## NOTES

1 The contrast with the conflict between different religious and ethnic groups back in Sarajevo was further highlighted with the participation of the Bosnian bobsleigh team in Lillehammer, manned by Muslims,

Serbs and Croats. Nizar Zaciragic, a 25-year old bobsleigher, offered a moving testimony of his time at the Games: 'We escaped briefly from hell on earth – a place where the starvation, the rape and the bloodshed are turning human beings into halfway animals. We came to a land of comforts yet we felt guilty when we ate.' Seeing the reaction to his speech, Samaranch made a special visit to Sarajevo in the middle of the Lillehammer Games and the IOC later created a fund to aid the rebuilding of Sarajevo's Olympic Ice Stadium.

2  According to Greek mythology, at the beginning of the 8th century BC, Iphitus King of Elis, asked the God Apollo at Delphi his advice on what he should do to save Greece, which was devastated by civil wars and plagues. Apollo, via the Pythia, recommended holding the Olympic Games as a celebration of peace.

3  'There's a fine and manipulative line that snakes through the five rings of the Summer Olympics,' observed *Business Week*. 'It's the line that tugs at people's nationalistic heartstrings or internationalist values while selling a product. In essence the IOC's sophisticated marketing programme charges its most exclusive multinational sponsors $55 million for the right to help promote world peace. "We'll make it all seem good and pure by convincing people that we are diplomats in running shorts – the physically fit UN." And boy does giving peace a chance sell.'

4  SRI research of 10,000 people across nine countries and five continents found that the Olympic rings enjoyed recognition levels of over 90% (99% in Japan) – compared with Shell 88%; McDonald's 88%; Mercedes 74%; Christian Cross 54%; United Nations 36%; World Wildlife Fund 28%.

5  A USOC promotion repositioned the breakfast cereal Cheerios as official edible Olympic rings. A 1988 commemorative spoon programme in Korea included a souvenir china spoon celebrating Olympic history, and each Olympiad. For 1944, when the Games were cancelled, the Koreans developed an artistic rendition of the atomic bomb rising out of the Olympic rings.

6 Lee Clow explained: 'This is not about advertising in the traditional sense, it is about reminding the world of the values and dreams the Olympics represent. The Olympics are the ultimate celebration of humanity; we want the whole world to be able to participate in that celebration.'

7 Bud Greenspan produced the official films and TV specials for the 1984 Los Angeles, 1988 Calgary, 1988 Seoul, 1992 Barcelona, 1994 Lillehammer, 1996 Atlanta and 2000 Sydney Games.

8 Referring to the silver medal spot, where Yoto Yotov from Bulgaria expressed his delight at winning the silver medal for weightlifting, Bob Garfied, the advertising critic for *Advertising Age*, wrote: 'Mr Yotov was clearly no Carl Lewis prima donna. He was a little guy who reached his maximum potential before the whole world and gloried in the experience. It is a very charming, very poignant spot that can't help but move and inspire you. Because – oh yeah – for all the scandals and ugly compromises, the Olympics are moving and inspiring. Also exciting, beautiful, vivid, often dramatic and sometimes breathtaking. It's no wonder that, quadrennially, the world suspends its disbelief and swoons under the spell of the Olympic euphoria, we buy into the silly methodology that politics are set aside, that competition trumps commerce, that sportsmanship reigns, not because we believe it, because we wish to believe it. It is a spectacle so grand and so rich with majestic moments, we are prepared to forgive it nearly everything ... thus does TBWA succeed so well, because this wonderful footage corroborates the myth. It validates our optimism. It permits us, against a large body of evidence, to feel good'.

9 Prior to the sale of Cayton's library to ABC, the IOC advised the network that the ownership of any Olympic material in the collection was a matter of some dispute. ABC nevertheless proceeded with the acquisition, and the IOC was forced to commence legal proceedings to claim back all Olympic material, including material from the Melbourne 1956 Olympic Games which, as broadcasters had boycotted the Games, was the only known film of the event. After a long drawn out legal battle, the Australian courts eventually ruled in the IOC's favour.

10  The Olympic Television Archive Bureau was finally established in 1995, as a 100% IOC owned and controlled organisation, based in London with TWI having a management contract to run and administer the operation.

11  Some moving images exist of Athens, and although it has been claimed that these date from 1896, subsequent research has shown that they came from the 1906 Olympic Games in Athens – a 'non official Olympic Games' staged by the Greeks, who felt that they should be given the right to stage the Olympic Games on a permanent basis and set about organising their own festival.

12  Leni Riefenstahl was born in 1902 and made her mark with her 1934 film, *Triumph Of The Will*, a hypnotic account of the Nuremberg Nazi party rally, where she glorified Nazi pageantry and Hitler's oratory. Goebbels saw the propaganda potential of an Olympic film and provided Riefenstahl with unprecedented resources. She travelled to Berlin with 30 cameras and hundreds of staff, shot over 400,000 metres of film (over 248 miles), around 250 hours – probably the largest amount of film shot at the time. The subsequent editing took more than 18 months. *Olympia* was a lavish hymn to sporting prowess and physical beauty and strength, and premiered in 1938 on Hitler's 49th birthday, with the Nazi leader attending as guest of honour.

Samaranch had long understood the importance of gaining back the ownership of this classic Olympic film. Early on in his presidency, he invited Riefenstahl to Lausanne to present her films as part of the Olympic Week celebrations, an annual festival for the local community. Riefenstahl came but the film presentation was cancelled at the last minute due to anti-Nazi protestors in the audience. Throughout her life, Riefenstahl was never able to shed the historical contamination of her connections with Hitler. Although her films have had enormous impact on world cinema, Riefenstahl found it difficult to gain public respect, remaining a controversial figure right up until her death in 2003, aged 101.

13  The Tokyo 1964 official film used 164 cameramen and 1,031 cameras – 59 just for the marathon.

14   Even the first torch relay of the modern Games had its official suppliers. Zeiss, the leading firm in the Greek market for optical products, was invited by the Greek Olympic Committee to provide the reflective mirror to light the flame. Daimler Benz provided the transport and Krupp Steel designed the torch.

15   The *New York Times* captured the true impact of the relay: 'Something unusual and unplanned is also happening as the Olympic torch makes its way slowly across the nation these days. For unseen by most of the country, as the flame moves through places like rural Missouri, communities like Useful, Linn and Knob Noster, Union, Sedalia and Festus, it seems to be igniting some special feeling tied less to the Olympics and more to patriotism. Some people, freshly roused by the flashing lights of the police escort, emerge from where they have been sleeping, on blankets in the grass or in the back of a pick-up truck. Others bring lawn chairs or stand for hours in the sun. This afternoon one farmer could be seen atop his distant tractor applauding silently in the middle of a giant soybean field ... it is in the countryside, out beyond the range and interests of the big city television stations, that the runners find themselves the most touched by efforts to become involved somehow: the crowds of 1,000 people in a town of 300. The little communities that line their sidewalks with scores of candles, their own glowing echoes of the travelling torch ... As a runner enters town, church bells sound, fire sirens blare, trucks blast air horns. Some people throw roses, offer beers or run alongside to touch someone, anyone involved with the torch. "Look at that runner, Honey," one mother urged her daughter, "Look at that runner and always remember him!" '

16   Several other Olympic commentators were advising Billy Payne around the same time as to who the final torch-bearer should be, including Dick Ebersol, chairman of NBC Olympics. Everyone came to the same conclusion, albeit maybe with a different logic.

17   The lighting of the Sydney Olympic cauldron did not go exactly as planned. A freak telecommunications signal caused a glitch in the computer that controlled the raising of the cauldron through the crowd. For 220 seconds, what would seem to the organisers like an

eternity, the cauldron was stuck above Cathy Freeman's head, with the band playing the same musical chord of Berlioz's *Te Deum* over and over again, until the engineers working in the bowels of the stadium were able to track the problem and override the safety mechanisms. Although the organisers had developed contingency plans of an extra 30 minutes of gas supply in the cauldron, last-minute weight restrictions had prevented the addition of the gas canisters and the Olympic cauldron had less than a minute of spare fuel when it did finally start moving again and the main gas burners kicked in. Ric Birch, the ceremony producer, later wrote: 'Imagine the symbolism of watching the cauldron ignite and start moving, only to see it stop and then a few minutes later to witness the Olympic flame die out.'

18  Unfortunately, not every torch relay ended so smoothly. In Seoul the legacy of the torch relay was seen by many international commentators to have more to do with roast pigeons than any community spirit. To the doves – read pigeons – that were released at the opening ceremony, the cauldron looked like a perfect bird perch from which to watch the rest of the ceremonies. While most of the pigeons immediately escaped from the stadium, about twenty decided to stay behind and enjoy the festivities. No sooner had they settled down to watch, than the final torch-bearers arrived, bringing the pigeon's relaxing afternoon siesta to an abrupt, and rather warm, end in front of three billion television viewers. For the following months, Samaranch's office was inundated by letters of protest from animal protection groups, distraught at what they had seen on live television. There was another problem – the pigeons, having been caged for the 24 hours prior to the opening ceremonies, are inclined upon release, to fly over athletes and spectators with an immediate urge to relieve themselves. The athletes, in their new parade uniforms, can quickly find themselves covered in pigeon droppings. As a result, the IOC Board decided to change to paper pigeons. This was deemed wise after it was established that if the Albertville organisers released their pigeons into the mountain air at night, they would get lost and freeze. Samaranch did not want another barrage of animal rights letters from around the world.

# Chapter 6

# BEATING THE AMBUSHERS

## IOC Marketing Operations Centre, Marriott Marquis Hotel, Atlanta, July 1996

Sports goods giant Nike launched its advertising programme for the Centennial Olympic Games by plastering downtown Atlanta with a series of cheeky billboards. Their theme: only winning matters. 'You do not win silver, you lose gold' trumpeted the Nike ads.[1] The win at all costs message was a clear attempt to upstage Reebok, the official Olympic sponsor. An ad campaign in the US magazine *Sports Illustrated* rammed the message home: 'If you can't stand the heat, get out of Atlanta,' and 'If you're not here to win, you're a tourist' (a quip apparently inspired by tennis star Andre Agassi).

Yet more Nike ads took a sarcastic swipe at the thematic-styled advertising popular among many of the Centennial Olympic sponsors. 'We don't sell dreams, we sell shoes,' said Nike, adding a further knock at one of the most popular pastimes of sponsor guests, 'I did not come here to trade pins.' Nothing seemed too sacred for Nike to take a dig at. The Olympic motto was modified to read, 'Faster, Higher, Stronger, Badder.' *Sports Business Journal* labeled Nike 'the Olympics' most high-profile party crasher'.

Nike's aggressive advertising was guaranteed to get a response – from the public, athletes and the IOC. Nike was trashing the Olympic ideals and undermining the overall Olympic brand message. No-one likes a party crasher. Besides, its campaign seemed a little two faced. After all, the Olympic Games are the sports goods industry's biggest showcase. The Games create heroes and role models that help Nike, and the rest of the sports industry, sell millions of additional shoes and motivate whole generations to take up new sports.

The IOC wasn't alone in questioning Nike's hardball approach. Athletes were irritated by the company's attempts to undermine the Olympic values and the devaluing of an Olympic silver medal. Olympic swimmer Amy White, a Los Angeles 1984 silver medalist, called the advertising a slap in the face to anyone who did not win gold. Olympic sponsors were also not amused. 'The ads are basically ridiculing us' was the commonly held view in the sponsor community.

Of course, Nike revelled in all the press coverage surrounding the campaign and the bad boy image it had carefully cultivated over the years.

The IOC though was not about to let Nike's ambush carry on causing trouble. As soon as I arrived in Atlanta and saw the billboards I got on the phone to journalists. My message wasn't malicious or anti-Nike. I simply pointed out that the feedback we were getting from athletes and spectators indicated that the campaign was backfiring. Athletes were very proud to be at the Olympics and likely to be uncomfortable when their shoe sponsor says they have failed unless they win a gold medal. In fact, by thumbing its nose at the IOC, Nike was crossing the very fine line between having an impact and biting the hand that creates tomorrow's heroes.

Our response paid off. The media were soon associating Nike with bad sportsmanship. The *Financial Times* headlined its story, 'Nike accused of trashing the Olympic ideal. Ruling body attacks the tone of group's advertising campaign.'

In a series of further interviews across the US media, we turned up the heat. Companies that ignored their social responsibilities did so at their peril, we said. Nike was a trendsetter for youth and often has as much influence over kids as their parents or school teachers, more sometimes. Society would not tolerate such behaviour from a leading multinational company.

We called for an urgent meeting with the Nike leadership to discuss their advertising and aggressive promotional activities – which included trying to get spectators to smuggle Nike promotional signs into the venues. Howard Slusher, the special assistant and long-standing 'fixer' to Nike chairman and founder Phil Knight, turned up at the IOC Marketing Operations Centre at the Marriott Hotel ready to do battle. Slusher, a straight-talking former sports agent, was in no mood for compromise. In the IOC corner were Dick Pound and myself, along with United States Olympic Committee marketing chief, John Krimsky.

The meeting did not get off to a good start. Within seconds Slusher and Krimsky were exchanging vitriolic verbal blows. This rapidly degenerated until the two of them challenged each other to settle the matter outside the room, in the hotel corridor, man to man. Both were of equal stature, similar egos and of questionable fitness. The impending boxing match had definite entertainment value, if doubtful sporting discipline, but was probably not going to resolve the issue.

As tempers subsided, Slusher tried to defend the Nike campaign. He said that in their research the message resonated with athletes and their desire to win. Phil Knight thought that the ads honestly reflected the competitive mindset of world class athletes who, with gold on the line, were not going 'to sing Julie Andrews songs together'.

Our position was equally clear. We did not care what their research said. We weren't going to sit back and let Nike's ambush marketing undermine and trash the very spirit and essence of the Olympic ideal.

For a while, the combative Slusher seemed unsure of himself as he weighed up the pros and cons of a head-on confrontation with the IOC. Thanks to the phone calls, the media coverage and headlines were starting to turn against Nike. Word had also leaked that the IOC might begin to play Nike at its own game of hardball public relations stunts. We were ready to round up a series of silver medallists from the Games for a worldwide press conference to let them express their views on the Nike campaign.

Meanwhile, as Slusher contemplated Nike's next move, the mood in the athletes' village towards the campaign was hardening. Athletes, who had devoted their life to training and just getting to the Olympics, were angry at being positioned as 'failures'. I initiated secret discussions with Brad Hunt, the agent of Nike's star athlete at the Games, 400 metre runner Michael Johnson, to see whether Johnson would be willing to stand up and speak out against the campaign. Hunt was open to the idea.

The IOC spelt out the situation to Slusher. Sport is played according to rules and the Olympic Movement was founded on a clear set of values and ethics. If Nike wanted to be part of this great celebration then the company had better start playing by those rules and respecting the Movement's ethical foundations. If not, the IOC would consider banning any form of Nike branding from all sports equipment at the Games, and immediately withdrawing all accreditation for any Nike service personnel, making it impossible for them to get through the security controls to look after their athletes. If they wanted to play hardball, we were ready.

Slowly the message started to sink in. Thoughts of fist fights in hotel corridors were forgotten as Slusher agreed that it would be much better if we all got around the table to see how we could work together. Nike stopped circulating advertising signs for spectators to take into venues, reined in its public relations team from the more aggressive stunts and, where possible, toned down the remaining advertising.

After the Games, I went to Nike's headquarters, a 175-acre campus in Beaverton, Oregon, to meet with Slusher and the Nike leadership. I wanted to start a dialogue that would try to get Nike to be a champion of the Olympic ideal, not an enemy. Nike soon understood that there was far more to be gained by working with the IOC and the Olympics than against us. Later, when Reebok reneged on its contractual partnership with the Sydney organisers a few months before the 2000 Games, Nike showed it was an Olympic convert.

Just to remind Nike that it had met its match when it came to advertising and public relations, the IOC had its own gentle dig at Nike's earlier 'silver medal' advertising, when the IOC's first ever global brand marketing campaign, Celebrate Humanity, was launched. One of the spots focused on the bantam weight Bulgarian weightlifter Yoto Yotov hoisting a gigantic barbell over his head at the Barcelona Games. Upon holding the weight aloft for the required interval he drops it, and starts jumping up and down, falling eventually to his knees in triumph. The voice-over then takes a sly shot at Nike's early ad, stating that 'Someone once said: "If you don't win the silver, you lose the gold." Obviously, they never won the silver.'

## Raining on the parade

Nike was not the only company to engage in such opportunistic marketing in Atlanta. There was another incident during the opening ceremony. The Greek team is, by tradition and Olympic protocol, always the first nation to parade into the stadium. As they came over the ramp that had been created to bring the athletes into the stadium (a dramatic visual effect for the broadcasters for the first team, but a total disaster for the remainder, as it interfered with any attempt for an orderly parade), my mobile phone rang.

'Have you seen the broadcast image of the athletes coming over the ramp?' screamed the brand protection manager. 'What are we supposed to do about the McDonald's sign?'

I ran around the stadium to see the problem for myself. There, as the athletes marched over the ramp, in the distance was a large elevated McDonald's neon sign. It provided a perfect backdrop for each nation as they came into the stadium. The sign might have been in the distance, located by the temporary McDonald's restaurant at the Olympic Park, but on television it looked like it was attached to the main stadium. The sign had to be switched off – and fast.

The McDonald's restaurant was near the Olympic sponsor hospitality village. I called the IOC manager at the village, Julie Osborne, and told her to get over to the McDonald's restaurant and find someone to turn off the lights.

Julie got to the restaurant, by the time the athlete parade had reached the letter c and Cambodia was stumbling down the ramp. She found it closed and locked up. Understandably, all members of staff were in the stadium watching the ceremonies.

'Then break in,' I yelled to Julie – by now we were up to Denmark in the athletes' parade, and there was no way for the television cameras to avoid the neon advertising sign. 'They will arrest me,' pleaded Julie.

'They will arrest all of us if we do not get that sign switched off now.' So an IOC manager proceeded to break into a partner's restaurant to get their sign switched off.

Straight after the ceremonies, I met the McDonald's management back at the IOC sponsor hospitality club, and 'apologised' for having to break into their restaurant. No one ever discovered how the sign had been 'accidentally' winched to its full height just before the start of the ceremonies and left on so that billions of people could see it.

## Keeping the Olympics clean

It is one thing understanding what your brand stands for. But it is meaningless unless you protect your brand. Defending your rights, your image and what you stand for is central to what the Olympic Movement has achieved over the last two decades. The Olympic Movement survives in large part because of its value proposition and the financial support it receives from the business community. If the IOC did not robustly defend that value proposition, or the exclusive rights of its partners, there would be no basis or logic for anyone to invest in or become a partner.

Exclusivity has been one of the cornerstones of the Olympic Movement's marketing programmes. The knowledge that a company can invest in the Olympic movement and be certain that they are not going to be undermined by a last-minute surprise promotional campaign by their competitor, was a key factor in driving the value of Olympic sponsorships.

The TOP programme was designed to be as ambush-proof as possible, providing partners with one of the highest levels of protection of any major sports property. The company not only sponsors the event, but all the teams participating in the Games and becomes a partner of the governing body, the IOC.

What many people do not realise is that the Olympic Games have a strict clean venue policy. This is unique among sports events. One of the fundamental tenets of the overall Olympic presentation is that the competitions take place in a field-of-play clean of all advertising. Athletes are similarly forbidden from having any sponsorship or commercial identification on their uniforms, other than a small trademark for the clothing company. The Olympics are unique in this. No other event in the world takes the 'clean venue' concept to such a level. Considering the global television audience for the Games, and the growing commercial pressures, it is no small achievement that the IOC has been able to hold the line.

In the 1980s, Samaranch was worried that, in the end, we would not be able to develop a marketing programme that could sustain the Olympic Movement, without finally having to give in and accept stadium advertising. All other events around the world had conceded and allowed not only stadium advertising, but extensive athlete advertising to help fund the teams. It was somewhat ironic that the champions of commercialisation within the IOC were the greatest advocates of the clean venue concept, explaining to Samaranch that to accept stadium advertising would destroy the image of the Games. It was also now questionable, having established TOP, whether significant additional revenues could be generated.

It was clear that any compromise on the clean venue principle could undermine the commercial position of the Olympics. It was an issue I felt passionately about. I am not sure that Samaranch ever truly believed me. Right up to the end of his presidency, he wondered whether there might still be a pot of hidden gold for the sports movement if we would just concede this last fundamental principle. He would test the issue regularly – even having Francois Carrard ask Coke's head of marketing, Steve Jones, how much extra the company would pay if we were ever to allow venue advertising.

Jones' reply shocked the audience and Samaranch. 'If the IOC ever introduced stadium advertising, Coca-Cola would withdraw from their

Olympic sponsorship, as you would have fundamentally changed what made the Games so special.' Finally all parties understood the marketing value of maintaining the 'clean venue' concept. It provided a key point of difference from all other events and, over time, added enormous value to the Olympic brand.[2]

Over the years there have nevertheless been various attempts to undermine the clean venue concept – both by sponsors and non-sponsors. The confectionary company Mars, an early TOP partner, never really understood that when the IOC said it wanted to keep the venues clean of advertising, it meant it. Mars executives saw it as a game, to see how they could get round the IOC rules and controls, and try to grab some opportunistic branding moments in front of the world's TV audiences. The company's tactics were fairly blatant. On one occasion, Mars dressed staff up in their M&M character suits. It then lined them up along the Olympic marathon route, with instructions to jump out onto the course as the runners went by, and wave madly at the TV cameras. Mars tried to argue that it was just creating some fun and cheering the runners on.

On other occasions, Mars dressed corporate guests with clothes bearing a series of large advertising messages. The hundred or so guests sat in the stands jumping up in front of the TV cameras each time the athletes passed by.

The IOC first tried to plead with Mars. This was not how we wished the Games to be presented, we explained, and we politely requested that Mars refrain from such presence marketing activities. Jacques Guertz, general counsel for Mars and 'special advisor' to the secretive Mars family, who oversaw their Olympic sponsorship, told the IOC that it 'did not understand the basics of marketing'. We listened and then calmly suggested to Guertz that if that was the company's attitude, then it was clear that this partnership was not working. We promptly offered to give Guertz back all the TOP money the IOC had received from Mars. At the same time, we would tear up the contract that had been negotiated for Atlanta and was close to execution.

Guertz was shocked that the IOC would walk away from so much money – we were talking about a $50 million partnership. He was convinced that in the sponsorship world, you could buy anything, including the IOC's commitment to clean venues.[3] The fact that the IOC was prepared to walk from such a huge deal sent a clear signal to the market. We would protect the clean venue policy at all costs.

## Zero tolerance

As the IOC developed its overall marketing strategy, a three-pronged protection programme was designed to protect us from ambush marketing of the Nike variety, accidental incursions and more opportunistic presence marketing – as practised by Mars.

Our basic philosophy was that the best defence is a good offence. If a company deliberately overstepped the line we would take no hostages, to set a clear example to the rest of the industry.

The second element was to build a fortress around the rights package and block all loopholes. We needed to get the house in order long before a host city was even appointed. We needed to invest in prevention, rather than being caught in a highly expensive and high profile cure.

Third, we designed an advertising communications campaign to educate the public on who the sponsors are and let the marketing industry understand the risks and consequences of taking on the Olympic Movement with any unauthorised campaign.

There is no question that the IOC adopted a very aggressive attitude in protecting its rights and those of the Olympic partners. The IOC's declared commitment that it would go to any length to protect its rights sent a strong signal to the market place – helping to increase the overall value for Olympic sponsors. If the IOC had sat back and taken the easy option, turning a blind eye to the occasional borderline promotion or partner presence marketing indiscretion, a cluttered market place would have rapidly followed. Sponsorship fees would have stagnated at 1980 levels. Sponsors had to be protected so that they could 'own' the Olympic promotional rights, without always having to look over their shoulder to see whether their competitor was developing some opportunistic last-minute promotion. Sponsors needed the confidence to invest – in Olympic promotions, in Olympic airtime broadcast buys, in a long-term Olympic marketing strategy.

Taking a hard line was never an easy option. It took time and attention to detail. In 1996 the Atlanta Organising Committee (ACOG) tried to sneak some branding for their automobile partner, General Motors, into the opening ceremonies. Although the IOC had reviewed and approved the details of the ceremonies, we were unaware of the intention to create a major branding opportunity for Chevrolet. Then, a couple of days before the opening, General Motors' John Middlebrook, Chevrolet general manager at the time, was quoted in newspapers proudly bragging that: 'Those who view the ceremonies will recognise that we elevated the GM and Chevrolet brands way above the field.' General Motors simply could not contain its excitement. Its over-excited spin-doctors had dropped their guard.

The IOC immediately demanded to know from ACOG what was going on and went to inspect all of the props and equipment to be used. The IOC already knew about the plan to use some flatbed trucks to carry lighting onto the field. What had not been agreed was that the trucks would be rebranded, with large chrome Chevrolet signs down the side of each truck. The IOC told ACOG to get the branding off. General Motors explained that it was chrome indented into the side of the trucks, which meant it was impossible to remove, hoping that this would be the end of the matter. The IOC responded that it would be, simply advising ACOG that that section of the opening ceremony was to be dropped. General Motors found a way to remove the brand on the trucks overnight.

There are many other similar examples. Some were more inadvertent than others.

In the early years of its TOP partnership, before it truly understood the value of the IOC's clean venue policy, even Coca-Cola would occasionally let something slip through the system. In Calgary, Coke agreed to help the local organisers out by providing 60,000 coloured ponchos as part of the opening ceremony kit for spectators. When worn, the ponchos would help form a series of patterns around the stadium.

As recognition of Coke's contribution, it was agreed that Coke could have a small credit on the inside of the poncho. The credit was to be visible to the spectator when they put the poncho on, but not to the TV cameras as they presented the opening ceremony to the world. The only problem was that someone 'forgot' to remind the manufacturer to print only on the inside.

A few days before the Opening Ceremony, the 60,000 ponchos were delivered to the McMahon Stadium, each one neatly packed in a plastic wrapper. Only by luck did an organising committee executive take one out to have a look and, in dismay, saw the Coke logo emblazoned on the outside of the ponchos. Coke executives were duly summoned and, along with some organising committee volunteers, spent the next few nights unfolding 60,000 ponchos, turning them inside out and then repacking them again, with the hope that the spectators would not tell which was inside and which was outside.

Similarly, in Sydney, four days before the Opening Ceremony, it turned out that the catering services company, Aramark, had provided 30,000 uniforms to all the food service personnel with its logo prominently displayed on the left side of the chest. This was a technical breach of TOP sponsor McDonald's exclusive rights. After a short, one-way discussion between the IOC and the Organising Committee, a team of seamstresses was sought to begin sewing new patches on.

An obsessive attention to detail? Absolutely, but it was this single mindedness that showed the partners the IOC's commitment to protecting the rights and the integrity of their exclusivity. Over the years, this policy has paid dividends in building and sustaining Olympic values.

## Off message

In order to maintain the clean venue policy, the IOC, together with the organising committee, puts together teams of trained executives to monitor all venues and control all athletes and spectators before entering the venues. The goal is to ensure that they are not carrying unauthorised advertising messages or promotional materials. It is not just about prohibiting commercial messages, it is also about ensuring that no one tries to make some political statement from the stands. This is paramount, but does not stop people with commercial or political agendas from trying it on.

In Lillehammer, for example, 60 Norwegian spectators turned up to the cross-country events, with the name of an insurance company emblazoned across their clothes. This was not accidental. It was a clearly orchestrated attempt to gain free publicity, with the insurance company probably paying for the cost of the spectator tickets. The spectators were told that in order to enter the venues they must either cover up the advertising, or take off their clothes. As it was minus 20° Celsius at the time, they were quickly able to find new jackets to cover up the offending advertising.

For all our vigilance, occasionally something slipped through the net. In Barcelona, at the basketball final between America's 'Dream Team' and Croatia, I arrived at the stadium after the game had already started, only to be greeted by Coke's sports marketing boss, Gary Hite, in a mild state of panic. Members of the Croatian team were drinking from green branded bottles – Gatorade bottles! The Croatian coach had been 'encouraged' to take some branded water bottles to the final. He thought that if the IOC questioned the issue, it would only do so after the event, by which point it would be too late.

As the IOC's clean venue policy did not even allow Coke to take branded bottles down onto the field of play, Gary Hite felt that a major injustice was underway. I walked down to the Croatian benches and started to collect up all the bottles. The coach came running, screaming at me. A brief exchange ensued. I told the coach that if his team wanted to finish the game, then the Gatorade bottles were leaving the field now. The IOC would replace the bottles with clean water bottles. If he wanted to keep the Gatorade bottles, then he should make an appointment for 8.00 am the next day with the IOC Executive Board, when it would be discussed whether they would be allowed to keep their medals. All the bottles were quickly exchanged.

Nearly all athletes and coaches know and respect the rules of the clean venues and advertising-free uniforms. For many, it is a relief not to have to worry for once whether they are wearing the right commercial t-shirt and standing the right way in front of the cameras to maximise the exposure for their sponsors. For once, they can just focus on the competition and the Olympic experience. They, too, recognise that the advertising-free policy makes the Games special.

In Atlanta, one athlete did not see it that way. Her underhanded advertising message came close to costing her country its first ever gold medal. Claudia Poll, from Costa Rica won the women's 200 metre freestyle event. The flag of Costa Rica looks remarkably like the logo of Pepsi-Cola – a red, white and blue wave. Everyone thought that Poll was swimming with a head cap proudly bearing the national flag. Only on close examination of the press photographs after the event did it become clear for all to see that the cap was also an advertisement for Pepsi.

Costa Rica was in uproar claiming that Coca-Cola had brought the matter to the IOC's attention and that because of Coke, Costa Rica would now lose its gold medal. Coke knew nothing about the issue, until the IOC began investigating. The company was now in a real bind. It was torn between, on the one hand, wanting the IOC to come down hard on such a blatant case of ambush marketing and, on the other, not taking the rap in Costa Rica and seeing its market share collapse through an incident that it had nothing to do with.

After a formal apology from the Costa Rican Olympic Committee, it was decided, that in view of the fact that this was the country's first ever medal, the IOC would not press for the ultimate sanction. Ms. Poll was not allowed to compete again wearing similar headgear.[4]

The clean venue concept was even expanded to include the airspace over the host city, to prevent air ships and planes towing adverts from flying over the venues. Even sponsor airships were expected to cover up their branding. Occasionally we would allow a related friendly message that people could recognise as coming from the sponsor. Goodyear, for example, was allowed to re-brand its airship in Sydney with the colloquial 'G'day' and 'Good luck'.

It was not always easy to enforce the grounding of airships. Fuji and Reebok airships turned up in Barcelona. They fully expected to be allowed to fly over the city for the duration of the Games, ambushing Kodak and the local sports brands. No legislation was passed forbidding air ships from flying over the city. But it was rumoured that the local air traffic controllers obtained the Games tickets they needed, while the requisite permissions for the offending air ships to take off languished in an in-tray for 17 days. No doubt the Fuji and Reebok executives were left wondering what on earth had happened. They probably didn't enjoy explaining to their senior management why they had spent millions of pesetas on a grounded air ship.

Every Games brings new and innovative attempts to circumvent the rules.[5] Today, there are specialist agencies to try to exploit opportunities. In Salt Lake City, one agency called GoGorilla sold Nescafé the idea of broadcasting its ads onto buildings from a vehicle. The idea was that the vehicle would move on as soon as the police turned up. Craig Singer, the founder of the GoGorilla agency, boasted that as the Games progressed the campaign would get even more aggressive – projecting onto the Ice Centre. In the end, no one ever saw any ads. You wonder how much Nescafé paid for such an opportunistic promotion and whether its headquarters in Vevey, Switzerland, was ever aware that its marketing budgets were being wasted.

## Fix it or we pull the plug

A similar attention to detail was applied to the broadcast presentation of the Games. After Albertville in 1992, the IOC decided to introduce a global monitoring programme to follow the telecast live around the world to ensure broadcast sponsorship and advertising guidelines were respected. Once again, the guidelines are designed to protect and maintain the unique nature of the Olympic presentation, making it stand out from all other sports broadcasts.

Broadcasters are allowed to maintain their normal commercial advertising breaks, and develop broadcast programme sponsorship. But they are restricted from overlaying any commercial message or logo over the actual broadcast of any sporting action, athletes or medal ceremonies. The only permitted logos are the credits provided to the companies supplying the timing and results services to the Games and these are tightly controlled directly by the IOC.

The practice of introducing sponsor logos and other advertising gimmicks into the middle of a telecast has becoming increasingly popular in recent years. It reflects the scramble among broadcasters to come up with new ways to generate advertising revenue, but can be intrusive and distracting for the viewer.

When the IOC first announced that it was to undertake a global monitoring exercise of Olympic telecasts, there was outrage among certain broadcasters. 'Didn't we trust them?' they demanded. The monitoring exercise in 1992 demonstrated to the IOC the importance of the programme. It soon became clear that broadcasters were starting to engage in some creative advertising practices which were in breach of the IOC guidelines.

In Albertville, within minutes of the start of the men's downhill on the first day of the Games, French Television flashed up logos for France Telecom across the screen every time a skier crossed the finishing line. By athlete number three, the monitoring control centre had called in to report the breach. By athlete number five the IOC was on the phone to the French producer and before the end of the first group of skiers the logo had been withdrawn, permanently.

Meanwhile, German television was found blanking out the IBM Results logo and replacing it with the name of another computer company, implying that it was running the results services. In South America, one broadcaster was caught superimposing the mascot of a new food company into the athletes' parade at the Opening Ceremonies, with the mascot dancing around the flag bearers of each nation, and even sometimes marching with the team!

By 1996, all the broadcasters knew that the IOC was monitoring so there were few infringements of the IOC's guidelines. It was nevertheless a major surprise when the report came in that Swiss TV was superimposing logos for Coca-Cola next to the timing clock. Coca-Cola head office denied that it was anything to do with them – it knew the rules and it had to be some local decision with Swiss TV.

The IOC immediately contacted Swiss TV to ask what was going on. After the initial surprise that we were able to follow the Swiss telecast in Atlanta, the broadcaster acknowledged that it had sold Coke a local advertising package that included these credits. The fact that this was counter to all the advertising rules had missed everyone's attention. What was stranger still was that it was in the country where the IOC is headquartered. Surprisingly Swiss TV refused to back down and pull the credits, saying the advertising contract with Coke was binding. I pointed out that the contract with the IOC was also binding and that, if the logo was not pulled immediately, the IOC would consider pulling the broadcast signal for the Swiss market.

Still Swiss TV did not budge. By now, Nicolas G Hayek, chairman of Swatch had woken up to what was going on and the interference to his official timing credits, and was not happy. Whoever was calling the shots back at Swiss TV was playing a strange game, acknowledging that they were in breach of their Olympic broadcast agreement, but refusing to do anything about it. As the issue escalated, wiser counsel finally prevailed. Swiss TV realised that there was a real risk of the IOC pulling the TV signal and finally closed down the infringing commercial credits.

But the action was too late to appease Hayek, who promptly filed a multi-million dollar damages suit against Swiss TV, for interference with Swatch's timing credits. This meant one of Switzerland's leading companies suing the national TV station, not in Switzerland but in the American courts. The issue was eventually settled after Swiss TV realised that it was in serious trouble and asked Samaranch to intervene and mediate. Swatch got a lot of free television advertising in Switzerland in 1997. Hayek's timely action helped to put everyone on notice that IOC rules were to be followed.

## The battle of the credit card giants

Some ambush marketing campaigns have involved long-term rivalries. Perhaps the most celebrated case is the guerrilla war waged by American Express throughout the late 1980s and 1990s to combat Visa's status as exclusive Olympic marketing partner. Amex never recovered from losing the Olympic rights to Visa after the 1984 Los Angeles Olympic Games. American Express 'may do nicely' in most places, but not at the Olympics.

In response, American Express embarked on an aggressive and highly creative programme, that pushed the trademark rules to the very limit, to undermine Visa's rights.

In 1986, American Express launched a promotional campaign in Asia, offering Olympic medallions from the Olympic Heritage Committee in Switzerland. There was just one problem, they neglected to point out that no such organisation even existed. American Express had either failed to do its due diligence with their promotions agency, or was sailing far too close to the wind.

The IOC immediately faxed a short note to American Express chairman, Jim Robinson, simply telling him what the IOC would do if the campaign was not totally withdrawn in the next twenty-four hours. The IOC explained that it would take out full page newspaper adverts in each territory advising the public that this was a bogus promotion and that they were being deceived by American Express into believing that Amex supported the Olympic Movement.

Furthermore, the IOC threatened to hold a press conference in each country with a cross-section of Olympic athletes and the sports minister. Aside from letting the athletes talk about the damage that American Express was doing to grass roots support for sport, we would provide a media photo opportunity of athletes cutting up American Express cards. Robinson's office called back in two hours desperate that we put a hold on the campaign. There had been some terrible misunderstanding, the company said, and they would investigate immediately. A few hours later they called back again, announcing that the whole programme was to be withdrawn immediately.

Visa's Olympic campaign inflicted such a heavy toll on American Express that Amex continued to come up with programmes to try to undermine Visa's position and lessen the impact. In Seoul in 1986, American Express took pictures from the 1986 Asian Games opening ceremony, and doctored them to look like the Olympic opening ceremony for a poster campaign, 'Amex welcomes you to Seoul.'[6]

Jerry Welsh, the American Express head of marketing, who had lost the Olympics rights, tried to justify ambush marketing. 'There is a weak-minded view that competitors have a moral obligation to step back and allow an official sponsor to reap all the benefits from a special event,' he said. 'They have not only a right, but an obligation to shareholders to take advantage of such events. All this talk about unethical ambushing is so much intellectual rubbish and posturing by people who are sloppy marketers.'

The battle between the two credit card giants rumbled spitefully on through 1992. In the build up to the Barcelona Games, American Express became ever more infuriated with Visa's comparative advertising. In the US, Visa's tagline was 'the Olympics don't take American Express', with images of ticket windows being slammed shut in the faces of American Express card holders. This time American Express responded with more style, pointing out in its own ad campaigns that 'to visit Spain, you don't need a visa'.

With an increasing escalation in the war of words between the companies, starting to interfere with the broader Olympic message, the IOC decided that the time had come to negotiate a truce. If American Express would withdraw from all forms of ambush marketing and promotional activities surrounding the Games, the IOC would no longer allow the Olympics to be used in hard hitting comparative advertising campaigns.

All parties agreed. But unfortunately, like so many truces, it did not last long. By Lillehammer in 1994, American Express was back with advertising referencing Lillehammer and flooding the market with promotional pins, stating 'American Express – Norway 1994'. Would American Express have ever produced such pins if the Games were not in Lillehammer? Of course not. So, the IOC immediately allowed Visa to resume comparative advertising, in an even more aggressive manner. American Express finally accepted that it had lost the battle. Since 1996, the company has refrained from any further ambush activity surrounding the Olympics.

## Getting your house in order

The second element in the IOC's strategy against ambush marketing was to build a fortress around the rights packages and block all potential loopholes.

Ultimately, if you don't build the proper rights architecture and management structures at the outset, no amount of aggressive advertising and public relations campaigns will ever protect you.

Early incidents of ambush marketing were often more a case of the sports organisation failing to get its own house in order, allowing competitors to pick off opportunities between the various sports bodies. One of the most celebrated examples involves Kodak. The company was desperate to get back into the Games after it lost the rights to the Los Angeles Olympics to Fuji. Kodak proceeded to tie up all the rights to the US track and field team. The ensuing images of the US Olympic team sponsored by Fuji, together with similar images from Kodak as sponsor of the US Olympic track and field team, showed the industry the dangers of an uncoordinated and unstructured marketing rights effort.

The primary focus of the IOC's protection programme for its partners starts long before any city is ever elected to host the Games. The philosophy is: get it right upfront – don't try and scramble to fix it after the event.

Now cities bidding for the Olympic Games are put through an extremely tough series of challenges to plug all loopholes long before they are elected. Time and experience has taught the IOC to take full advantage of the competitive dynamics of the bidding process and to apply maximum leverage to all stakeholders to get their houses in order. Once a city is elected, all leverage from the IOC and the local organisers evaporates.

Requirements to create a single marketing programme – where all the rights are bundled together into a single centralised package – have done much to reduce the overall risk of ambush marketing.

But once a city is elected, solidarity among the various authorities quickly disappears as each body decides it is pay day for them. Getting control after election, as the Atlanta organisers learned to their cost, is an almost impossible task. Commitments to pass special legislation to control advertising and street vending during the Games have become a key part of the bid review. Athens, a city with one of the most uncontrolled outdoor advertising markets in Europe, where zoning regulations are widely flouted, understood the importance of reigning in the billboards to ensure that it could present a clean, uncluttered look to the world. The government and the local city authorities used the occasion of hosting the Games to push through new legislation, removing thousands of outdoor advertising signs from key sites like Syntagma Square and around ancient monuments.[7]

After the problems in Atlanta, with various sporting goods manufacturers and their aggressive presence marketing activities, the IOC decided to engage the World Federation of Sporting Goods Industries (WSFGI) in a code of conduct. The code recognised the unique contribution that all the sports goods manufacturers made to the sports movement, supporting athletes, clubs and sports federations 365 days a year, but at the same time bound the manufacturers to a special marketing code when it came to Games time activities.

The Olympic Games are the biggest showcase for the sports goods industry. The IOC did not want to see an all-out escalation of the brand wars breaking out between manufacturers that would detract from the event. In Barcelona, the basketball competition was all but overshadowed by the high profile, and often aggressive, debate between Nike and Reebok over what the athletes would wear on the medals stand, with both Nike and Reebok claiming rights. In the end, the US team came out to collect their gold medal wearing the official USOC team uniform but with the American flag draped over their shoulders, covering the Reebok logo.

The first code was signed in December 1997 between the IOC and the president of the WSFGI, Stephen Rubin, along with representatives of five of the biggest manufacturers, Adidas, Asics, Mizuno, Nike and Reebok.

Over the years the media has often singled out Nike and other sports goods manufacturers as some of the biggest ambushers of the Games. I have always argued that the sports goods industry is not an ambusher, at least not in terms of ambushing Olympic rights. The leading manufacturers are probably providing as much, if not more, financial support to the Olympic teams, as any of the major sponsors. As such they are fully paid up partners, entitled to communicate their support to the athletes.[8] To think that only the sports goods sponsor of the organising committee can claim a presence at the Games is unrealistic, when the other manufacturers are all providing key support to the 202 Olympic teams. Where manufacturers do have to be careful is that they do not ambush the Olympic ideal or the process of fair play, as both Nike and Reebok have done over the years.[9]

## The PR battlefield

The media initially saw ambush marketing as something of a game between corporate titans. The coverage was about who could outmanoeuvre whom? How can one brand upstage the other? How do you get around the rules? It was a David and Goliath scenario with popular support often going to the underdog – the gung-ho Robin Hoods taking from the wicked corporate giants.

The final element in the IOC strategy, therefore, was to change media and public perceptions about ambush marketing. It was important to show that it was not a game, but a deadly serious business that, if left unchecked, had the potential to destroy the fundamental revenue basis for all sides. Left unchecked, ambush marketing would see the funding basis for the Games and Olympics teams shrivel and die. Ambush marketing had to be positioned as an unethical activity. Few issues strike at the heart of the legitimacy and credibility of the marketing business as the issue of truth in advertising.

The IOC decided to embark on an aggressive public relations campaign, taking a leadership position within the industry to change perceptions about what some were depicting as an imaginative and legitimate marketing practice. We set about challenging the thinking that ambush marketers were inspired marketers; neutralising the competitive advantage, by confusing the consumer as to who the legitimate sponsor of the event is underpinned by the notion that all is fair in the cut and thrust of the marketing battlefield.

Instead, ambush marketers were positioned as thieves, knowingly stealing something that did not belong to them; parasites feeding off the goodwill and value of the organisation that they are trying to deceive the public into believing that they are supporting. I compared them to leeches, sucking the lifeblood and goodwill out of the institution.

The decision to change the terminology from 'ambush marketing' to 'parasite marketing' was critical in helping to reposition the practice. This was an idea we came up with while brainstorming with our public relations agency at the Albertville Games. There was nothing cute or clever about being a parasite. A parasite is an organism that lives off another, with no benefit to the host.

For the IOC, a strong public relations programme has probably been as effective as any legal initiative in deterring ambush marketing. Over the years the IOC and the organising committees have developed a series of advertising and public relations programmes designed to educate the public and focus the debate on the broader ethical issues of ambush marketing.

Campaigns on 'How do you feel about cheating at the Olympic Games?'; embarrassing corporate leaders with a shame campaign; and proposals to induct CEOs who ambush the Games, into the 'Olympics Hall of Shame' soon began to get the message across of the pitfalls of ambush marketing. Threats of pictures of the offending CEO, under a banner headline of 'Stop Thief!' have helped to deter ambush activities and make CEOs and their agencies think twice before embarking on such a high-risk strategy.

Keynote addresses were given to advertising and marketing conferences around the world. 'An insidious, parasitic disease is spreading among our amateur athletes ... robbing generations of the very best athletes of the ability to compete at world class level,' Darby Coker, Atlanta's marketing communications director announced. 'The disease I am talking about is parasite marketing.'

*Advertising Age*, the advertising industry standard bearer, took up the debate with a tongue-in-cheek contest for its readers to design suitable sanctions for ambushing CEOs. A cross section of suggestions flooded in, ranging from the CEO 'having to clean the athletes village' to overprinting all the company's advertising, with 'I am a parasite'. Other suggestions included 'Wanted for Parasite Marketing Activities' posters, with a picture of the offending CEO, and a give-away of t-shirts to all spectators with the company logo and slogan, and a message that 'this company is a parasite marketer ... it lies and cheats'.

The strategy was simple: discredit any company and the agencies that create such campaigns, while placing both in jeopardy of litigation and significant damages. Make ambush marketing be seen as an unacceptable tactic by the media, the public and business peers. Slowly the IOC began to win the battle, as the media faithfully reported the IOC's position. 'Cute?

Street Smart? You must be kidding,' Dick Pound sounded off to the *Financial Times*. 'This is uncreative, unethical and unprofessional.' However, any publicity generated needed to be precisely and accurately directed, otherwise there would always be the risk of a 'blow back effect' leaving the public with the view that the little guy was being squashed.

It was important not to be seen as 'crying wolf' too often. Sponsors would often see any form of advertising activity by his competitor as ambush activity. A sponsor would fail to buy airtime on the Olympic broadcast and a competitor would step in with its normal commercial spots, and the sponsor would scream 'ambush'. A company that had a long-standing partnership with the sports movement, and continued to communicate its support for sport, was a totally different case to the company that, having lost out in the bid to acquire Olympic rights, would suddenly discovered a remarkable passion for sport, creating artificial and tenuous links to athletes and the Games.[10]

## Reebok plays poker – and loses

For me personally, one of the most satisfying parts of the IOC's efforts to police the Olympic brand was when a former poacher turned gamekeeper – as happened with Nike at the Sydney Games.

In the run up to Sydney, Reebok's marketing team informed me that they were pulling out of the sponsorship deal. Reebok claimed that the Sydney Organising Committee had breached its contract, and wanted to stop all rights fee payments. The truth was that Reebok, under financial pressure, was trying to cut back on all its sports deals around the world and was attempting to renegotiate the terms of several of its agreements. In order to apply pressure, Reebok threatened to hold a press conference in Sydney to announce it was pulling out of its Olympic sponsorship. I had been in Sydney the previous week and endeavoured to broker a solution between Reebok and SOCOG. From my perspective, SOCOG had not breached its contract – a fact that two years after the Games an Australian court confirmed.

Discussions were being held with the local Reebok representatives. To ensure that they did not take a decision on a local basis that would have clear global ramifications for the image of the whole Olympic Movement, still reeling from the effects of the Salt Lake City scandal, I called the new global head of marketing at Reebok in Boston to advise him that the IOC would be willing to assist in brokering a solution. Reebok thought that it was in the driving seat, that it could unilaterally walk away but still be able to provide the uniforms for the Australian team – enjoying all the promotional benefits of outfitting the home team. It believed that, with less than nine months to go before the Games, no other manufacturer would have the time to step in, design and outfit an entire team. Reebok had already produced many of the items for the team.

Reebok appreciated the offer of help from the IOC and assured me that there would be no press conference or press release about any withdrawal – and that, before any such action was taken, it would come back to the IOC to see if we could finally arbiter a solution. I left Australia, taking the 28-hour trip home, safe in the knowledge that the problem, at least for the time being, was under control and there was no risk of a new media firestorm about sponsors withdrawing just before the critical IOC Session.

I landed back in Geneva and all hell had broken loose. Reebok had reneged on the agreement. Its local office had proceeded with the press conference the moment I had left the country and promptly announced that they were withdrawing from their sponsorship of the Games.

I was jet-lagged and angry – not a good combination. In spite of everyone saying that it would be impossible for another manufacturer to outfit a major team at this short notice, I decided to try. I called Tom Harrington, head of marketing at Adidas. His initial response was that he doubted that they would be able to do it in the time left but he would check with his Australian colleagues. My next call was to Ian Todd, head of sports marketing at Nike and one of the most experienced and toughest operators in the business. Ian had a reputation of always stepping up to the big high profile deal and doing it quickly.

'Ian, have you seen what's happening in Australia?' I asked.

'Yes.'

'You interested in playing?'

'Don't know – give me 30 minutes to speak with my people – call me back.'

I called back 30 minutes later. Ian's opening remarks did not bode well.

'My team says they are not sure that there is enough time to pull a uniform programme of this size together.'

'I know, but are you willing to try?'

'Yes – if you can get your people on the plane and in Oregon, Portland within 24 hours.'

I called Craig McLatchey, secretary general of the Australian Olympic Committee to tell him that we were going after Reebok and to respond in a way that it would not know what had hit it, but that we had to do it quickly and in total secrecy. Six hours later, he and Rod Read, head of marketing, were on their way to Nike headquarters. On arriving they went straight to meet Todd who, by now, had formed a team to see what it would take to design and manufacture a uniform, and negotiate the agreement. We set ourselves a target of 48 hours, so that we could make a major announcement during Samaranch's final press conference for the IOC Session. Negotiations went round-the-clock – with conference calls between the teams in Portland, Michael Knight, president of SOCOG, and John Coates, president of the Australian Olympic Committee in Sydney, and the IOC in Lausanne.

Negotiations seemed to be falling into place, but over the final 12 hours they became bogged down in legal issues and everything began to unravel. By the morning, the deal was off and the Nike communications team who had come to Lausanne for the press announcement, left to go back to Amsterdam. It looked like Reebok would win after all. I took Dick Pound and Kevan Gosper, the IOC vice president for Australia, aside to tell them that sadly the deal had unravelled over night. We all looked at each other in disappointment. Dick asked me if I was really sure it was dead. I told him it looked like it but that we would have one final try. Dick instructed me to do whatever it would take.

The final day of the IOC Session had started; there were two hours left to make this work. Todd was also disappointed that we had not been able to pull the coup off. I called Ian again.

'Ian, this is not worth losing – for either of us – come on let's find a way. Let's take the risk.'

Samaranch had already started his press conference when we finally found a way through the outstanding issues. We had our deal.

Nike, which four years earlier in Atlanta was attacking the Olympic ideals with its advertising campaigns and marketing activities, had formally come on-board and joined the Olympic fold. The first Reebok knew of the deal was when it read the wire reports announcing the fastest Olympic marketing deal in history, and how Reebok had made a huge tactical error. Aside from its pending lawsuit with SOCOG, Reebok now had to work out what to do with all the uniforms it had produced for the Australian team – uniforms that carried the Olympic rings, so could not be sold, and that would have to be destroyed. Reebok was left to ponder the full consequences of taking the IOC on and going back on its word.

Nike shocked the world's media by immediately stepping into the void. We had come full circle. Nike, the antithesis of the establishment, had finally come inside. The bad boy of Atlanta had turned into an Olympic champion.

Nike's quick decision gave it some of the most defining moments of the Sydney Games, with the outfitting of the whole Australian team, including the Games' heroine, Cathy Freeman. When she won the 400 metre gold medal, wearing a suit emblazoned with the Nike swoosh, Reebok could only look on in dismay. The situation was all the more poignant when Reebok saw its one remaining chance to upstage Nike literally disappear – its star athlete, French woman Marie-Jose Perec, vanished 48 hours before she was to face Cathy Freeman, in what was being billed by many as the race of the Games. Reebok had to scramble to pull its advertising in France that had naturally focused on her. It was a salutary lesson on the pitfalls of individual athlete endorsement![11]

The Olympic Movement had come to cherish its brand – and learned how to protect it. But the next lesson was about managing a franchise. In particular, we had to find a way of controlling overzealous franchisees in the form of the host cities and national organising committees. Failure to do so could lead to the hosts ambushing their own Games and damaging their own image – something we discovered the hard way.

## NOTES

1 The Nike advertising slogan 'You do not win silver, you lose gold' apparently came from a focus research quote from US basketball player, Lisa Leslie.

2 Jones followed up with a letter to the IOC: 'In our opinion the value of the Olympics is increased only when every aspect of the Olympics is different, better and special. This need for differentiation is heightened by the fact that you are out of consumer sight between the Games and you face ever increasing competition for the public's share of mind and spirit. A clean field-of-play, where no visual distractions can detract from the drama of the athletic competition, can help make the fans' experience even more memorable. It's pure, honourable and distinguishable. More importantly I think it is what the fans expect. A clean field of play is an Olympic equity ... One of your core assets. The field of play is an important branding space that you own. Own every inch of it! Sharing your branding space dilutes the Olympic brand. Don't compromise your greatest opportunity to build brand power. There is no valid loss of revenue argument when the risk is loss of brand equity. The Coca-Cola Company may be better known for field-of-play signage than any other company. We consider the signage and presence to be a core Coca-Cola equity. But I think that we (and other sponsors) derive more associative value with strong Olympic branding created by a clean field of play than we do sharing signage on the Olympic field of play.'

3 Mars was a sponsor for the TOP II programme Albertville/Barcelona. After its excessive activities at Barcelona, the IOC withdrew from any renewal discussions for Atlanta. In many ways this was a pity as, outside of the Games, Mars ran some of the best promotions and marketing of any of the partners.

4 A similar incident occurred a few years later in Salt Lake City. Ales Valenta from the Czech Republic was competing in the aerial freestyle competition, wearing a crash helmet in the colours and trade mark of the energy drink Red Bull. Valenta did not have any other crash helmet, and this was clearly a case of accidental branding. In between jumps, sticky tape and paper were applied to the helmet to cover up the

offending trade marks. Valenta went on to win the gold medal with his record-breaking quintuple twisting triple somersault, a jump never before performed in competition.

Of course, sometimes ambush incidents occurred through plain bad luck. The big media story of the first week of the Salt Lake City Games was 'Skategate', when Canadian figure skaters, David Pelletier and Jamie Salé only won the silver medal when many thought that they should have won the gold. At the press conference, the pair rushed out of the Canadian television studios, grabbing whatever mineral water they found in CBC's fridge. Unfortunately, it was not a Coke brand. So when the world's press met the figure skaters, the images that went around the world the next day were with the wrong mineral water. Coke was not happy – and much of the rest of the Games, was spent trying to make amends.

5  One of the first ambush marketing incidents occurred at the 1932 Los Angeles Games. The Helms Bakery won the right to be the exclusive supplier of bakery products to the athletes' village. Another bakery, Weber, decided to gain some local promotional advantage by supplying bread to one of the competing nations. Helms, anxious to protect his exclusive rights, a marketing concept way ahead of its time, promptly threatened to sue the Organising Committee for $1 million for interference in his exclusive contract.

Helms became a major thorn in the side of the USOC president, Avery Brundage. As a result of USOC negligence in properly registering its marks, a 15-year lawsuit with Helms ensued, finally being settled in 1950.

6  The Asian Games has stadium advertising. The American Express ads had all the advertising removed, so that the stadium looked as if it was the Olympic stadium.

7  Under regulations first introduced in 1999 in Athens, fines on illegal advertising – levied on the billboard promoter and the advertiser – can reach $118,000 with jail sentences up to one year.

8  Nike spent $1.422 billion in 2002 on athlete and team endorsements, excluding equipment and clothing provided, Nike 2003 SEC Filings.

9  The success of the Sports Goods Industry Code led the IOC to consider developing a number of other codes to bring further discipline

to the marketplace and to further protect the rights of marketing partners. The most significant of these was a Code of Conduct for ticketing agents. Although the Olympic ticketing distribution procedures were probably far more disciplined than for any other major event, there was still a considerable black market in tickets and hospitality opportunities to the Games. Hospitality at the Games is one of the most important rights and benefits for sponsors. If any company could simply pick up tickets from an agent and use them for their own sales promotions and key guest invitations, then the benefit to the official partners would be significantly undermined, to the extent that some companies might even question the value of the sponsorship and whether it was not better to just buy some tickets directly from an agent, and put their own programme together.

10 This is perhaps best illustrated by the cases of Qantas and National Australian Bank (NAB), two companies which lost out on the rights to become Olympic sponsors for the Sydney Games. Qantas lost out to then number two Australian airline Ansett. Qantas had a long-standing tradition and heritage of supporting Australian athletes and sporting events, and was perfectly entitled to continue, even though the company lost the Olympic bid. Qantas was nevertheless anxious to avoid any risk of being branded an ambush marketer, and with a bit of help from some strict IOC marketing guidelines and local legislation, withdrew from any form of sports-related advertising or marketing during the Sydney Games. NAB, on the other hand, had no tradition of any involvement with sports and, when they lost out to Westpack to be the official sponsor of the Games and the Australian Olympic team, they immediately formed their own artificial sports team called 'Team NAB', a collection of Australian athletes with the sole objective of undermining Westpack's Olympic programme. After a few months, NAB's efforts fizzled out.

11 The media were brutal on Perec for leaving Sydney. Headlines referred to her as 'Mademoiselle La Chicken'.

## Chapter 7

# OPERATION PERFECT HOSTS

© Getty Images

## Office of the Mayor of Salt Lake City, Rocky Anderson, City Hall, 7 August, 2001

The 19th Olympic Winter Games in Salt Lake City are only months away. Salt Lake is a hive of activity, as the final plans and preparations to host the world are pulled together. IOC executives are visiting Salt Lake on an ever more frequent basis to work through last-minute issues. The final count-down has begun.

I am concerned. There are rumours that the city authorities plan to create their own separate identity and celebration plan, rather than collaborate with the organising committee to ensure a single unified programme. The IOC can ill afford a repeat of Atlanta, where the city's commercial agenda was allowed to run amok, damaging the image of the host city and undermining the Olympic values in the process.

Organising committee president, Mitt Romney, and chief operating officer, Fraser Bullock, are far from comfortable that they have things fully under control with the mayor and city hall.[1] The city council is starting to dream up various celebration and fund-raising programmes – many of which compete directly with the efforts of the organising committee.

Romney asked if I would come along to a meeting with the mayor, Rocky Anderson. The mayor opens the proceedings with a comprehen-sive overview of the broad marketing programme he's planning. These include a special celebration park which would compete directly with the organising committee's efforts for Olympics medals plaza. Romney and the Salt Lake Olympic Committee (SLOC) delegation look pale. Fraser Bul-lock starts to argue about the problems that this parallel programme could create for traffic circulation and other key logistics. But the mayor is not budging. The longer the debate continues, the more we seem to be heading for a repeat of Atlanta, where the organising committee's agenda and that of the city collided head on, leaving the Olympic Movement caught in the middle and badly bruised.

Watching the drama unfold around me, I know something has to give. With no end to the deadlock in sight, I turn to Mayor Anderson and politely but firmly point out that if the city insists on proceeding with the programme they will be in breach of the host city contract they signed with the IOC when Salt Lake was elected. The IOC will be left with no alternative, I say, but to sue the city for breach of contract. It would be the only way to protect the image of the Games.

Until this point, the IOC had never threatened to sue any host city, and the mayor may have assumed mine was just an idle bluff. He nevertheless turned to his legal counsel and asked whether the IOC could sue. The answer was clear: if Salt Lake proceeds with its city marketing programme, it risks being in breach of the IOC's contract.

## Angelic hosts

No one needed reminding about the headlines of the world's media after Atlanta. They were damning. The city failed to live up to its responsibilities to host the Centennial Games, because it elected to put short-term profit over any enhancement of its image.

Whether the IOC would have ever sued Salt Lake is open to debate. But the mayor decided not to take the risk and quietly allowed the city's marketing programme to fade away. From that moment on, SLOC and the city started working closely together. At the closing ceremony, Rocky Anderson came up and thanked me for threatening to sue them, bringing the city to its senses. Salt Lake went on to develop one of the strongest visual identity programmes ever, and in the process lay to rest many of the ghosts of Atlanta. The organisers proved that America did understand the true ideals of the Olympic Movement and could stage a magical Games.

Hosting the Olympic Games can provide one of the most powerful platforms for any nation. Governments spend billions of dollars every year managing their national image around the world. They seek to influence how they are perceived by other nations. National images, they know, affect political and economic relationships. Whether it is to increase tourism, change foreign and domestic policy, attract investment or aid, or boost international trade, the goal of national image management is to cast the nation in a more favourable global light.

Tokyo in 1964, for example, signalled a change in both the world's and Japan's own view of itself, and its place in the world. Seoul was a monumental step forward in modern Korean history – showcasing the fact that the country was no longer a poverty-ridden nation but ready to evolve from years of military dictatorship into a true democracy. In Barcelona in

1992, the city succeeded in catapulting itself into the top tier of Europe's tourist and business destinations. Similarly, the Games in Beijing in 2008 provides the perfect stage for China to redefine its place in the modern world.

It is no coincidence that the Games have become an international showcase for the host cities, or that the Games themselves continue to grow in stature as a result. When Samaranch became president, he immediately identified that the IOC was missing a great opportunity to brand the Olympic venues and competition sites with Olympic imagery. He had a clear vision and became very committed to the development of a consistent brand experience. Over the next two decades, he led a concerted campaign to develop a programme, called 'Look of Games', to reinforce the unique nature and presentation of the event.

By Sydney, the Look of Games project had become one of the key success factors of the Games. Samaranch often said that a $300 million stadium is not complete, until the Look of Games has been applied to it. Why throw the world's greatest party, and not bother to get dressed?

In 1980, the Olympic branding at any of the venues was very limited. The competition field of play was clean but sterile. By 2000, the field of play had become a vibrant dynamic stage, reinforcing the message that this event is different from all others. In Salt Lake City, an athlete was overheard to say that he was going to treat this as just another competition, until he stepped onto the ice and saw the giant Olympic rings at the end of the arena. At that moment it hit him: this was not just any other event; this was the Olympic Games.

Although working with a limited budget, in 1984 Peter Ueberroth and his team in Los Angeles had already identified the potential of venue presentation to raise the Olympic bar. They developed a visual presentation for their venues that differentiated them from all previous Games. They used an unusual combination of colours, including magenta, vermillion chrome, vivid green and aqua. This colour palate became known as 'festive federalism'. The eclectic mix of colours had Ueberroth claiming to be colour blind, but it worked.

# The world's longest commercial

Despite such isolated moments of brilliance, it wasn't until Barcelona that the IOC succeeded in significantly raising the bar on the presentation of the overall visual Games identity. Barcelona understood from the outset what the potential of hosting the Games meant – and how the Olympic celebration could be used to present a new identity for the city and country as a whole.

The fact that Samaranch was a native of Barcelona, and was on the organisers' and the mayor's case every day, helped. Samaranch challenged the organisers to establish a new standard in the visual presentation of the Olympics and in the process to add a totally new dimension to the Olympic brand. But it did not happen overnight.

The initial indications of Barcelona's design vision were not promising. From a city associated with brilliant artists like Antonio Gaudi, Salvador Dali and Pablo Picasso there were high expectations. The organising committee for each Games is always responsible for creating a series of emblems and designs to identify the specific nature and character of their Games. The IOC does not interfere in the creative process other than rubber-stamping the final design. At least that was the case until Barcelona came to present its mascot to the IOC for approval.

Samaranch looked on in utter disbelief as the proposed mascot for the Barcelona Games was presented to him for approval. Barcelona designer Javier Mariscal had designed a dog, called Cobi, to represent the Games. Cobi was a very avant-garde dog. It needed a lot of imagination to be even recognised as a dog. Even Mariscal was unsure about his design, later noting that, 'It is hard to fall in love at first sight with a dog that looks as if he has been run over by a heavy goods vehicle.'

Few people jumped to Cobi's defense. One who did was Spanish novelist Manuel Vazquez Montalban, who unhelpfully announced, 'I am pro-Cobi. He is a tribute to all dogs that have been run over at the tolls on the Barcelona motorway.' Eventually Cobi fired the collective imagination and, with his endearing nature and offbeat sense of humour, became an important contributor to the success of the Games, and perhaps the most successful Olympic mascot ever created.

In their presentation of the Games and their city, the Barcelona organisers showed that they grasped the basic ground rules of theatrical and stage management. A top advertising executive, Luis Bassat, was hired to produce the opening and closing ceremonies. Bassat, a Barcelona native and European creative director of global advertising agency Ogilvy and Mather, described the ceremonies as 'the longest commercial spot' in his career.

The mayor of Barcelona, and president of the Barcelona Organising Committee, Pasqual Maragall, set Bassat a simple challenge: 'Put Barcelona on the map. Put Catalonia on the map. Make the Games, Catalonia's coming out party! The image of Barcelona, Catalonia and Spain depends on the opening ceremony. The 100 metre sprint is the same in Seoul and in Barcelona … The big difference we can offer in comparison to other past and future Games, is our opening ceremony and perhaps our closing too.'

Luis Bassat came up with a number of simple iconic ideas that stamped their mark on the Games and the city. From the dramatic lighting of the Olympic cauldron by a flaming arrow, through to the symbolic unfolding of the Olympic flag over 10,000 athletes, he produced dramatic and highly effective visual images.[2]

The world, and in particular the media, was quick to praise. The Games took place against the backdrop of a new world order. The Soviet Union was unravelling, the Cold War was over and the Berlin Wall had fallen. The Germans were reunited and apartheid in South Africa was crumbling. Reuters observed that for those moments 'it was possible to imagine that the world was a perfect place and that Barcelona was at its fulcrum. Barcelona became the only place one could imagine ever wanting to be'.[3]

Barcelona won gold for its staging of the opening and closing ceremonies. Mayor Maragall noted that in the space of five short years the Olympics allowed the city of Barcelona to undergo a transformation that would otherwise have taken it 30 years.

How would Atlanta shape up? Billy Payne, the chairman and CEO of the Atlanta Organising Committee (ACOG) came to Barcelona with his team. They were not expecting to learn much from the Spanish organising committee. He left town, with four years to organise his own Games, with headlines saying that the Barcelona Olympics would be a tough act to follow. And they were.

## Arctic circles

Before Atlanta took centre stage, the Olympic circus moved to a small Norwegian town of just 22,000 people, closer to the Arctic Circle than the Games had ever been staged before. Lillehammer won the Games at the 1988 IOC Session in Seoul, as the rank outsider. It went on to stage one of the greatest Winter Games in living memory. [4]

Norway was anxious to avoid the same mistakes it had made hosting the World Nordic Ski Championships in 1982. Then, the prevailing image among the foreign media, was the staggering price of the cost of living and how no one could ever afford to holiday in the country. The Lillehammer Olympics showed a different side of the country.

The leadership of the Lillehammer Organising Committee (LOOC), and its COO Petter Ronningen, soon realised the importance of image. Under the direction of their design director, Petter Moshus, they built the first truly integrated design programme of any Olympic Games. Moshus created a concept that focused on Norway's distinctive features and national character. It combined the motifs of wood and stone, closeness between people and nature. The designers deliberately chose 'materials with an emphasis on solidity, honesty, authenticity and environmental awareness'. The pictograms were inspired by Norwegian petroglyphs – rock carvings thousands of years old. They reinforced the idea of the Games returning to the birthplace of winter sports.

The organisers also recognised the critical role of the spectator in creating atmosphere. In Albertville two years earlier, most of the spectators had been placed behind the television cameras, and therefore were not visible to the television viewers. But the Lillehammer producers decided to place the spectators as a backdrop to the athletic performance. The effect was dramatic.

The importance of the spectators had long been recognised by Samaranch. He repeatedly fought to ensure that the Olympic stadiums were full, arguing that if they looked empty on television the viewer would not fully appreciate the importance of the event. It was an honour to be able to attend the Games in person, he insisted, and if no one turned up then the event appeared second rate.

During the 1988 Seoul Games in Korea, where athletics is not a popular local sport, Samaranch berated the local organisers for the empty athletic stadiums. He argued that no one outside of the country would understand why the stadiums were empty. Samaranch instructed the organisers to fill the stadium with soldiers, school children – anything just to fill up the venues.

Lillehammer turned the spectators into part of the spectacle. This and the overall look of the Games exceeded everyone's expectations. The media heaped praise on their Norwegian hosts. The Games, they acknowledged, provided an unrivalled platform to promote the culture and image of the host country around the world. Norway and the Norwegian people had taken full advantage of the opportunity to host the Olympic Games; to change certain perceptions of the country and dramatically enhance the country's global standing.[5]

'The truth about the Olympics is that they are almost impossible to ruin ... Any damage Atlanta might do will only harm Atlanta,' was how the *International Herald Tribune*, with uncanny foresight, closed its commentary on the Winter Games.

## Atlanta shoots itself in the foot

Two years later the headlines around the world told a very different story. The world's media were united in their condemnation of the Atlanta Games.[6]

Atlanta won the privilege to host the Centennial Olympic Games, in a contentious election at the 1990 IOC Session in Tokyo by, 16 votes.[7] Atlanta, the frontier town of modern capitalism, beat the sentimental favourite Athens, the cradle of civilisation and birthplace of the modern Games.

The seeds of failure were soon apparent. The city of Atlanta embarked on a contentious relationship with the Atlanta Organising Committee and its president Billy Payne. When Bill Campbell took over as mayor of Atlanta from Maynard Jackson in 1993, things went from bad to worse. Campbell never understood his responsibilities as mayor of an Olympic host city. He set Atlanta on a collision course with the organising committee.

The organising committee also caused raised eyebrows with some of its early design decisions. Atlanta's mascot, Whatizit, with its bulging eyes and dangling feet, received a similar welcome from the world's media as Barcelona's mascot, Cobi. The IOC again briefly pondered whether to veto the design. But, recognising how Cobi had eventually become such a hit, the IOC elected not to intervene. Looking back, this was a mistake.

Unfortunately, Whatizit, or Izzy as the mascot became officially known, never rose to the challenge. In the lead up to Atlanta, the media had a field day. The *Los Angeles Times* kicked off the debate shortly after the mascot's launch describing Billy Payne's pride and joy, as: 'A little mutant monstrosity that was born in the toxic dump of somebody's imagination.' The reviews only got worse with the world's media referring variously to the 'blob', 'the sperm with legs' and suggesting alternatives including, in the spirit of Lille-hammer's human mascots, Haakon and Kristin, that Atlanta should adopt Ted and Jane – after media mogul Ted Turner and his wife Jane Fonda.

Atlanta City Council seemed intent on squeezing the Olympic opportunity for every cent and be damned with the consequences of what it would do to Atlanta's image. The city's marketing director, Joel Babbit, a well known *enfant terrible*, soon began to show what might be in store when the world arrived in Atlanta. He talked of his plans to sell sponsorship to the city's parks and buildings, streets and street signs. He even proposed to bounce laser beams off the moon and round up all the stray dogs in town, using them to display advertising messages. Not all of his ideas were practical, but they were bound to spark a reaction.

The IOC reacted strongly to the proposals. A letter to the mayor stated that the proposed activities would be inconsistent with the terms of the Host City Contract and could compromise the successful financing of the Centennial Olympic Games. The mayor was invited to attend the next IOC board meeting. Mayor Jackson backed down over the proposals, responding that 'Atlanta will take no action which will jeopardise the success of the Games.' Sadly, his successor, Bill Campbell, was less far-sighted and pressed ahead with a damaging commercial agenda.

The city soon approved a new revenue-generating plan, through the Atlanta Economic Development Commission, chaired by Campbell himself. An associate of Campbell, Munson Steed, developed a programme to lease and manage street property during the Games. Steed's plan was to raise up to $50 million for the city and himself, selling to whoever would pay, be it Olympic sponsors – or their competitors. The sponsors were apoplectic with rage. George Fisher, chairman and CEO of Kodak, threatened to pull his company's operations out of Atlanta. Even this did not bring the city's officials to their senses.

The original plan was to sell an initial batch of around 350 stalls for $10,000–20,000 each. But after pressure from local lobby groups, the programme was opened up, with the price dropping to as low as $150 per stall. Some 6,000 'entrepreneurs' jumped at the opportunity. The operation was a total commercial flop, with Munson Steed sued by angry stall-holders for $25 million. Some unfortunate stallholders lost their life savings.

The result was chaos. ACOG's own managing director of communications, Dick Yarborough described downtown Atlanta as looking 'like a small town carnival on steroids. Tacky is too nice a word to describe the city during the Games. The city looked like a third-rate flop house when the world came to see us ... Atlanta paid dearly for its reputation.' Olympic historian Robert Barney described a scene of 'roving street hawkers and frenzied vendors preying on residents and Olympic tourists like a horde of locusts.'

My own memories are equally vivid. The street market initiated by Atlanta City Council created traffic grid-lock around the centre of Atlanta, preventing everyone from travelling around town. The media couldn't get to the main press centre. Media buses would finally make it through the traffic, only to have drivers speed right past the entrance, refusing to stop and pulling up some 800 metres further on. This was because the city council refused to issue a special temporary permit, to allow the buses to stop in front of the press centre.[8]

Journalists who actually made it to the press centre considered themselves lucky. The bus drivers, who were brought in from all over the country to drive the press around, often had no clue where they were supposed to go. One group of journalists found itself visiting one of Atlanta's scrapyards, instead of attending the opening ceremony.

By the time the press did make it to the press centre, they were ready to tear the city and the organisers apart. The Atlanta organisers had forgotten Samaranch's dictum that the media are the last to judge the Games. Despite repeated pleas by the IOC, ACOG never understood that the media could make or break the Games.

Media management became ACOG's Achilles heel and the leadership became paranoid in their dealing with the media. 'They never got the idea that we were a necessary evil. We were just evil,' was how long-time Olympic journalist, Associated Press sports chief Larry Siddons saw things. One commentator later noted, when analysing 'Why Atlanta missed out on Olympic Glory', that 'the organisers must be regretting not taking better care of the people writing their epitaph.'

After years of grating encounters with ACOG's leadership, knives were sharpened. 'We'd been lulled into this myth of this wonderful American organisation,' noted veteran Olympic journalist Morley Myers, UPI's international sport editor. Myers was an experienced Olympic hand, having attended every Games since Mexico 1968. 'When we got there, it plainly wasn't the case. We were expecting high-tech, and we got Third World. Basically nothing was working.'

Mayor Campbell had absolutely no appreciation of the damage that his actions were doing to the image of the city that he had been elected to promote and safeguard. His reaction to the media onslaught was to suggest that 'they should take the critics out to the shooting venue and get rid of them.' The *International Herald Tribune* noted that the 'statement revealed more about the parochial weakness of the Atlanta leadership than any of the transportation or computer problems.'

Billy Payne lost the plot. His response to media criticism about how tacky the city was looking as the hawkers descended on downtown Atlanta, was that this was just a case 'of Atlanta getting ready to party'.

By the third day of the Games, Samaranch was well aware of the damage that ACOG's lack of media management and the city's self-absorbed revenue-generating programmes, were doing to the image of the Games. Dropping his usual diplomatic guard at the daily Co-ordination Commission meeting between the IOC and ACOG, Samaranch laid into Billy Payne. 'You have to provide the media with a full mechanism to successfully do their work', he said. 'You are killing the Games.' Samaranch went on to tell both Billy Payne and Mayor Campbell that if things did not improve within 48 hours, Atlanta's image would be tarnished forever.

During the years planning the Atlanta Games, it had become apparent that there was a totally dysfunctional relationship between the city and the organisers. But nothing truly prepared the IOC for the fact that the host city would go out of its way to ambush the Games and to do untold damage to its own image. As *The Wall Street Journal* noted, 'the IOC was prepared to repel the usual corporate ambushers but not a host city ambush.'

At the very least, we had perhaps naively expected the city authorities to be co-operative and supportive of the Olympic effort, not to effectively sabotage the Games. After all, not only were the city authorities not being asked to contribute to the cost of the Games, ACOG was going to spend nearly $500 million in construction projects for the Games.[9] This included a new $207 million baseball stadium that after the closing ceremony would be given to the Atlanta Braves, guaranteeing that the team would not move out of the city. All of this was in addition to being relieved of $11 million of debt on the old baseball stadium.

This though, was not enough for Campbell. He wanted more. Campbell set about trying to shake down the organising committee for every conceivable cost. Atlanta became the first ever host city to charge for extra policing and sanitation costs – some $9.5 million. This was a cost that ACOG could ill afford, forcing it to cut corners elsewhere in the operations and push its marketing efforts beyond the limits of what the Olympic image could sustain.

The original financial model for the staging of the Games in Atlanta was, with hindsight, fundamentally flawed. Billy Payne promised the local authorities that not a single cent of taxpayer or city funds would be spent on the Olympics. All costs, including the construction of all the venues, would be covered by the Games marketing programme. Ultimately this proved too steep a mountain to climb. As funds started to dry up, ACOG became increasingly desperate.

The marketing programmes had no problem in funding the costs related to the actual staging of the Games. But it was too much to ask them to cover the $500 million of capital costs for building all the venues. The idea that they could recoup all these costs over 17 days was madness. Unfortunately the number one priority for the ACOG leadership was how to balance the books, rather than finding the time, and the budget, to set about enhancing and perpetuating the Olympic image.

The initial reactions after Atlanta was awarded the Games were positive. The Governor of Georgia, Zell Miller, noted shortly after Atlanta's election in early 1991, that the 'failure to fund [these Games] would send the wrong signal from the state honoured to host the Centennial Games.' But within a few months, ACOG was scrambling to raise the necessary funds. Soon it was slicing the cake very thin. 'To say that we had a short-term view was an understatement', Yarborough, ACOG's communications chief joked. He described ACOG and the city's revenue-generating philosophy as 'Show me the money', a catchphrase taken at the time from the hit movie *Jerry Maguire*, based on a struggling sports agent.

## A play in three acts

The Atlanta Games were three quite distinct events. The Games that were seen on television generated global TV audiences that established new records.[10] The television cameras, for the most part, avoided the tacky downtown street images and focused on the sports venues and athletic competition. As a result, the world saw some of the best sports competition ever, and was shielded from the trashing of the Olympic ideals in the city streets. Broadcasters simply averted their eyes, and the eyes of the world, from the shameful spectacle. For this, the Olympic Movement owes it a great debt of gratitude. But something else was also lost: the soul of the Games.

It was interesting to note that in research conducted in the US after the Games, people commented on how wonderful the Games were but that there was, nevertheless, something missing. When pressed, they would ask where were the waterfalls of Montjuic in Barcelona? Where were the festival street scenes of the host city celebrating? The Games needed the magic to extend beyond the sports venues, to make them the Olympics.

And then there was the media view. Even Atlanta's own press had to admit that it had blown it: 'The "greed Games". That's the knock we heard often during the Atlanta Olympics, as critics complained that commercialism ruined what should be a celebration of the nobility and dignity of sport for its own sake.'

And finally, there were the Games you attended as a spectator. Atlanta attracted record crowds – selling 8.6 million tickets, more than Los Angeles and Barcelona combined. On the whole, these spectators had a wonderful time, their enjoyment fuelled by the success of the US team, who won a record set of medals. It was no small achievement for ACOG to pull together an operation that could cope with such large crowds. But in the end all this was lost in the comments of the vocal, but critical and highly influential, 4,000 print journalists attending the Games.

ACOG's Dick Yarborough reflected after the Games: 'The city couldn't live up to its hype and showed it to the world.' He continued, 'the city of Atlanta government blew the Games – pure and simple. What could have been an opportunity to show the world we were the major league city we claim to be, was instead an embarrassing display of tacky shacks blocking sidewalks and impeding traffic flow.'

The *Financial Times* wrote: 'This was the chance for Atlanta to show itself to the world, but for the sake of a few thousand dollars (raised from letting land to small business) it has allowed people to go away with a poor image of the city. It's a crying shame when the sport competition and the enjoyment of the crowds have been such a phenomenal success.'

And therein lay the tragedy for both ACOG and the IOC. Billy Payne, and his senior operations team at ACOG led by A.D. Frazier, had done an excellent job, staging some of the best sports competitions ever seen. They had pulled together a very committed team but, in the end, were let down by the local authorities and a weak mayor. They had taken their eye off the ball in dealing with the media, and failed to engage the mayor and the city in a collaborative effort.

My own emotions after Atlanta were mixed. Initially, I felt a sense of failure that the IOC had not been able to prevent such a disaster. My colleagues and I had allowed the Olympic image to be undermined. But it also led to a hardening of our resolve to protect the Olympic brand. The IOC resolved to never let it happen again. Never again would we let a politician take control of the Games for some personal short-sighted agenda.

## The wake-up call

Atlanta became a major wake-up call for the IOC and a watershed for the Olympic Movement. It was abundantly clear that the world did not like what it had seen in Atlanta and felt that the Olympic ideals had been tarnished while in Atlanta's possession.

The *Wall Street Journal*, in its closing report on the Games, noted that 'the IOC feels its sacred rings have taken some significant dings, and Atlanta's legacy may be more pronounced in the realm of how not to do things ...

To remain effective, [the IOC] must retain an aura of international amity, patriotic intensity and dewy-eyed Olympic hopefuls. Much of it is hooey, but it is what every enterprise needs: a point of differentiation.' Atlanta was a warning for future host cities.

The journalists were right. The Olympic image took a major hit in Atlanta. It did not matter that for the most part the sponsor programmes were a success, and developed in a manner totally complimentary to the Olympic ideals. The actions of the city with its street vending programming, along with a mismanaged souvenir licensing programme, had done significant damage to the Olympic brand.

Atlanta had totally missed the opportunity to use the Games as a platform to enhance its image and promote itself around the world. Mayor Campbell and the city council's short-sightedness and greed not only scored a major own goal for his city, but, in the process, distorted the Olympic values. [11]

Even before the Atlanta Games were over, the IOC sat down with officials from Nagano and Sydney to make sure that they fully understood why Atlanta had slipped up and what steps could be taken to prevent a repeat exercise at subsequent Games. Atlanta provided both Nagano and Sydney with a cautionary lesson in the issues of image management.

## Lessons learned

Michael Knight, the New South Wales Minister for the Olympics, and the Lord Mayor of Sydney, Frank Sartor, left Atlanta with some important lessons. There was no sense in putting on a perfect sports presentation, they realised, if you did not manage how the city presented itself on the world stage. For Sydney to succeed, and the Olympic Movement to rediscover the Olympic values that many believed were lost in the cluttered streets of Atlanta, the IOC and Sydney must find ways to rein in the rampant commercialism. Knight and Sartor knew that the venue for the Games is not just the sports venues, but the whole city. This is what the world would see. As with Barcelona, this would be the true payback for hosting the Games.

Immediately after the Atlanta Games, Samaranch tasked the IOC management with reviewing the structures and relationship with host cities.

A 30-page list of new marketing conditions was drawn up, designed to ensure that the local organising committees, and in particular the host cities, would not work at cross purposes with the IOC, or with each other. The IOC could not afford a repeat public relations disaster by a host city. The IOC set about reviewing how it could manage and control the whole visual presentation more tightly. The Olympic Games were to be seen as a franchise, with the IOC as the franchisor doing a much better job at controlling its franchisees – the host cities and local organising committees.

One of the first actions was to develop a standards manual for the overall presentation of the Olympic imagery at the Games, both within the venues and throughout the city. The Olympic symbol had to be made 'the hero' of the overall presentation of the Games. In every picture and every television shot, the Olympics and the host city must be clearly branded. The design team of Copeland Hirthler was hired to start working with Nagano to review the whole look of the Games' presentation.

Meetings were held with all the partners to review the Atlanta experience and decide what lessons could be learned from the overall presentation. Although most partners had developed successful programmes leading up to the Games, many were insulted by the naked commercialism on the streets of Atlanta. They recognised the damage that this would cause to the Olympic brand, if left unchecked. 'The United States brand has suffered badly', was John Hancock's CEO, David D'Alessandro's judgement of the Atlanta Games. *Advertising Age* in a lead editorial shortly after the Games, pointed out that 'Sponsors stand to gain the most from close association with a well-run event and lose the most from over-commercialisation.'

The headlines confirmed what I already knew: the Corinthian spirit and the commercial value of the Games were not in conflict – they were symbiotically intertwined. By protecting the former, we enhanced the latter.

Although Nagano was only 16 months away, the IOC and the Organising Committee, NAOC, set about reviewing all aspects of the visual presentation, sponsor presence at the Games and, most importantly of all, the co-ordination between the city, the local prefecture government and the organising committee. This time, there was to be no parallel city marketing programme – the Japanese understood the importance of presenting a single, unified image and tightly controlling the overall commercial presentation.

Samaranch took an even more hands-on approach to the Look of Games programme, poring over architectural plans and making suggestions as to where the Olympic rings and other branding elements should be added. Even once the Nagano Games had begun, Samaranch stayed focused to the multi-screen TV feed in his office at the IOC headquarters hotel. In one incident he called up in the middle of a race to inquire how quickly we could add the rings to the ice of the luge run. The Japanese organisers, who had planned for every contingency other than the IOC president becoming chief 'look designer' during the Games, were left scrambling to find out how to sink the rings into the ice, whilst not interfering with the running of the sleds. The technicians screamed that it was impossible, but by day two of the competition the rings were there. Samaranch turned his attention to the next venue and more small details and adjustments that improved the overall visual presentation.[12]

Even if Nagano, an industrial city of over a million people, could not always present the most beautiful visual backdrop, it won over the world with the charm of its people. A long-standing Olympic commentator wrote in the *New York Times*, how 'the Japanese hosts were open and capable, and visitors like me felt honoured to live three weeks in a very different culture, walking down narrow lanes and peeking into tiny houses.' The press left Nagano in decidedly better spirits than they had Atlanta.[13]

## Raising the bar in Sydney

From an early stage, the Australian Tourist Commission recognised the potential of hosting the Games. Initial research by the Commission suggested that the Games would attract an additional 1.74 million visitors between 1997 and 2004, generating Aus\$ 3.5 billion in foreign exchange earnings. John Morse, managing director of the Commission was clear on the potential benefits: 'The media coverage will add depth and dimension to Australia's image, by looking at every aspect of our lifestyle and culture, including travel, the arts, business entertainment and cuisine. The unrivalled exposure we receive on television, radio, print and on the internet will change forever the way the rest of the world sees us.'

The Australian media were less sure. Following the euphoria of Sydney's election, the local press embarked on a campaign fretting about everything that might go wrong with the Games.[14] There was concern that the organising committee might embarrass the nation in front of the world. Bill Bryson, the award-winning author, compared the Australian attitude to hosting the Games, with that of the Americans: 'Australians are ace fretters, which in a context such as this, is no bad thing. The American approach to a big event like the Olympics, is to expect everything to go right, to be dumbfounded when it does not, and then to move swiftly into denial.'

Bryson went on to talk about the huge amounts of newspaper space devoted to all things that might go wrong: 'It is literally not possible to name a catastrophic contingency, short of asteroid impact or nuclear attack, that hasn't been mooted and exhaustively analysed in the nation's press in the long run-up to the Games.' The Australian population enjoyed seven years of cynicism and backbiting before they were able to sit back and enjoy their Games.

Michael Knight, Sydney's Olympics Minister, understood that if the city was to be treated as an Olympic venue, the Games would need special legislation to manage the downtown precinct. New laws were needed to deal with everything from the control of streets, to limitations on billboards and city advertising, through to special police powers to prohibit unauthorised street vending and hawking. Knight drove the Sydney Olympic Arrangements Act through the New South Wales Parliament.

Although Knight moved to ensure tight control of Sydney's image while staging the Games, he was still struggling to balance the books and was reluctant to allocate the necessary financial resources to completely dress the city. It was to be an ongoing budget battle between the IOC and SOCOG.

Shortly after Sydney had been awarded the Games, Ric Birch, who had been appointed to produce the ceremonies, came up with the idea of placing a giant icon of the Olympic rings on Sydney Harbour Bridge. Knight decided that this would be an unnecessary extravagance, and repeatedly refused. Others though, believed that the idea had the potential to become the overriding image of the Games and kept quietly working away on the plans. By February 2000, it was clear that if Sydney did not take a decision on the rings on the bridge, it would be too late to undertake the manufacture. Knight was still refusing to allocate the budget and it looked like the idea was not going to happen. Either the IOC was going to have to 'volunteer to pay', or Knight would have to be 'tricked' into agreeing.

The IOC Executive Board held its final meeting in Sydney prior to the Games in February 2000, and Knight reported to Samaranch and the Board. I scribbled a note to Samaranch, telling him to read out the message, as part of his concluding remarks, at the end of Knight's presentation and after all the questions. Samaranch looked at me, asking what on earth this was all about. I just said, trust me, please do it, it will be worth it.

'Mr. Knight, I understand that you are considering applying the Olympic rings to Sydney Harbour Bridge for the Games', said Samaranch, squinting at my handwriting, 'but are not sure if you need the IOC's approval. I think it is an excellent idea and I am pleased to approve it. Thank you, meeting closed.'

Knight looked on not quite sure what had happened. His right-hand man, David Richmond, head of the Olympic Co-ordination Authority, knew exactly what had happened – he had just had $1 million knocked out of his dwindling contingency budget. Richmond cornered me the moment the meeting broke up, asking what I was up to. I just smiled and told him that the IOC was pleased to approve the project. After the Games, everyone – even Knight – agreed that the rings on the bridge had been one of the best investments they had made in the presentation of the Games.

Construction immediately began on the largest Olympic rings ever produced. Made out of 35 tons of steel, the rings were 75 metres wide and 35 metres high. Erecting them on the bridge presented its own set of engineering challenges. The job was completed just a few days before the Opening Ceremony, only to cause mild panic within NBC's Olympic studios.

Dick Ebersol, NBC's Olympic head, had designed his main studio at the international Olympic broadcast centre to appear as if it overlooked Sydney bay and the bridge, and had gone to great expense to create a photographic backdrop to achieve the effect. Ebersol arrived in Sydney the day the rings were being added to the bridge, only to realise that his expensive set was now out of date. NBC scrambled to hire helicopters and arrange for the rings to be secretly switched on at night, so that the whole studio scene could be re-shot, this time with the rings on the bridge.

The rings dominated the skyline throughout the Games and identified Sydney as a remarkable Olympic host city. The Sydney organisers knew that they really were hosting the world. 'Our objective has been about making sure that not only are the venues looking absolutely fantastic,' Bridget Smythe, Sydney's director of Games Look and Design observed, 'but to make sure that Sydney as a city and the public spaces surrounding the venues are really bought to life for the Games, they are really dressed up to make sure that everybody gains the Olympic experience. It's all about making the precinct sing. We have branded this city Olympic.'

## Party time

Sydney introduced a number of other projects that had a major impact on how the world experienced the Games. These included creating six 'Olympics Live' sites around city, to entertain the public who might not be able to afford or have the time to go to the venues. The effect of the six sites around town was to create a dynamic festive party atmosphere. The spirit carried through to the athletes and the media who could be found watching large video screens of the competition, and listening to local bands late into the night. The Olympic spirit transcended the whole city.

When the Olympic flame was extinguished on 2 October, as an Australian airforce F-111 jet swept over the cauldron, no one wanted to leave Sydney, least of all the media. Sydney insiders referred to the last day of the Games as 'Sad Sunday', not wanting their party to end.

The headlines around the world were effusive in their praise for the organisers, Sydney and the Australians. 'No city on Earth will outshine what we have experienced here,' was how the UK's *Daily Mirror* summarised their experience, 'they were the best Olympic Games of everybody's lifetime. For two weeks a nation that truly loves athleticism elevated sport to a plane none of us thought attainable in this cynical world.' 'Sydney restored something to the Olympics you can't measure on a balance sheet: Humanity', reported the *Observer*.[15]

Bill Bryson, writing in *The Times*, summed up the general mood. 'Congratulations Australia. You did it. From start to finish, it's been wonderful ... I invite you to suggest a more successful event anywhere in the peacetime history of mankind.'

'Australians can now allow themselves the quiet satisfaction of know-ing that they have thrown the best party of the planet,' was the accolade from *Time Magazine*.

Inevitably Sydney's accolades led to direct comparisons with Atlanta. More than once Sydney was described as the antithesis of Atlanta, thanks in part to keeping the commercial agenda on a tight leash.[16]

The media also gave the sponsors credit for their programmes. 'If the Olympics are remembered for one thing – besides the splendid setting and spectacular athletic feats – this could be the Olympics that forever changes the nature of how sponsors speak to visitors', was how *USA Today* reported on the marketing efforts of the Games, recognising how the sponsors had worked hard to develop programmes that enhanced the visitors Olympic experience.

## Lighting the fire in Salt Lake

With the close of Sydney, it was only a few months before the Olympic Movement was scheduled to return to America, this time for the Winter Games in Salt Lake City. Among the world's media, the jury was very much out about whether the Sydney presentation was a mere anomaly, a one-off, courtesy of the Australians. Would the Olympic organisers in Salt Lake return to the commercial problems found in Atlanta, or had the IOC and the organisers learnt their lesson to build on the brand strengths found in Sydney?

And, on top of these challenges, Salt Lake would have to work hard to overcome stereotypes about polygamy and to demythologize the Mormon religion, as well as dispel the lingering odour of the bribery scandal linked to Salt Lake's bid to host the Games. There were many misconceptions about the region, prompting journalists to joke in the lead up to the Games, 'that most of the visitors pouring into Salt Lake for the 2002 Winter Games will have heard just two things about Utah; that it can be tough to get a drink, but no problem looking for three wives.'

Although Mitt Romney, president of the Salt Lake Organising Commit-tee, understood the importance of avoiding a commercial free-for-all on the streets of Salt Lake he, like Billy Payne, a few years earlier, faced many of the same challenges in balancing the books and bringing the Games in on budget. Romney was unsure that he would have the necessary resources to develop a strong image programme for the Games. And as SLOC was effectively once again a private organising committee, Romney also did not have the legislative authority that Knight had in Sydney to ensure control over the city.

Romney, nevertheless, left Sydney with a much better appreciation of the importance of Look and Image as one of the key success factors in defining the Games. Slowly, over the coming months, the Look budgets would be increased and the SLOC creative team, led by Scott Givens, was given an ever freer hand to push the envelope and develop a series of dramatic visual presentations.

Givens, and his director of design, Bob Finley, came forward with the idea of wrapping all the skyscrapers around the centre of Salt Lake in twenty-storey high images of athletes to provide a unified backdrop against the Wasatch Mountains. The team also decided to challenge Sydney in producing various interpretations of the Olympic symbol. To the northeast of the city, they constructed the largest Olympic rings yet built. At an elevation of 1800 metres the rings, measuring approximately 150 by 90 metres (imagine a 14-storey building on its side), and composed of over 1500 florescent lights, lit up the mountainside at night and shone down on the Games below.

If there was one single moment that best captured the difference between Salt Lake and Atlanta it was during the opening ceremony, when the Olympic flag was marched into the stadium. Traditionally, the flag has been paraded in either by athletes from the host nation, or a military guard of honour. In Atlanta, Billy Payne had broken with tradition by inviting seven friends, the original members of the bidding team to march the flag in with him. Many Olympic traditionalists were appalled. All the more as these had been the Centennial Games.

Romney, though, showed that he understood the true power of the Olympic brand and the symbolism of the rings, and their ability to inspire. Romney came up with the powerful idea of inviting eight living legends to march in with the Olympic flag, representing the five continents, and the three pillars of the Olympic Movement: Sport, Culture, Environment.

Triple Olympic gold medallist and skiing legend Jean Claude Killy was chosen for sport, filmmaker Steven Spielberg for culture and activist Jean-

Michel Cousteau for environment. They were joined by astronaut John Glenn, representing the Americas; Nobel Laureate and former President of Poland, Lech Walesa, Europe; Nobel Laureate Archbishop Desmond Tutu, Africa; Nagano 1988 ski jumper and gold medallist Kazuyoshi Funaki, Asia; and the last person to light the Olympic cauldron, gold medallist, Cathy Freeman, Oceania.

After some soul-searching at city hall, Mayor Anderson finally realised that it would be suicidal to embark on the same strategy as Atlanta, going head-to-head with the organisers over the visual presentation of the city during the Games. Anderson backed down from embarking on a broad programme of street vending and, by the time the athletes and media arrived in Salt Lake, the world found what it wanted: a city and an organising committee that fully understood its responsibilities in staging the Games; that they were mere custodians of the Olympic brand, and were tasked with nurturing it, polishing it and eventually returning it back to the IOC – stronger, and in better shape, than when they had received it. Given some of the issues that Salt Lake faced along its journey to stage the Games, with the scandal surrounding it's election, the final positive result was all the more impressive.

When the torch was extinguished, the press were once again generous with their accolades and the image of Salt Lake City and the Mormon religion would be changed forever.[17]

Polls run by the *Salt Lake Tribune* after the Games underlined just how far public local opinion towards the Games had changed, with nearly 60 per cent of the population feeling exceptionally well about the Games, and another 29 per cent better than expected. Only one per cent saw the Games as worse than expected. The big winners were: the Mormon Church, with 51 per cent believing that Games had improved its image; the Utah people no longer perceiving themselves as boring (80 per cent); the state's natural beauty (91 per cent); and Utah in general (92 per cent). As with Barcelona and Sydney, the setting would linger in the collective memory long after everyone had forgotten who had won the ice dancing.

Eighty-seven per cent of the population saw it as a good thing to have bid and won the Games, and over 74 per cent had not had enough and wanted to bid for a future Olympics. Fraser Bullock, the chief operating officer of SLOC talked about the theme of the Games, 'Light the Fire Within', and how it proved 'that the power to inspire is the power to change. More than anything else, these Games showed that this vision is perhaps humanity's greatest untapped resource. Well after the medals were awarded and the champions crowned, it was this spirit that Salt Lake City left to the world.'

## The tourism dividend

'The Olympic Games are the best thing that has ever happened to Australia's tourism industry,' John Morse, managing director of the Australia Tourist Commission said a few months after the Sydney Closing Ceremony. 'The Olympic Games have changed forever the world's view of Australia.'[18]

Although tourist boards in previous host countries had set about benefiting from the glow of staging the Olympic Games, strategies were more often than not developed after the Games had actually taken place. Australia was perhaps the first country to truly realise the potential benefit of being an Olympic host nation, from the moment of Sydney's election they developed a strategy to maximise the return. The mere fact that Sydney won the right to host the Olympic Games helped Australian destinations capture the ear of convention organisers. The Australian Tourist Commission's goal was to make the Olympics a two-week documentary on Australia for the global TV audience of 4 billion, creating a lasting legacy for their industry.

Australian tourism marketers wanted to divest Australia of the Crocodile Dundee image by which it was perceived in many international markets, and project an image of a diverse and modern country with a unique look and feel. Back in the early 1990s, Australia was rarely on the world stage. The Games became the hook the media had been waiting for. 'The media were saying – the Games are on in Australia, let's find out more about this country ... The Olympics added to the depth and dimension of the world's knowledge of Australia and will make us a contemporary destination.' The Games took Australian tourism to places it could never otherwise have afforded to go.

Morse grasped the potential benefits of promoting Brand Australia with the Olympic brand. And the IOC saw the value of a host country taking the benefits of hosting the Games to a new level of excellence, which in turn could lead to an even greater roster of cities applying to host the Games in the future.

The Australian Tourist Commission had only limited budgets to fully realise the opportunity and although the government provided an additional $6.5 million grant for specific Olympic-related promotions, Morse understood that the real potential was to gain access to the marketing budgets of the Olympic partners and connect with the producers of the Olympic broadcast rights holders. The IOC also believed that a partnership between the Olympic sponsors and 'Brand Australia' could add a new dimension to partner marketing programmes.

John Morse and his team were invited to attend sponsor and broadcast workshops, and explain to the partners how the ATC could help with film, images, story ideas, contact for talent, logistics and shoot location guides. Over time, the sponsors started to listen, and began to integrate Brand Australia into their Olympic programmes, eventually leading to an additional $170 million in additional publicity and promotional programmes for Australia. Visa alone generated over $20 million in destination spend advertising, from television commercials in the US through to bus shelters in Shanghai.

The torch relay was also turned into a series of video postcards for the host country broadcast around the world, from Uluru (Ayers Rock), the world's largest monolith and an Australian icon, through to an underwater dive along the Great Barrier Reef.

Tourism has always been an important objective for cities bidding for the Winter Olympic Games. The promotional campaign for the first Winter Olympic Games in Chamonix in 1924, was undertaken by the PLM Railway Company, which wanted to increase the number of visitors to this resort now that it was connected by train.

Lillehammer and Norway, benefiting from the stunning broadcast images and glowing media reports, saw the number of guest nights in hotels grow from 1.6 million in 1988 to over 2.22 million a decade later, with similar increases in overall number of visitors to Norway up from 11.85 million to 16.42 million.

Barcelona has seen some of the most dramatic benefits of any recent Olympic host city. In economic terms, Barcelona in the early 1990s, was ranked 11th according to a survey carried out among 500 businessmen.

Today, it has risen to sixth place after London, Paris, Berlin, Frankfurt and Amsterdam.

The growth in tourism between 1990 and 2002 truly illustrated how Barcelona benefited from being in the world's spotlight in 1992. Total overnight stays more than doubled from 3.8 million to over 8 million and the number of conventions nearly tripled to over 270,000.

## The global stage

The Olympic Games are unique in their ability to present a host nation and a city to the world. No other sports event, or any other type of event for that matter, offers such a global stage. Recent host cities have begun to appreciate the true potential of hosting the Games. How a host government takes advantage of its brand identity internationally is critical in terms of future trade and investment. The nation and the city need to define the image, what it wants to tell people about itself, in the brief time it is under the spotlight. It must also develop a post-Games strategy to help build a long-term business legacy.

The IOC's vision of developing a strong Look of Games identity has significantly expanded the potential benefits for any nation in hosting the Games, and is one clear reason today why more cities than ever before want to host the Olympic Games. The decision to brand the whole city 'Olympic', has taken the branding potential beyond anything previously achieved. The football World Cup is a great event, but look closely and all you will see is a football match, like any other match, with no point of differentiation that makes it *the* World Cup, or image payback to the host.

For any nation, the economics of staging the Olympic Games are best understood as a Herculean re-branding campaign. The aim of any re-branding exercise is to take a product with a certain image and turn this perception around. The Olympics have the effect of focusing the world's attention, for a very brief moment, on a single city and the culture and character of the host nation.

Hosting the Olympics can be an expensive path to self-esteem – but one that, correctly managed, is one of the most cost-effective, powerful and rewarding undertakings that a government and a nation can embark on. Only once in the last twenty years, has a city got it wrong. The mistake at

Atlanta was one of short-termism over long-term investment. Even then, within the local community, Atlanta was seen as a great success, leaving a tremendous legacy of new facilities.

What the IOC has learned from its experience of working with host cities is the importance of maintaining strict brand discipline. This means negotiating and finalising many of the arrangements in advance of the host city being chosen. The danger, otherwise, is that the local politics get in the way. A city that is one of several on a short list is altogether easier to deal with than the same city once it is confirmed as the next Olympic host. The IOC learned this in Atlanta. But it also learned other lessons.

Chief among these is the importance of getting the technology right. Technology and the Olympics have grown up together over the years. As technology has advanced, it has enhanced the Olympic experience. But, in Atlanta we discovered that technology is a double-edged sword. Ironically, it was in the US, which has hosted so much of the technological revolution, that the lesson was graphically brought home. No matter how good the physical infrastructure of a host city, if the technological infrastructure fails, the Games can fail too – and that is what happened when IBM's systems crashed in 1996 in Georgia.

## NOTES

1  Mitt Romney, a Harvard MBA and law graduate, became Governor of Massachusetts in 2002, and founder and chairman of private equity and venture capital firm Bain Capital. Scion of a prominent family, his father was president of American Motors Company and governor of Michigan. Romney is touted as a possible Presidential Republican nomination in 2008.

2  The idea for lighting the cauldron came about practically by accident. The judging panel for the design of the cauldron, selected the winning design and then realised that they had not worked out how to light it. They called the designer back and asked how he planned to light the Olympic flame. He told them that he had no idea but, after a moment's reflection, jokingly suggested that they might consider firing an arrow. The idea was nearly dismissed but over the coming weeks Bassat kept coming back to it. After the Games, people asked what would happen

if the archer had missed. It has been suggested that there was so much gas being pumped into the air around the cauldron that, even if the arrow had gone in the opposite direction, it would still have ignited.

3 The *Financial Times* wrote that the Games 'were brilliantly organised, executed and hosted by Barcelona, (and that) Spain will bask in the afterglow of the Olympics for some time.' *The Times* noted how 'the Spaniards confounded all the sceptics, by staging the Olympic Games with a spirit that was a model of its kind ... These were the relaxed Games, the friendly Games and, above all the fair Games; where for all the commercialism and drugs, the world saw that top-class sport could be fun and exciting ... The Olympic torch that is now handed onto Atlanta in the US burns as brightly as it has ever done. The success of the Games should have a lasting effect on Spain itself, as the Seoul Olympics left their beneficial legacy in Korea.' *The Japan Times* made its own homage to the host city: 'Brilliantly staged. The Games won high praise with many commentators calling them the best ever ... Few cities have been able to display the architectural monuments in the way Barcelona repeatedly did ... Never was this truer than during the diving events. The world was entranced by the vision of graceful divers catapulting into the rays of the dazzling Mediterranean sun over the Barcelona skyline, only to plunge past Antoni Gaudi's unfinished masterpiece, the Church of the Holy Family, into a blue splash of competitive excellence'; the *International Herald Tribune* ran the banner headline, detailing how 'The Real Winner was Barcelona, Not the Athletes. The athletes never had a chance. No matter how well they jumped and ran and rowed, they could never dominate these Games. The City won the Games. The people of Catalonia won the Games ... At their best, the Games are a celebration of the people who stage them – every trilingual official, every volunteer'; *Sports Illustrated* reported how the 'Games were pure Gold', 'There was more pleasure to be found at the Barcelona Games than any other Olympics in living memory. This was due to the elegance of the city.'

4 Even the Lillehammer bid committee did not really expect to win the right to host the 1994 Olympic Winter Games, sending all of their promotional material home the night before the election. The favourite to win was Ostersund, Sweden, but it lost momentum in the final

48 hours when certain voting blocks, especially the South Americans, were rumoured to have switched their allegiance, as a result of losing the election to the IOC Executive Board of their candidate to the Swedish IOC member. When Samaranch announced that Lillehammer had won, the Norwegian delegation looked on in utter disbelief. The King of Sweden, who was sitting in the first row of invited guests, looked up in disbelief as well, but for very different reasons. Samaranch was totally surprised, subsequently joking as to whether he had in fact opened the right envelope.

5 'These were the Games that touched the heights and hearts. The bidders who were 1000–1 outsiders. The Norwegians whose cheers steamed into the air – loudest for home skiers but still loud enough for foreign competitors. They presented a positive image of the host country that is beyond price.' (*The Independent*); 'Norwegian warmth knows no boundaries. As we head home, Norway and its people are in our hearts ... we give you one more gold medal for a winter Games as perfect as your Christmas-card snow' (*USA Today*); 'These Games have enabled Norway to present their face to the world and to enjoy a collective identity that brings a national sense of confidence and well being' (*The Times*); 'Lillehammer showed the Norwegians in the best possible light: polite, organised, adaptable, mature in their snow culture and with consciences alert to the world's trouble spots such as Sarajevo and the preservation of environmental balances' (*The Guardian*). The accolades continued for years to come, leaving a lasting legacy. *The New York Times*, in an article previewing the Salt Lake Games, fondly reflected back on Lillehammer, 'with [its] bright sun, frigid air, quaint buildings, rolling farmland under a clean coat of snow, idealistic Norwegians burning candles on the sidewalk for sister Olympic city of Sarajevo. It all worked.'

The Norwegian press, which had spent six years lambasting the organising committee, undertook a 180 degree U-turn following the opening ceremony, talking about how 'the world had never seen anything more beautiful ... and that ... heaven [Lillehammer during the Games] was a place where one can still be, while still alive.' Humourists like Dave Barry became enchanted with the Norwegian people, explaining to his readers back in the US, that Norwegians 'LOVE cross-country skiing. This is a huge event for them, very much like our Super Bowl, except that, at the Super Bowl, you can actually see the Game' (*Seattle Times*). It was, perhaps, *Sports Illustrated* that paid Lillehammer and Norway the greatest compliment: 'The XVII Winter Olympics did not exist. Norway did not exist. These were the fairy tale Games, drawn from the imagination, staged in the pages of a children's book. They could not exist. Reality cannot be this good.'

6 'Gold medal for chaos' (*Sports Business Journal*); 'Atlanta has blown it big time' (*France Soir*); 'The Greed Games' (*Los Angeles Times*); 'Greed eclipses Olympic creed at Olympic flea market. Atlanta promised the greatest Games of all time, but never mentioned that they would be the tackiest too' (*Atlanta Constitution*); 'Scorned Atlanta [has been] brought down to earth' (*The Times*); 'The ideals [were] left behind in the Atlanta gold rush ... Atlanta will go down in the history of the Summer Games as the city that failed to produce an enlightened strategy' (*The Independent*).

7 Six cities applied to host the Centennial Olympic Games: Athens, Atlanta, Belgrade, Manchester, Melbourne and Toronto. The final round of voting saw Atlanta gain 51 votes to Athens' 35.

8 Journalists eventually found out how to make the buses stop. They all lit up cigarettes in front of the press centre, forcing the driver to eject them from his non-smoking bus.

9 In addition to the new 49,714 seat baseball stadium, ACOG also funded a new tennis centre at Stone Mountain Park, a new shooting complex at Wolf Creek and contributed towards many other construction projects including new housing, used as the Olympic Village, at the Georgia Institute of Technology. Construction costs accounted for nearly 29 per cent of ACOG's overall budget – revenue that should have been allocated to other critical areas like technology testing and transportation.

10 The Opening Ceremony was the most watched Olympic Ceremony in US broadcast history.

11 The rest of Campbell's time as mayor of Atlanta was fraught with controversy, with the FBI investigating him and his administration in 2000 for alleged corruption.

12  Samaranch's eye for detail also prompted the adoption of blue tables
    and yellow balls in table tennis. Other bodies changed their scoring
    protocols to make them easier to follow.

13  'Thanks a Million and Sayonara,' was the lead headline in Time:
    'Nagano's warm hospitality will be a tough act to follow. Host cities
    put their marks on the Olympics ... The Japanese organisers have res-
    cued the Olympic spirit that was so deeply shaken after the disaster of
    the 1996 Atlanta Games ... The question we were all asking, when we
    fled Atlanta in disgust back in 1996 was whether the Olympic Games
    had become so big and so complex that they were unmanageable ... In
    Atlanta there was no way to escape the relentless commercialism of
    the street hawking vendors ... In Nagano, the problem was the stores
    had run out of stuffed replicas of the snowlets, the overtly cute mas-
    cots ... In the end, Sydney must remember that it is hosting the Games
    for the world.'

14  The *Sydney Morning Herald* alone published more than 8,000 articles
    on Olympic preparations between January 1995 and the Opening
    Ceremony. After the success of the Games, some of the most critical
    elements of the Australian media claimed that the success was because
    of their repeated criticism, having kept the organisers on their toes.

15  In Germany, *Hamburger Adenblatt* noted 'the Olympic Movement could
    not have found a better place for its rebirth'. The *International Herald
    Tribune* talked of 'how the unmitigated success of the Sydney Games
    came at a most opportune moment. It has restored faith in the rele-
    vance of the Olympics'. In Spain, *El Pais* quoted Jacques Rogge saying,
    'A friend of mine said that Sydney had raised the bar (for future cities)
    from a high jump to a pole vault.'

16  'It was noted time and again that while Atlanta which has become a
    byword for the antithesis of the Olympic spirit ... Sydney gave it back
    to the world,' was how *The Times* closed its report on the Games.

    'After the commercial excesses and failures of technology and
    transportation in Atlanta,' wrote Jerry Longman in the *New York
    Times*, 'the Sydney Games revived the idea that the Olympics can
    be organised smoothly, and that they remain in reach of ordinary
    people. Sydney has little of the flea market ambience that made the
    Atlanta Games a byword for crass commercialism.' 'What the Aus-

tralians have done so magnificently is to just once again make the Olympics seem worth all the trouble. They redeemed the shame of the Atlanta Olympics,' concluded *The Independent*, while *USA Today* noted how, 'Atlanta's Games were a monument to corporate crassness. Sydney never made that mistake.'

17  *The Guardian* in the UK, wrote that 'Salt Lake has emerged as the biggest winner ... The Wasatch Mountains provided a gorgeous backdrop and the city extended a friendly hand, belying its reputation as a Mormon-dominated enclave where it is tough to get a drink. The Mormon Church kept its promise to curb its missionaries' zeal while the Games were on. "We have taken a giant step forward in correcting some of the misconceptions people have about the church," said M Russell Ballard, a church elder, "I think that we have made a lot of friends." ' 'Yes, Salt Lake City definitely did it,' said the *Washington Times*, '2002 Winter Olympics were as good as gold.' All this was a far cry from the headlines that closed the Atlanta Games.

18  Morse claimed the Olympic Games advanced Australia's international tourism brand by ten years, attracting an additional 1.74 million visitors to the country between 1997 and 2004 – visitors who generated over $3.5 billion in foreign exchange earnings. In 2000, visitor arrivals to Australia increased by 11 per cent and the International Congress and Convention Association predicted that Australia would be ranked as the number one country for meetings in 2001 – overtaking both the United States and the United Kingdom. In the 12 months following the Games, Sydney saw its convention business increase by 71 per cent.

# Chapter 8

# MAKING IT HAPPEN

## The elephant stumbles

Over the years, the Olympics Games have become an important global showcase for new technology. In 1984, the Los Angeles Games introduced e-mail to a wider world. Back in 1964, Seiko's Quartz timing system debuted at the Tokyo Games, and Matsushita used the Seoul Games in 1988 to break into the professional broadcast market.

For technology companies, the Games offer a unique platform – a world stage to demonstrate state-of-the-art technological sophistication and vision. Abby Kohnstamm, IBM's head of marketing, described the Olympic Games as 'the ultimate showcase of technology'.

The technology is not decorative. World records require accuracy and reliability, otherwise their entire credibility is undermined.

The Games have become increasingly dependent on technology. IBM sent 2,000 people to run the computer systems at the Sydney Games, aided by a further 4,000 volunteers – creating the largest temporary computer network ever built on the planet. The network was designed to process three trillion bytes of data – the equivalent of the amount of information contained in an average newspaper every day for 30,000 years; enough paper to stretch from here to the moon. Also at Sydney, Xerox brought in over 600 employees to help run the Games document management systems made up of over 800 copiers, 800 fax machines, 400 printers and eight publishing centres, working around the clock, to help deliver the results and key information to the media and sports officials. Anne Mulcahy, chairman and CEO of Xerox said the Olympics 'serve as a competitive benchmark and as a showcase for talent, teamwork and excellence'.

Technology costs now represent upwards of 30 per cent of the total operating budget for the Games. According to Tom Furey, general manager worldwide for Olympic technology, the Games have become 'the largest, most complex information technology challenge in the world'. Should the technology ever fail, the Games face great difficulties. The IOC and IBM learned this to their great cost and embarrassment at the Centennial Games in Atlanta.

# The blues

IBM's involvement with the Olympic Games dates back to the 1960 Winter Games in Squaw Valley. It was the first time a computer was used to help compile the results (35 technicians working on an IBM Ramac with punch cards). Four years later in Tokyo, IBM had to place its computers in fridges to prevent them from overheating.

In the early 1990s, the IOC and IBM began exploring ways to simplify the technical operations for the Games. By the 1992 Barcelona Olympics, the IOC was concerned about the growing cost of technology. It set out to find a way of formally transferring the complicated and unique Olympic systems from one Games to the next.

IBM was also rethinking its approach. It was having a torrid time in its traditional markets, experiencing losses for the first time in its history. As a company, Big Blue was in the process of changing its overall strategy, shifting its image from a manufacturer of boxes to an overall solutions supplier and systems integrator. IBM's market was changing, with companies like EDS becoming a far greater threat to its core business.

Until Atlanta, the computer network and results systems were run by a consortium of different technology companies. IBM provided the hardware, while others, like EDS, provided the systems integration, and specialist companies, like Sema, provided specific niche solutions for accreditation and other systems. IBM, however, came to the conclusion that from its own marketing and business standpoint, it needed to take over the whole operation. Big Blue had to 'own' all aspects of the Games' computer network and related systems.

IBM's head of European marketing, Paul Wipperfurth, came to Lausanne to see me. He explained that a consolidated solution would not only meet IBM's overall business objectives, but provide the IOC with a safer and more cost effective way to handle the required technology. Rather then entering into individual agreements for each Games, why didn't the IOC consider a long-term strategic alliance for a multi-Games deal? This would allow IBM to create new state-of-the-art systems from which the company could then recoup its investment over a longer period.

For IBM, the Games would become the centrepiece of its strategic marketing programme. This would help the company's change of image by showcasing new integrated solutions to a global audience. IBM's proposed strategy, Wipperfurth said, would help increase the IOC's overall management of the Games, reducing operational risks and helping to control escalating technology costs. Dick Pound and I took IBM's plan to Samaranch and the IOC Board, and it was quickly approved.

The IOC and IBM teams then got together to begin thrashing out the details of how to create a permanent technology transfer team. Recognising the investment that IBM would now be making in the Olympics, the IOC proposed to upgrade IBM to full TOP programme status. Jack McMahon, who was leading the IBM negotiating team, told us in no uncertain terms that what they wanted was a strategic partnership with the IOC, not to be part of the TOP programme. 'We are not interested in putting the Olympic symbol on our products. If you insist on continually pushing TOP, we will withdraw our offer of support for the Olympics – TOP is not right for IBM,' he said.

We couldn't understand IBM's position. The IOC was offering the company the highest level of Olympic sponsorship, to become a member of the most elite marketing club in the world, and IBM didn't want anything to do with it. IBM wanted all the rights and benefits, but not membership. The IOC had no choice but to accept McMahon's dictat and the negotiations dragged on. Months went by and we did not seem to be any closer to closure. The contract simply grew in length. The longer it became the further away we seemed from concluding anything.

In April 1993, John Ackers, chairman of IBM, suddenly resigned to be replaced by Lou Gerstner. This seemed to be the worst news possible for the IOC. Gerstner had been a senior member of the American Express executive team that had turned down the Olympics. It looked like two years of negotiations with IBM were about to come to an abrupt and unceremonious halt.

I flew to New York to meet with Gerstner's new head of communications, David Kalis, expecting to be told that the whole deal was off. But, before I could begin to explain the deal, David promptly announced: 'Lou told me to tell you, that he has made the mistake once of losing the Olympics and TOP and he is not about to make the same mistake a second time. The only way we are prepared to go forward, is if we are a full TOP partner – nothing else.'

Having spent the previous 12 months of negotiations with McMahon and his team removing any reference to TOP from the draft IBM contract, it was amusing to watch McMahon do a complete U-turn. At our next meeting, he explained how all the TOP references had to now be reinstated. With Gerstner in the driving seat, soon to be joined by Abby Kohnstamm, who also came over from American Express as his new head of global advertising, the deal was quickly concluded.

## Hot technology

IBM set about preparing for the Atlanta Games, putting all its technological and marketing muscle behind the programme. Senior IBM executives touted the challenge they faced to their customers and to the press. 'Imagine the largest hotel chain in the world, the largest restaurant chain, the largest medical facility and on top of that, two Super Bowls a day for 17 days, then you have something like the operating environment for the Olympic Games,' Dennie Welsh, general manager of IBM Global Services, explained to his customers.

Ron Pamlich, an IBM veteran and core member of its Olympic team, acknowledged the challenges of an immovable deadline. 'We could always defer a space shot or big projects of this type. The Olympics are different. July 19, 1996, and the Games begin. It's show time. We have to perform. We have a sacrosanct deadline. It's like hide and seek. Here come the Olympics, ready or not.'

Palmich continued the media rounds, talking of Olympic 'computer and technology requirements that surpass those of 95 per cent of businesses. The Olympics mimic a client environment that has rigorous requirements, like tough deadlines and a huge scope. We want our potential clients to leave the Games and think – How can this model work for me?'.

Eli Primrose-Smith, the former chief operating officer of the 1994 Soccer World Cup in the US, was brought in to be IBM's overall Olympic project director. She said their partnership with the Atlanta Organising Committee (ACOG) gave the company a chance to demonstrate that 'if we can help to plan, manage and run much of the Olympic Games, we can provide the technology infrastructure for any size'. John Patrick, vice-president of IBM Internet Technology, announced that 'IBM's goal is to come to the Olympics with the image as the world's hottest internet company.'

Atlanta's technology director Bob Neal also continued to raise the stakes. 'The reliability, accuracy and productivity of systems and telecommunications technology will be a critical element in attaining the Organising Committee's goal of providing the best Games ever,' he said.

IBM's publications explained how their products had been chosen exclusively, 'because they provided the only industrial strength solution'. IBM's results system promised to deliver information to broadcasters between 3/10 and 7/10 of a second after reporting. The Info 96 System, a 60 gigabyte warehouse, contained a century of history and Olympic results, the biographies of some 10,500 athletes, event schedules and an e-mail system for the 150,000 accredited members of the Olympic family.

The hype was insistent. Lou Gerstner, meeting with a group of shareholders in Atlanta a few months before the Games, acknowledged: 'We both have a lot on the line. It's a chance for your city and our company to show the very best of the world stage. I don't need to tell you there's an element of risk in stepping on to that stage.'[1] Gerstner's declaration proved prophetic.

## Crash test dummies

One year out from the Games, the IOC felt that the technology systems were not coming together as they had in previous Games. For the first time, broadcasters and the international press agencies were starting to express concern, calling the IOC and saying they were nervous. We raised the issue with IBM and ACOG, only to be told bluntly not to worry and that everything would be OK. After all, this was the United States, the world capital for technology, and this was IBM, Big Blue.

The IOC kept its own counsel and looked on wearily. Who were we to question one of the world's largest computer companies and the world's technological capital? Every now and then we checked in with IBM and ACOG, asking how the technology testing was going and was there anything we should be aware of? We were told to stop worrying, everything was fine and to, basically, mind our own business.

Two weeks before the Atlanta opening ceremony, it was blatantly clear that everything was far from fine. The Games results system – the most high profile and critical of all of the Olympic information systems – was not behaving itself. Everyone involved started to seriously worry; everyone that is except IBM. ACOG, and its blunt, no-nonsense, chief operating officer, AD Frazier, still trusted that IBM would eventually come through. But IBM was not listening, especially to the real experts – the international press agencies that had the most to lose if the results system did not work. There was still time to create a back-up system. Kevan Gosper, an IOC vice president and chairman of the IOC Press Commission, pleaded with ACOG and IBM to develop a simple back up with the agencies.[2] IBM would have nothing to do with Gosper's proposals, and proceeded blindly on. July 19, 1996, arrived and the stage was set for a record-breaking Centennial Olympics. For the first time in the history of the Olympics all the recognised NOCs were present – 197 countries. While the Games started in style, the technology did not. The words of Paul Wipperfurth, the IBM executive who had pioneered the broader Olympic strategy, came true: 'If you can handle the Olympics, you can handle anything. [But] if we fail, the Olympics fail.'

In time-honoured tradition, when things start to go wrong they go wrong big time. The results from IBM's much hyped information results system never appeared. Actually some results did appear – and the information only served to highlight the extent to which IBM had lost control of the system. It had a life of its own. The IBM results systems started producing stories of one metre high boxers; 900-year-old pole-vaulters; a 12 centimetre tall Nigerian ping-pong player pitted against a 19 metre tall Chinese competitor; and Danes and Australians setting new world records for events that had not yet taken place.

No doubt much of the information – or misinformation – was the result of human error in the inputting of data. But with no effective results coming out, it was the press, and in particular the international press agencies, who were embarrassed in front of their clients. They were rightly furious and swift in their condemnation. Some of the world's largest and most influential newspapers, which had been planning to run full-page results from the Games, were left with blank pages. IBM could not have found a more important or influential audience to disappoint. IBM's failures provoked a barrage of negative headlines around the world.[3]

IBM was reduced to faxing the results to the major news organisations, even sending runners carrying paper results, which then had to be fed into the media's own computers. By day three of the Games, the press were in a state of rebellion. At the daily morning meeting of the IOC Co-ordination Commission Samaranch told the ACOG that their mistreatment of the world's press, was 'killing the Games'.

IBM had made a huge mistake by failing to run enough simulated tests on a system that they knew was about to embark on possibly the most ambitious exercise in integrated communications ever attempted. IBM's head office was in a state of panic, as they watched their carefully planned advertising and public relations campaigns collapse around them.

Advertising boasting of IBM's work in Atlanta was immediately pulled. Senior IBM communications experts were flown in to try to defend IBM's reputation. To be fair to IBM, six out of the seven major systems the company had developed for the Games were working perfectly. Only one was not. Unfortunately it was the one providing the results to the world's press.[4] IBM spokesman Fred McNeese admitted, 'We fouled up with the people who buy ink by the barrel'. The press reported the story ad nauseam, even blaming IBM for things that it had nothing to do with. *The Philadelphia Inquirer* even suggested that an IBM system might have contributed to security lapses.

Slowly the IBM and ACOG engineers addressed the basic issues facing the results system, and the media moved on to criticise other aspects of Atlanta. But, it was almost a week before the results operation was running smoothly. Lou Gerstner in Atlanta for the Opening Ceremony was not amused and stormed around reading the riot act.

Immediately after the Games, post-mortems were held on the Games technology systems, to understand why they had failed and to make sure that the same mistakes were never, ever made again. Unfortunately, all that seemed to materialise was a major exercise in finger pointing. IBM claimed it was not allowed by the Atlanta organisers to speak directly to various end users about their needs. So it was unable to fine tune the systems. It did not seem to dawn on IBM that the head of ACOG technology was actually an IBM employee and that other technology partners like Swatch had no problem contacting key stakeholders.[5]

What should have happened, in my view, especially in light of the major public relations hammering that IBM took from the world's media, was for Lou Gerstner to have called for a major inquiry by an independent auditor. But Gerstner never tried to find out why the system collapsed. No external inquiry was ever called and no one ever really knew where to place the blame.

Even so, IBM's own post-Games research produced an interesting conclusion. Among the company's technology savvy business customers, there was considerable empathy towards IBM's predicament and the fact that systems can and do fail. These customers were more interested in how IBM reacted and got things fixed.

Even the critical press did not seem to diminish IBM's enthusiasm. 'We have found no residual downside whatsoever,' IBM's Eli Primrose Smith told *Business Week*. 'Our customers and potential customers understood we were working in a high risk environment.'

## Twice shy

Going into the Winter Olympic Games in Nagano, IBM took no chances. It went back to square one to review all systems and, where necessary, develop totally new ones. Big Blue added dramatically to the number of employees working on the project, building back-up systems to the back-up systems and testing everything again and again and again. The systems worked perfectly in Nagano, but the costs had soared. So much for keeping costs under control by transferring the same operating system from one Games to the next.

Things were starting to get out of hand. IBM processed one terabyte of data (one trillion bytes) during the entire Nagano Games, or five times as much as the Lillehammer Games, four years earlier. The information system logged more than six million requests – triple the volume at Lillehammer. IBM stepped back and took a long, hard look at the costs. The IOC took a similar look. It was not a pretty picture.

Rather than creating a structure to control costs, the situation was spiralling out of control. With all sides paranoid about repeating Atlanta's technology disaster, Sydney saw its information technology budget escalate to over $375 million. This was against the $75 million spent eight years earlier in Barcelona. The number of athletes was basically the same and there had been no dramatic increase in the number of events. But the demands of the end-users and the need to create multiple back-up systems had driven costs through the roof.

When the IOC and IBM sat down to talk about the future and whether to renew their long-standing partnership, the parties were hundreds of millions of dollars apart on what the true cost of the Games technology should be. The IOC had an obligation to keep technology for the Games at the forefront of information management systems, but at a sensible price.

The other new development was the advent of the internet. IBM was convinced that it should exclusively 'own' internet access to the Games as part of its TOP sponsorship. For the IOC, the internet was a new medium and one that different stakeholders and partners had a legitimate claim to. There was no way that one company could claim all the rights. Kodak with its digital imaging business, Visa's electronic payment systems, Samsung's mobile phones with internet access – all were involved with the internet in one way or other. IBM did not see it that way. On one occasion, for example, Xerox wanted to give its web site details in an Olympic advertisement, only to have IBM object. There was intense frustration among the sponsors at IBM's attitude

Over the course of months of renewal negotiations, it slowly dawned on both sides that we were not going to be able to make this work. The IOC was convinced that the best way to manage costs and reduce risk was to return to a technology consortium of best of breed companies that had proved so successful and efficient up to and including Barcelona. For IBM, this was counter to its overall strategic positioning. Regretfully, after a 40-year Olympic partnership, the parties agreed that the time had come to go our separate ways. [6]

IBM still faced the responsibility of delivering a flawless results system in Sydney and going out in style. The press watched closely, as nearly 13 million lines of software code were put to the test, and 6,000 IBM and technical support personnel were drafted in. Even then, it was not until just a few weeks before the Games that everyone was really comfortable that all systems were go, and IBM got the headlines it so strived for: 'Glitches to Gold'. IBM flew in over 1,000 customers from around the world for its final

Olympic party. And, in spite of all the problems the company had faced in Atlanta, 'the Olympics', according to Rick Singer, IBM director of world wide marketing, 'really did enhance how people thought of us'.

## The integrated mousetrap

With the decision not to renew with IBM, the IOC decided to return to the tried and tested, and much more cost-effective system, of a technology consortium led by a systems integrator. We approached Sema, Europe's second largest computer services company, to take on the role of overall systems integrator for the Games. Sema had already run many of the systems back in 1992 at the Barcelona Games, and had quietly worked since then as a subcontractor to IBM for a number of key Games systems, like accreditation.

The IOC was anxious to turn to a more flexible technology arrangement. Sema would be able to select the best and most cost-effective solutions. The Games would not be hostage to marketing people imposing whatever new system was to be showcased that month, whether it was suitable or not.

Sema's chairman, French industrialist Pierre Bonelli, told the *Wall Street Journal*, 'I don't intend to use the Olympics to market products like IBM does. All I care about is showing the world this company has the knowledge to get the Olympic job done on time and on budget. We are a company of engineers not a company of marketers. There is zero tolerance for error'.[7]

Sema set about preparing the systems for the 2002 Winter Games in Salt Lake City. Members of the organising committee were nervous as they watched Sema turn up with a fraction of the number of engineers IBM had sent to the Games. But as Sema senior vice president Tidu Maini kept pointing out, 'the bar may look high, but that's just because of the way the previous partners chose to jump'.

The Salt Lake organisers became even more nervous when, in April 2001, Sema was suddenly acquired by Schlumberger, an oil services conglomerate looking to diversify its operations. Would Schlumberger, which had shied away from any form of publicity, continue to support the Olympics with the same enthusiasm as Sema? Would the key technology executives stay with the company? Salt Lake did not have to worry – Schlumberger jumped into the project with even more enthusiasm and commitment than before.

SchlumbergerSema calmly and methodically built a new set of systems. It then devoted 100,000 hours to testing. Nothing was left to chance. The company opted for a low-key marketing campaign to support its Olympic partnership. It wanted to first prove to the world that its systems and methodology worked, earning it the nickname of 'the invisible sponsor'.

SchlumbergerSema's attitude was to let its services, and its successes, do the talking. This was less to do with any global brand-building programme, and more to do with a carefully targeted communications programme to build trust within a specialist and very select group of customers and potential customers.

Irwin Pfister, chief operating officer of SchlumbergerSema, became more bullish as the Games progressed and the technology systems continued to perform flawlessly. This, he said, is 'the largest, most complex sports related information technology project in the world; and we're the best, so we wanted to be able to demonstrate that, and being able to pull off a project of this magnitude just establishes the level of credentials that's unparalleled.'

The Games results and technology management systems went off without a hitch. SchlumbergerSema sat back and relished the glowing media coverage. 'Right now good editorial gives me more credibility with our business than does any advertisement I could buy,' was how Michele Bernhardt, Schlumberger's director of communications summed up the results of their post Games press.

Bill Cottam, one of SchlumbergerSema's project directors, recalled: 'If the systems failed ... It was our name that was going in the paper. The team worked 24 hours a day. There was no room for error of laxity. We have an "a" system, a "b" system and a "c" system. Failure was not an option. The unexpected also posed challenges. The decision to award two gold medals in one event – the figure skating, after a judging controversy was not something that had been tested on the system.'

Schlumberger had delivered. Jacques Rogge, presiding over his first Games as IOC president, succinctly summed up the result when he wrote to the SchlumbergerSema team after the Games. 'All of this was achieved with significant cost and operational savings over previous Games. SchumbergerSema achieved all this without any way increasing the risk of technology operations. On the contrary, they reduced it.'[8]

With Schlumberger handling the overall systems integration, the IOC looked to bring on board other key technology partners to complete the consortium. As Swatch was already handling all timing and scoring, they were perfectly placed to handle the critical area of 'in-field results management'. Nicolas Hayek, chairman of Swatch, jumped at the opportunity to expand his company's Olympic involvement.

## Chinese computing power

The third key pillar of the consortium, was to find a computer partner and, by late 2002, the IOC had begun negotiations with Chinese computer giant Lenovo to join the TOP programme. [9] The Chinese Government was very keen for one of its key industrial leaders to step up onto the global stage and take full advantage of the 2008 Games to showcase their technological potential.

Lenovo had seen how Samsung quickly built a global brand position through Olympic sponsorship, but remained uneasy about whether it had the international resources to take on the global responsibilities of a TOP partner, especially servicing the IOC's global computer needs, and the not insignificant requirements of the Torino 2006 Winter Games.

As much as the IOC was attracted to the potential of bringing a Chinese company into the TOP programme, the Games technology experts were anxious to ensure that Lenovo was up to the challenge. Months and months of testing took place, as the marketing negotiations continued on. With Lenovo passing the technical evaluations with flying colours. Mary Ma, Lenovo's head of corporate marketing, announced that Lenovo would in due course make a major international acquisition to build up its international presence. Lenovo formally joined TOP in March 2004, and less than nine months later, Mary Ma delivered on her earlier promise of a major international acquisition. Lenovo aquired IBM's PC division, overnight becoming the world's third biggest PC manufacturer.

## New media, false dawn

Technology is not only critical to delivering the Games, communications technology is also key to the Olympic's financial well-being. In January

2000, the IOC called a meeting of key broadcasters in New York to discuss how to manage the growing challenge of the internet. If we were to believe the press, the broadcast industry – the principal source of funding for the Olympic Movement – was under threat, and within a few years would probably be extinct. One forecast had advertising on sports-related websites growing to $6.27 billion by 2005.

Gathered around the conference room table in New York were the representatives of some of the world's most powerful 'old' media conglomerates: General Electric's NBC; Channel 7 from Australia; Canada's national broadcast network, CBC; the European Broadcasting Union; and a cross-section of broadcasters from Japan. Everyone was concerned. The Sydney Games were scheduled to take place in a matter of months. New media technology was challenging the governing principles of the sports broadcasting industry, which was founded on the basis of clear territorial definitions and exclusivity. The internet was no respecter of the boundaries of exclusivity or territory.

Change was in the air. A start-up company, iCrave TV, had already begun to broadcast live US network television into Canada on the internet for the first time. *USA Today* welcomed the upstart's arrival as 'a move that threatens to blow holes in the TV industry as we know it'. The traditional media and sports property giants, including Disney, Rupert Murdoch's Fox Network, CBS and the NFL, along with ten other entertainment industry superpowers, proceeded to carpet bomb iCrave with a barrage of lawsuits. It became the largest ever legal attack on an internet company. Reflecting the mood of the time, a Federal Communications Commission official said, 'Broadcasters have told me, that if they lose this case, it's the end of the world'.

The broadcasters at the New York meeting had been gathered together to discuss whether we should put Olympic footage from Sydney on the web. They agreed that while the internet might offer interesting new opportunities to expand the viewers' experience, it was not possible to control the territorial footprint of the transmission. If all broadcasters could not agree to a new global protocol, then there would be no broadcasting of video images or audio on the internet for the Sydney Games. This decision was greeted with dismay and shock by the rest of the world's media industry.[10] The condemnation of the IOC's perceived short-sighted view was almost universal. The *Sun* in Malaysia reported that 'the Olympic Committee is treating the net with the same suspicion they did the television 44 years ago'.

## Discovering the internet

The first Olympic Games to encounter the internet was Atlanta, with the official site attracting some 200 million visits, a record at the time. Although several companies had approached the IOC with various internet proposals, none had been able to show that it truly understood the sports world or could explain how sport could be enriched by this new medium. None, that is, until two Australians founded a small specialist company called Quokka.[11] Its sole focus was the creation of the interactive sports experience and how to bring the spectator closer to the athlete experience.

One of the founders of Quokka was John Bertrand, the legendary Australian yachtsman who had skippered Australia's challenge for the America's Cup in 1983. Bertrand's victory had broken the US's continual 132 year run as Cup holder. Bertrand and his America's Cup team had been one of the first sports team to truly realise the value, power and potential of technology as a tool to assist them in design of their boat and analysis of weather and wind conditions. The other founder was Alan Ramadan, chief technology officer for the Australian Syndicate in 1992.

Ramadan got his brainwave during Australia's 1995 attempt to win the America's Cup, when he realised that the experience for the sponsor guest could be greatly enhanced by being allowed to follow the data pouring into his computers from the boat, detailing wind speeds, weather conditions and other statistics meant that the difference between winning and losing. Ramadan also saw that this sponsor experience could be expanded to a much broader audience if it could be made available in a user-friendly format over the net.

Bertrand and Ramadan teamed up and created the concept of 'total immersion sports'. The traditional armchair viewer was transformed into his own producer, surfing hundreds of channels, and in-depth data, permanently clicking his or her computer mouse. Their objective was to create the leading sports entertainment company in the digital world, and in the process trigger a revolution in the comfortable, simple world of the armchair sports fan.[12]

Quokka was not alone in its conviction that the new media world would own and control the future of sports presentation. IBM felt that it was also sitting on a goldmine. (As noted, Big Blue had convinced itself that it owned all Olympic rights to the internet.)

The fact that the word 'internet' did not appear once in the Olympic partnership agreement with the IOC was of little consequence. From IBM's perspective, it made all the bits and pieces that ensured the internet worked, so, therefore, it owned the category. The logic was baffling.

I responded that it was similar to one of the other TOP partners, like Panasonic, claiming it owned the broadcast rights to the Games, just because it made TV sets and video recorders. My arguments fell on deaf ears.

IBM refused to accept that the internet was a medium. Its executives refused to acknowledge that the internet was much more than a sponsorship category. This difference of opinion led to a breakdown in negotiations between the IOC and IBM, precipitating the eventual collapse of any renewal discussions post-Sydney.

As the internet continued to gain momentum – or at least continued to generate a lot of hype – the IOC, like many other organisations, began to consider how to take control of the various Olympic domain names, as an investment for the future. The IOC identified some 1,800 names that had already been registered with some form of Olympic related prefix – mostly by individuals with the sole aim of then re-selling the URL to the highest bidder. Under new anti-cyber squatting legislation introduced by the World Intellectual Property Organisation, the IOC proceeded to launch the largest ever lawsuit against cyber squatters to take back control of the Olympic terminology. Eventually, when the US District Court ruled on US Olympic Committee v 2000Olympic.com, it affirmed an earlier magistrate's ruling cancelling 36 domain names and transferring 818 back to the IOC. By the time of the 2003 ruling only 45 of the 1800 domain names originally listed remained.

There was no question that the internet was empowering a whole series of new stakeholders, who until now had been solely dependent on the traditional media to gain any exposure or profile. The new medium was embraced by sports agents and managers. They saw the potential to build their athletes as commercial brands by taking their message directly to the public.

At the US Olympic trials, 400 metre runner Michael Johnson, reportedly ignored the media at the post-race conference, preferring to post his comments about the race, his injury and his supposed rivalry with Maurice Green on the NBC.Olympics.com site run by Quokka. The public, however, only learned of Johnson's views when a wire report picked up the story from the Quokka site and repeated it through traditional media.

## Sink or surf

In preparation for the onslaught of the new media world at the Sydney Games, the IOC began preparing its defences. In the midst of a digital revolution, it was suggested that the IOC should change its official languages of English and French to zeros and ones. Prior to the Games, some 25,000 different sites were identified as having some form of Olympic content. Of these, close to a thousand might have the capability to transmit video images.

A specialist legal monitoring team was formed led by Net Results, with a group of lawyers surfing the web around the clock, ready to serve injunctions at short notice.

During the final contingency risk management training exercises, run by the Sydney Organising Committee with the IOC before the Games, everything from security procedures for terrorist attacks, to food poisoning at the athletes' village was reviewed. But there was one scenario that completely threw the operational planners.

What would we do, I asked, if a website in India started taking the broadcast signal live and streaming it to the world? And then, the scenario continued, the fax came in from NBC announcing that it was withholding the final multi-hundred million dollar rights fee payment for breach of rights. There were some long blank looks around the table. Finally, Michael Eyers, the deputy chief executive of the Organising Committee, shot back at me, that as the television contracts were signed and negotiated by the IOC, then it was clearly the IOC's problem to fix.

It was, therefore, with some trepidation that the IOC entered the Sydney Games, wondering whether we would see the meltdown of the broadcast industry. 'In today's Wild West environment, NBC's huge investment in Sydney can be chipped away at by competitors, athletes or anyone sit-

ting in the grandstands with a digital camera, cell phone and personal web page, an investment of about $500,' observed one article. The sports industry would either learn to surf the web, or drown.

The media were convinced that the power of the internet could eventually undermine the economic foundation of the modern Olympic Movement. 'The 27th Olympic Games may be remembered for many things – world records, peacetime logistical planning,' wrote the *New York Times*, 'but it will surely be a benchmark in the struggle between those who hold intellectual property rights in sporting events and those seeking to cover sports, especially for the ever expanding universe of news outlets on the internet.'

Yet, in spite of all the media hype and IBM's marketing push that these were the 'Olympics of the internet', it simply didn't stack up. Within the internet industry, everyone was used to talking about billions of hits, but no one was asking how many individual users this actually meant. When the final numbers came in, everyone, including the most optimistic champions for the new media world, experienced a rude awakening.

IBM claimed that the official Olympic.com site had attracted 11.3 billion hits and had set a new industry record for a sports site at the time of 1.2 million hits per minute.[13] But this only translated into 8.7 million unique visitors. NBC–Quokka, with its complementary site to the US network broadcast, attracted some four million visitors. Such was the scramble to push the numbers up that IBM was even accused of misdirecting hits from the NBC site to its own to beef up the final result.

Other broadcasters, like Channel 7, anxious not to get left behind in the new media rush, felt it necessary to put their own stake in the ground, only to find that the numbers fell far short of expectation. Channel 7 attracted over 16 million television viewers at home for the opening ceremonies, and another 2.7 million in pubs and big screens throughout the country, against only 200,000 clicking onto the web.

The most optimistic estimates of the global internet audience, across all the official sites, was less than 20 million people. This amounted to just 0.5 per cent of the global TV audience of over 3.7 billion. The average TV viewer was spending upwards of ten hours in front of the TV screen, and a lot more time in major markets like US and Japan. But the average internet surfer was spending less than 50 minutes over the 16 days in front of his computer screen on Olympic sites.

Quokka spent over $30 million building and promoting the NBC Olympics site, attracting some $12 million in ad revenue. IBM and the Sydney Organising Committee were estimated to have spent over $50 million to produce their real-time results official site.

It did not take long for the accountants to examine the numbers and realise that the business model, despite all the hype, was just not there. Global Olympic broadcast advertising revenue had exceeded $1 billion; global internet ad revenue connected to the Olympics had barely reached $20 million. The broadcasters made a respectable profit on their Games telecasts. The internet made a substantial loss. Within a few months this would drive many of the industry leaders over the cliff into bankruptcy. The internet bubble burst.

## Casualties of hype?

There is no question that the Sydney Games were a watershed in the relationship between sport and technology. For many, the 2000 Olympics were regarded as the first true internet Games. The Games were also a clear watershed for the ambitions of many of the dot.com companies. Depending on where you stood, the Games were either an encouraging signal of the brave new world that lay just around the corner, or a salutary lesson about the limits of new technology.

Recognising the threat, the IOC staged the first ever world conference on sport and new media. Over 1,000 people came. The *Wall Street Journal* likened the event to the Congress of Vienna which carved up Europe after the Napoleonic Wars. The broadcasters argued that Sydney was an acid test for new media that by and large failed. NBC Olympic's vice president of business affairs, Gary Zenkel, warned, 'the value of our rights is totally locked up in exclusivity. We can not run the risk that other web casters working in other time zones are going to put video on the internet'.

Not all broadcasters supported the internet ban. Those, like the BBC which had been actively developing a broader internet strategy, felt locked out. 'Our Olympic experience left a nasty taste in my mouth,' was how BBC's head of Sport Online Pete Clifton recalled his Sydney experience. 'The millions of pounds that the BBC spent to be in the Olympic family worked against us when it came to our internet coverage.'

The BBC had been given a yellow card for breaching internet guidelines. Clifton had not taken kindly to being woken up at 3.00 am by BBC controllers back in London, pointing out that the BBC was in danger of having all of its Olympic access withdrawn, for failing to block out Olympic coverage from their regular news bulletins. In the end, BBC Online had to employ a team of eight people for the duration of the Games just to press one button, so that any Olympic streaming video was blanked out of the regular news reports.[14]

And not everyone subscribed to the idea that separating out the new media rights was the best way forward. Philip Melchior, managing director of Reuters, pointed out that 'the more you divide rights, the more you disenfranchise people'. Kerry Stokes, chairman of Australia's Channel 7 network, made the simple observation that 'before anyone starts cannibalising the rights, it might actually be a good idea to look at the opportunities to bring it all together'.

But, for all of the new media hype, it was clear that the internet industry was far from ready to take up the challenge. The basic Olympic experience was built on moving images. Streaming video was not a problem for the broadcasters, but for the new media industry it remained a very expensive and somewhat far-fetched option. Streaming a mass event, at that time, would have absorbed half the world's telephony capacity. The lack of telecommunication infrastructure was proving a very real barrier to what the internet was really capable of – at least in terms of its ambition to become an entertainment medium.

The advertising industry was also far from certain of the true potential of the new medium. Coke marketing boss, Steve Jones, made all the right noises, challenging networks to work with other technology suppliers, in order to make the content effective for the consumers: 'The business model has changed from brand-centric to people-centric so we must leverage the power of new media to stay alive. The new media tailors messages to one person at a time. Fans want more experiences, they want interaction and to share information with friends and talk back to athletes.'

Jones went onto envisage an Athens Olympics where Coca-Cola sent the previous night's action direct to the individual, dictated to by the users' sporting preferences, and sent wireless video messages throughout the day, which the consumer could then send on to family and friends.

'Coca-Cola is a multimedia entertainment brand,' continued Jones, and 'Coca-Cola wants credit from fans for enhancing the Olympic experience. You can deliver totally different messages online – and provide the person with more value. The more people I have a relationship with, the more money Coca-Cola makes'.

There was just one problem. For all of the hype and promise of the new media, for all the talk about the opportunity, money talked. The bottom line was that Coca-Cola was spending less than two per cent of its global media and marketing budget on internet related advertising and promotions. Nike, a leader in pushing the boundaries of marketing and communications, was spending over $1 billion per annum on athletes and marketing, but allocating less than two per cent of its marketing budget to new media.

What the internet did prove in Sydney was that it could deliver incremental value to sponsors – although maybe not at the levels that were first envisaged. The ability of the medium to expand the marketing opportunities, because of its multi-directional scope, rather than the single direction of television, did start to deliver the results in Sydney. General Motors with an extended advertising campaign through the official NBC.Olympics.com web site, was able to deliver an additional 500,000 direct potential customer leads.

A few brave new media players hung in trying to paint a promising picture for the future. Rick Gentile, who had produced several Winter Olympic telecasts while at CBS, was now heading up a New York-based company, WeMedia, that specialised in streaming video from sports events on the web.

WeMedia had acquired the rights to broadcast the Paralympic Games from Sydney, and Gentile argued that 'you can webcast and broadcast without hurting either medium,' and that they had successfully delivered three simultaneous streams over 12 days from the Paralympic Games.

The issue here though, was that no broadcaster in the US was even interested in taking Paralympic coverage, and the web became the only way the event was going to get any exposure. WeMedia entered into a multi-year agreement with the International Paralympic Committee as their global broadcast partner. But WeMedia would soon be going the same way as Quokka – the costs of webcasting far outstripping any potential revenue source.

Quokka's Ramadan had already sadly begun to see his vision slowly slipping away, acknowledging to the conference that they had all been 'starry-eyed two years before the Games, and none of us really understood what we were saying'. Within a few months, Quokka sadly filed for Chapter 11 bankruptcy protection.

And the biggest technology players of all, like Samsung, which was investing hundreds of millions of dollars in the future, quietly warned against getting too carried away on the technology hype.

What became increasingly clear was that, although the internet could offer important operational and communication benefits for the sports movement, it was far from being an entertainment medium. For all of the attractions of Quokka's deep immersion sports concept, people wanted to be entertained and, when they came back from the office or the school, they wanted to put their feet up and relax, not to have work hard clicking down through hundreds of pages to find some unique additional piece of information about an athlete's heart rate and then watch a grainy picture on a small computer screen.

The advertising community slowly began to realise that straight banner ads across the top of a page were not delivering their message. The business model, at least for the first iteration of the internet, began to dry up. While the appeal of the internet is that there is not supposed to be any barrier in cyberspace, advertisers realised the real world is awash with barriers.

## New media, new mission

By the Salt Lake City Games in 2002 things had changed. The number of sites carrying Olympic information had dropped from 25,000 to less than 6,000.

But while the internet had failed to become an entertainment medium to challenge the broadcast industry, it was starting to establish itself as a key operations and communications partner of the Games, helping to both reduce operating costs, and in some cases create genuine additional revenue opportunities.

Nothing better illustrated the true role and value of the internet than its support in ticket sales. In Sydney, around ten per cent of the ticketing inventory had been sold online. By Salt Lake City, 80 per cent of all public ticket sales were purchased online – not only dramatically helping to reduce the costs of managing and processing ticket orders, but through specially designed navigational software, helping spectators to complete their Olympic experience, by offering them additional opportunities for extra events during their stay in Salt Lake.

In volunteer recruitment, the Salt Lake organising committee was able to attract and process over 67,000 applications, 90 per cent of their overall volunteer needs for the Games. In communications, the IOC was able to develop online resources for the media, ensuring that they received timely and comprehensive information – removing the barriers that had so beset the IOC with various public relations issues over the years.

In marketing, with the development of specialist extranets, a whole new level of marketing and client service support was established, with online approvals for partner marketing programmes, and accessible data banks of market research and thirty years of sponsor television commercials.

The Olympic Television Archive Bureau established one of the first online search libraries of video images, allowing TV producers from around the world to trawl through 100 years of Olympic history and download key video clips.

And, after all the debate over moving images on the web, the IOC was able, with three partners – Swiss Television, SchlumbergerSema and Swisscom's Bluewin internet service – to test the potential of video-on-demand via broadband connections to a few thousand homes in Geneva.[15] Swiss TV presented multiple live video feeds and access to the Games commentator information system as a compliment to their traditional overall television coverage of the Games. The test proved a success. For the first time, it was possible to control the territorial footprint of the signal, and thereby respect the integrity of the rights of other broadcasters. And the sports fan was able to expand, on a supplemental basis, his viewing experience. The success of the test prompted several broadcasters working with SchlumbergerSema to expand the programme for Athens.

The results of the official Games time site nevertheless underscored the fact that the medium remained a supplemental information tool, and was never going to become close to being the primary or even secondary vehicle for people's Games time experiences. At its peak, the official site was only able to attract five million unique visitors per day, and average of just three million per day, throughout the Games.

## A brave new world

Technology has always played a critical role in the development of the Olympic Movement, expanding the Olympic experience beyond the confines of the spectator in the Olympic stadium. New technologies will continue to broaden the experience of the sports fan, allowing the individual to choose what he wants to watch, when he wants to watch, in what language and with what supporting information. But, at the end of the day, although people want information, they also want to be entertained, and technology has often underestimated the impact of the barriers it has placed in the way of the consumers' enhanced experience.

Quokka's immersion sports offering looked impressive to the analysts and investment bankers. But everyone became seduced by the promised-land and forgot the fundamental business dynamics of how to make it all pay. The advertisers were not queuing up and are still not for general sports sites.

The mobile telephone operators made the same mistake when they went on their wild spending spree to buy up 3G rights, only to begin multi-billion dollar write-offs a few years later. Sport was supposed to be one of the key drivers of this new medium – but who honestly is going to watch anything more than a news clip of a soccer goal on their mobile phone? (Data information and transmission is altogether another issue.)

'Old media' has regained the leadership, not that perhaps they had ever really lost it, except in the eyes of various commentators and the investment banking community. 'New technology' will continue to help the 'old media' to broaden the entertainment experiences for the fan, but television will, from the entertainment perspective, remain the engine for many more years to come.

The trouble with technology is that it is highly seductive. Many people thought that the dot.com bubble changed the world. The tangible world seemed to be altered by the creation of a parallel – and as we ultimately discovered, illusionary – world in cyberspace. The trick for an institution like the Olympic Games is to walk the fine line between what is possible technologically and what is practical and affordable. Fall behind and you risk looking out of touch. But get ahead of the curve and you risk failure and financial ruin.

With IBM, we learned an important lesson. Technologists have a tendency to believe their own propaganda. The technology tail was in danger of wagging the Olympic dog. The deal with Sema was one of the biggest and most important in Olympic sponsorship history, but the announcement was all but eclipsed by another story. The Salt Lake City scandal was, perhaps, the most serious crisis the IOC ever faced. It was a distinctly low-tech, old-fashioned tale of corruption. But it looked like breaking the IOC – and undoing all that we had achieved since Moscow.

## NOTES

1 The press also recognised the risk. The *Atlanta Constitution* wrote, with some understatement, that 'IBM has quite a bit riding on the Olympics'. The newspaper quoted a confidential report from business research firm the Aberdeen Group analysing IBM's plans. 'IBM needs to score a perfect 10 or risk worldwide embarrassment. If IBM scores a perfect 10, it will have sent a message to the world that it is still the premier supplier of complex systems. One slip and IBM gets the blame. If scores are late, wrong or mis-delivered to the 15,000 strong army of journalists and broadcasters, IBM dons the dunce cap.'

2 Kevan Gosper was a long-standing IOC member, a silver medalist at the Melbourne Olympics, and also a regional president of Shell – not exactly, therefore, technologically illiterate.

3 'IBM's Olympic Fiasco' was *Fortune's* take on events. 'Big Blue screwed up at the Olympics, no doubt about it ... multi-million dollar ad campaign touted reliability. If self parody were an Olympic sport, IBM have medalled.' 'IBM's frenzied race to save face in Atlanta,' was *USA Today's* view. Associated Press, which had paid IBM for additional special results services, likened IBM to 'an Olympic veteran which exuded confidence at the prospect of repeating past successes, but when it came to the crunch could not perform.

4 Other IBM and ACOG technology systems had dealt with 800,000 accommodation nights; a 10.5 million ticket inventory; a 265,811

person accreditation database; 131,000 workforce of staff and potential volunteers who, during the 17 days of the Games, log 5.5 million hours of service, and require over 1 million uniform pieces, and a 6,600 vehicle fleet – all without too much of a glitch.

5   Bob Neal, ACOG head of information technology, was a senior IBM executive on loan to ACOG, as were a large proportion of ACOG's technology department.

6   The *Wall Street Journal* reported that 'Divorce is never a pretty sight' and quoted Dick Pound as saying, 'IBM's institutional solution is to throw money at every problem ... IOC accused IBM of gold plating its Olympic computers, designing too fancy a system that the IOC could have bought a third cheaper elsewhere. IBM accused the IOC of being computer illiterate, failing to realise how complex the Olympic technical requirements had become since 1960, and refusing to pay up.'

7   Tidu Maini, Sema's senior vice-president, talked of the company's 'ability to web together different systems rather than push proprietary systems as IBM did, [and that] worked to our advantage'. 'We're not seeing the Olympics as a way to promote any hardware or software product,' he added. The media immediately recognised the potential for Sema. 'Victory over sexier US information technology companies will transform the little known European system integrator of 16,500 people, into one of the world's most recognised brands,' was how the *Wall Street Journal* greeted news of Sema's Olympic partnership. Associated Press commented that 'the high profile tie with the Olympics should put the company on the world map'. Bonelli proudly announced that 'this sponsorship would take Sema out of the shadows of the big US IT companies'. Analysts talked of how 'the Olympic association gives potential customers a warm feeling that you are up there with the leaders in technology and can also deliver'.

8   SchlumbergerSema's success in Salt Lake City was crowned when the Management Consultancies Association awarded the company the 'gold medal' for its work. The judges described SchlumbergerSema's challenge as a 'very complex project on an impressive scale'. The company had 'successfully managed a diverse group of stakeholders and partners. Client satisfaction was very evident. The fixed deadline required excellent management. It worked!'.

9 Lenovo was known as Legend until April 2003 when it changed its English brand name to Lenovo,in order to develop a global brand position. Founded in 1984 in Beijing by eleven scientists – including Liu Chuanzhi from the Chinese Academy of Sciences in Beijing – Lenovo, in the tradition of other great start-ups, began life in a small hut. When Lenovo acquired IBM's PC division in 2004 for $1.3 billion, its revenues shot up fourfold to $12 billion.

10 *The Financial Times* kicked off the pre-Games debate with the headline 'See no action, hear no action, click no action.' 'For the duration of the upcoming Olympic Games in Sydney, we're all supposed to plug our ears, cover our eyes and pretend the internet doesn't exist,' ran a *Chicago Tribune's* editorial. 'The IOC has refused to [sanction video images on the web]. If this sounds a little ridiculous, well it is. In this age of instant information, the IOC and NBC are trying to smuggle sounds and images of the Games past a worldwide network that's perfectly designed to distribute such data.'

11 Quokka was named after one of the first Australian mammals ever to be seen by Europeans. A quokka is a type of wallaby.

12 So powerful was Ramadan's vision that he was soon listed in *Time's* cyber elite. Venture capital funding poured into the company.

13 Olympics.com site attracted 1.2 million hits at 15.19 Australian EDT on September 17.

14 The problem was that broadcast rights were, and still are, sold on a territorial basis, but the internet does not respect territorial boundaries, and sites are available on a global basis. As such, any site broadcasting outside of its national host territory, breached the rights of all other broadcasters – and with the different time zones around the world could pre-empt key prime time programming.

15 The Salt Lake City live web-cast service was offered free to subscribers in Basel, Geneva and Zurich for the first three days, thereafter a charge of Sfr10 ($5.90) was levied for the remainder of the Games.

## Chapter 9

# TO THE BRINK AND BACK

## The city of saints

It all began quietly. On November 24, 1998 a Salt Lake City television station, KTVX-TV, reported that a scholarship had been provided to the daughter of an IOC member, Rene Essomba from Cameroon, to attend university in Washington. The news report was based on an unsigned letter, dated September 17, 1996, from David Johnson, one of the leaders of the Salt Lake bid team, to Sonia Essomba advising her that the Salt Lake Organising Committee (SLOC) was unable to continue its scholarship support.

The letter had been handed over by Stephanie Pate, the former secretary to SLOC President Tom Welch, who had been pressured by Olympic trustee, Ken Bullock to 'find dirt' on Dave Johnson. All this was unhelpful internal politicking, but then the letter reached KTVX Channel 4 reporter, Chris Vanocur, who broke the story. At this point it became clear that the payments were part of a larger scheme to woo the family and friends of IOC members to win votes for Salt Lake City to host the 2002 Olympic Winter Games.

At first, media coverage of the scandal was limited to the local press in Salt Lake City. But it soon had massive worldwide media coverage, with far-reaching repercussions that eventually threatened the very existence of the IOC. It was one of the biggest crises in Olympic history.

For the IOC marketing team, it meant a frantic exercise in shuttle diplomacy, involving a whistle-stop tour of the world's most powerful companies. At stake was the then still fragile Olympic marketing programme – and all that we had achieved. David Miller, the chief sports correspondent of *The (London) Times*, noted that 'this initially minor revelation was on a par with the Watergate break-in. The ramifications were to prove similarly far reaching.'

As is often the case, the seeds for the crisis were planted much earlier. The starting point was Salt Lake's original bid for the 1998 Olympic Winter Games which it lost to Nagano, Japan. Salt Lake officials were convinced that they had been cheated. In this they were plain wrong. It was unthinkable that the IOC would stage consecutive Summer and Winter Olympic Games in the same country. With Atlanta hosting the 1996 Games, there was no chance of another North American city hosting the 1998 Winter Games.

The Salt Lake team didn't see it like that. Utah Senator Orrin Hatch wrote to Salt Lake's bid leader, Tom Welch, shortly after they had lost to Nagano, stating: 'Had it not been for the prejudice and corruption in the system, we would have been winners.' Senator Hatch later told the *Salt Lake Desert News* that Salt Lake had lost its bid to host the 1998 Games, 'because Japanese leadership just basically bought the Olympics ... We were swindled out of it'. Ill feeling had bred a determination to win the next bid at all costs.

I first heard of the imminent crisis from the IOC director general, Francois Carrard. It was a passing comment at IOC headquarters. At first blush, it seemed a local story which would probably stay local. Samaranch, however, immediately recognised the potential gravity of the issue and instructed the IOC Juridical Commission and Francois Carrard, to begin a discreet investigation. Carrard contacted Frank Joklik, chairman of the Salt Lake Organising Committee, to establish what exactly was going on, and asked him to immediately bring a full report to Lausanne.

## The loose cannon

Things came to a head at the IOC's Executive Board meeting on December 11. This was the final meeting of the year. It was business as usual – the agenda included reports from the future Games organising committees, a debriefing on the Nagano Winter Games, along with regular reports from the various IOC commissions and the IOC administration.

For IOC Marketing, this was an important day. At lunch time, the new TOP partnership technology agreement was to be signed with the chairman of Sema, Pierre Bonelli, and senior vice president, Tidu Maini, who had led the negotiations over the past six months. Sema was to replace IBM as the overall systems integrator and provide the critical technology backbone to the Games.

At this stage it was still far from clear exactly what had happened in Salt Lake. The IOC had only read brief media reports and had not yet received any hard facts or evidence or a report from Salt Lake.

Straight after opening the meeting, Samaranch announced that a formal inquiry commission would look into the allegations. Samaranch asked Dick Pound, as an IOC vice president, to chair the commission.[1] This appeared to be a strong response, which would hopefully stop the problem escalating.

But any hope of a discreet inquiry was lost when veteran IOC member Marc Hodler rushed out of the meeting and into the lobby of the IOC headquarters to hold an impromptu press briefing. The usual crowd of around 15 or so journalists that follow the Olympic Movement were waiting for the standard mid-day board press briefing. No major decisions were expected, and the journalists were hanging around for odd bits of gossip and anecdotes of future Games preparations. They were surprised, therefore, to be confronted with the elderly Hodler in a state of considerable excitement.

Rather than waiting for the full report from Salt Lake, Hodler immediately started talking of bribery and corruption. He was not sure, he said, whether other Olympic cities had been elected cleanly – and talked of agents and secret encounters. 'The cities have been the victim and not the villain,' he insisted, pointing the finger of suspicion firmly in the IOC's direction. Within five minutes of Hodler starting his ad-hoc press interview, the journalists had a lot more than mere gossip to report – they had the makings of a global front page story that would stop the presses and run for months and months.

Hodler was then in his eighties, one of the elder statesmen of the IOC. On the occasions I had any dealings with him, he struck me as highly principled and dignified. Elected in 1963, he had served at the top of the Olympic Movement for several decades. A leading Swiss lawyer, he had presided over the International Ski Federation for 47 years – the longest serving president of any international federation. He had been the chairman of the IOC Finance Commission since 1989, and had served as chairman of the co-ordination commissions for the Calgary, Albertville, Lillehammer, Nagano and now the Salt Lake Winter Olympic Games.

Hodler was also a senior member of the IOC Juridical Commission and, with concerns about the cost of bidding for the Games spiralling out of control, had been appointed by Samaranch to come up with a set of rules for bidding cities. These became known as the 'Hodler rules'. Hodler had served three terms as a member of the IOC executive board and as a vice president of the IOC from 1993 to 1997. He had even at one stage been seen as a potential front-runner to succeed Lord Killanin as a future IOC president and actually ran for the post in Moscow. Hodler was highly respected, a major establishment figure within the Olympic Movement. Given this, his behaviour over the coming days and weeks was unusual to say the least. Hodler was not just some maverick outsider, he was the ultimate IOC insider.[2]

Not surprisingly, Hodler quickly had the media pack's undivided attention. Broadening the agenda, he started talking of Ferraris being given away so that Italy could host the World Ski Championships, and the role of the Agnelli family. (This did not please Evelyn Cristillin, Agnelli's niece, who was in Lausanne presenting Torino's candidature for the 2006 Winter Games. She threatened to withdraw the bid.) The journalists could not believe their luck. A trip to a quiet executive board meeting that had been hard to justify to their editors had suddenly become front-page news. The Sema announcement now seemed curiously unimportant – not to say embarrassing.

Eventually, Hodler was persuaded by IOC secretary general, Francoise Zweifel, to leave the press conference dais to make way for the formalities of the contract signing. Bonelli and Maini, along with the director general of Athens 2004, Costas Bakouris, and Salt Lake president, Frank Joklik, joined Samaranch, Pound and Carrard on the stage.

Bonelli talked about his pride in joining the most prestigious marketing programme in the world, and Samaranch talked of the importance of corporate support to the Olympic Movement. But, hardly were the set speeches over when the questions started. None were about the new technological partnership, the largest and most important Olympic sponsorship agreement ever signed. Instead, they locked on to Hodler's outburst. Did the recent revelations mean that the IOC would withdraw the Games from Salt Lake? Was this the first time that the IOC had heard of any bidding indiscretions? What action was the IOC going to take against the members implicated? Would investigations be launched into other cities? How would the other losing cities react?

This was only the beginning. Over the following days, the media interest began to mount. Hodler cast himself as the conscience of the Olympic Movement, claiming that Samaranch had muzzled him from speaking to the press. In reality, Samaranch had simply suggested that the impromptu press conference would do more harm than good. Christmas only provided a brief respite, merely allowing journalists to gather their resources and start the New Year with a renewed energy for the scandal. By this time, the story had been passed from the sports journalists to some mainstream investigative journalists.

Curiously, when Hodler appeared before the IOC Inquiry he revealed that his allegations were actually based on hearsay rather than concrete facts and much of the corruption he referred to had actually occurred in his own ski federation rather than the Olympic Movement. Even so, he continued being quoted extensively. The oxygen of publicity can become addictive.

## Bunny business

The Salt Lake Organising Committee freely acknowledged it had broken the rules. Ken Bullock, a SLOC trustee, said: 'The Games are an aphrodisiac. If you want something bad enough, you stretch the boundaries.' Visiting IOC members had been transported in private jets. Various IOC members had received support for education, their relatives had been given jobs, debts had been paid off and some had received hospital treatment. The SLOC had gone to imaginative – as well as excessive – lengths to gain support. It even spent $1200 on sending a dozen rabbits to Dick Pound after he had suggested that their bid was running out of inspiration and there were no more rabbits they could pull out of the hat. The story looked as if it had the potential – scandal, bribery, high powered corruption, sex – to run and run, and all connected with the clean-living lifestyle of the Mormons.

As the negative headlines increased, the IOC's main focus was to communicate directly with all partners to let them know what was happening.[3] There was just one problem – we did not really have a clue what was happening. By early January 1999, the rumour mill was running overtime. Allegations and accusations were coming from all sides, with no hint where the next grenade might come from.

Such was the media onslaught that, on more than one occasion, I arrived at the office for the daily 8.00 am crisis meeting and wondered whether the IOC, which had survived 107 years and two world wars, would even make it through the next 24 hours. The IOC simply did not have the internal media resources to deal with the growing media barrage. Sponsors were increasingly concerned by the escalating negative coverage.

Typical of the coverage was an article in the *Financial Times* which observed: 'Faster, Higher, Stronger is the Olympic motto – to which could now be added Deeper, as the IOC plunges further into the mire of the Salt Lake scandal ... The carefully constructed image of honour and probity has been shattered ... dragging the Olympic name through the mud.' Another newspaper reported: 'Bribes scandal reveals sham of Olympic ideal. The credibility of the Olympic Movement is shattered, the five inter-locking rings blown apart.' Jerre Longman wrote in the *New York Times*: 'The Olympic Games are as decayed as a bad tooth, perhaps facing perma-nent extraction sometime in the future.'

Hodler continued to throw even more fuel onto the fire and, after origi-nally defending SLOC, was now proposing that maybe the Games should be moved. Cities which had lost out to Salt Lake City in the election started talking of legal claims against the IOC. Rene Paquet, president of the Quebec bid, announced that the city, provincial and Canadian govern-ments, along with the private corporations which had supported the bid, deserved some recourse. 'We had a budget of $12 million ... that's a good place to start ... and then there is punitive damages.' Christer Persson, who led the Ostersund bid from Sweden, talked of Salt Lake being ordered to pay $14 million in compensation to its competitors.

## Who pays the piper?

But Salt Lake was not simply about acting decisively to regain credibility. The media soon identified the real risk to the IOC – sponsors jumping ship – and began to home in, arguing that the power had shifted in the Olym-pic world to the sponsors. Calls in the media for Samaranch's resignation began to mount. The *Financial Times* and others reported that the final word on whether Samaranch stays or not 'may well rest with the Olympic Movement's new masters in the corporate world'.

*The Economist* put the issue more bluntly in its lead article 'Saving the Olympic Spirit': 'The obvious risk for the IOC is that the public will be appalled, the sponsors will take fright and the TV companies will lose heart, in other words the Olympics will slowly die.' *The Australian* wrote how 'Sponsors will check Olympic corruption ... And how one concerned group can provide a modicum of accountability to the almost untouchable IOC – the Olympic sponsors'. *The New York Times* broadened the attack to question not only sponsor support but broadcast advertiser support, commenting that while 'NBC will deliver the audience, negative public vibes will cause advertisers not to shy away, but run away'. The next report was that the local Salt Lake telecommunications partner, US West, was considering withholding a $5 million payment to the Organising Committee.

Sponsors increasingly came under the media spotlight and, although most still refused to comment publicly on the situation, privately alarm bells were starting to ring, and ring loudly. Among those sounding the alarm was David D'Alessandro who, during 15 years at John Hancock, had quickly risen through the ranks from corporate communications to become chief executive. D'Alessandro was unsure whether the IOC would react quickly enough and believed that his own company's image – an image that in the world of life insurance was founded on 'trust and integrity' – would be tarnished if the scandal dragged on.

Three years before the crisis, D'Alessandro writing in *Fortune* noted that what 'we sell is trust. The credibility of the Olympics is very important to a company like ours'. As an old New York PR man, who had once handled publicity for an Ali–Frazier fight, D'Alessandro knew how to grab the media's attention with a short, sharp sound bite.

'We woke up one morning in late 1998 to discover we were now linked with a situation that represented the opposite of integrity ... and we believed that if the scandal had gone on too long without a resolution, it might well have hurt our brand,' he said. 'If they fail to investigate, the rings won't be tarnished, they will be broken. A failure to do so will cost the IOC its golden aura and the Olympics will become a mere mortal like the NBA and the NFL.'

## Message to our sponsors

All of this had an effect. Mud sticks. From a commercial point of view, the most worrying news was that Coca-Cola was reported to be reconsidering its sponsorship. Coke had been an Olympic sponsor since Amsterdam in 1928. If the company was to withdraw, then the end was potentially very close at hand.

Samaranch placed Dick Pound in charge of the investigative commission. This was a very public demonstration of the IOC putting its house in order. Carrard was dealing with the politics and communication. My brief from Samaranch was to meet with key sponsors to explain exactly what the IOC was doing to fix the problems.

Normally, giving CEOs of major corporations 72 hours notice of a meeting is not a good idea. They are busy people. This time, however, they were keen to talk – very keen. Such was the urgency that I flew by Concorde to meet with the public relations firm Hill & Knowlton and from there late at night chartered a private jet to fly to Atlanta to meet Coca-Cola's top management. At the meeting were Doug Ivester, Coke's chairman and chief executive, Chuck Fruit, senior vice president marketing, and Scott McCune, head of global sports. After a 30 minute presentation, they all reassured me that they were not going to pull the plug. While they were understandably concerned about the scandal, they had enjoyed a long-standing partnership with the Olympic Movement and wanted it to continue.[4]

The message to the sponsors was simple. The IOC understood the extreme seriousness of the issue. The IOC leadership was committed to getting to the bottom of the matter and would take whatever measures were necessary to restore confidence in the Olympic ideal. Overall, the partners were surprisingly understanding. I spent an hour in a one-to-one meeting with Paul Allaire, chairman and CEO of Xerox, and he gave some of the best advice. Acknowledging that every company and organisation goes through a crisis, the challenge, and the true test of leadership, he said, was whether you could use the situation as a catalyst for reform and change. If you did, a lot of good could come out of the crisis.

The US trip was followed by a two-day visit to Korea and Japan to meet with Samsung and Matsushita. Both companies pledged their continued support for the Olympic Movement, although you could see that they were also struggling with increasingly aggressive media coverage. The Japanese, in particular, hold the Olympics in high regard and any suggestion of its ethics and standards being tarnished was difficult for them to take.

## Managing the media

Although Samaranch had built the IOC into a highly professional administration, there had always been one major weak spot – the communications department. The IOC did not really have one. Samaranch was never comfortable dealing with the media and had failed over the years to engage or keep a senior communications director. As they had come and gone, Samaranch had simply shrugged his shoulders.

So, when the crisis hit, the IOC paid a terrible price. The failure to address the communications issue meant that the IOC was misunderstood and had limited goodwill to deal with the press. Samaranch himself paid a high price. The toll on his personal reputation for failing to properly court the world's press was significant. Even today many people associate Samaranch personally with the Salt Lake scandal, something that is both unfounded and unfair.

Francois Carrard formed a small crisis review committee with a few senior IOC directors. The group reviewed each day's media headlines and the latest batch of rumours, so that we could try and respond accordingly, and advise all of our stakeholders on where things stood, so that they would not be blind-sided by the headlines or media calls for comment.

The first objective was to build up the IOC's communication resources so that we could begin to respond to the media inquiries. At the peak of the crisis we had over 1,000 journalists following the story on a daily basis. We looked around for the best crisis communications team we could find, and chose a specialised unit from Hill & Knowlton. They spent much of the next few months living in Lausanne. Dedicated information lines were set up in New York and London for the media, at times pulling in several hundred calls a day. Hill & Knowlton later compared the level of coverage and global media attention to the Monica Lewinsky story.

## Next up

Then a new scandal arose. On January 22, 1999, John Coates, president of the Australian Olympic Committee, and the key strategist behind Sydney's bid campaign for the 2000 Summer Olympic Games, released a set of documents. They indicated that the night before Sydney's election, at the IOC Session in Monaco, he had offered $50,000 in athletic scholarship grants to two African members from Uganda and Kenya to encourage them to vote for Sydney. As Sydney had only won by two votes, the implications of Coates' revelations were dramatic.[5] Would the Chinese, who had lost to Sydney, demand that the Games be withdrawn from Australia? Would other cities come forward to sue the IOC over a mismanaged or perceived fraudulent election process? The drip, drip nature of the allegations looked like becoming a deluge that would kill the IOC.[6]

The Australian press were now on a witch hunt. They were soon digging up new stories about the IOC member Phil Coles and the number of times he had visited Salt Lake to inspect their facilities, with accusations of freeloading. In themselves, most of the allegations were pretty petty. But there was a conviction that there was much more behind all this, and the heavy mob of investigative journalists continued to weigh in. There was no let up.

Politicians, and especially those in the US Senate and US Congress, were soon starting to talk of special hearings, with a view to amending US Federal legislation on how broadcast and US sponsor payments might be remitted to the IOC. Senator John McCain talked of introducing a bill that would expand the Foreign Corrupt Practices Act to include the IOC. 'This legislation is in response to what I believe is a failure of the IOC to adequately respond to corruption in the selection of cities to host the Olympic Games,' McCain said.[7]

Meanwhile the Salt Lake Organising Committee and the US Olympic Committee had set up their own investigations.[8] The FBI, too, was allocating ever greater resources to the investigation. It was claimed that federal expenditure on investigating the Salt Lake scandal would eventually exceed the amount spent on the Oklahoma City bombing.

To make matters worse David D'Alessandro upped the ante by announcing that he was pulling the Olympic rings from John Hancock's advertising and marketing material until the scandal was resolved. Similarly he would not be buying any airtime on the NBC Olympic telecast. 'The IOC is not listening to the NOCs, or the press – perhaps they will listen to the people sending the money,' he said. On February 14, he sent the IOC a Valentine message with a difference. In a blistering piece for the New York Times, under the heading 'How to save the Olympics', D'Alessandro wrote: 'Every government forgets about the people who give it power ... it happened to Louis XVI, it happened to the Soviet Communists' and closed with 'a call for an immediate search for Samaranch's successor'.

I called D'Alessandro to explain that, in spite of the media comments, the IOC was a democracy and it would take time to get all the IOC members and countries on board to pass the necessary reform. D'Alessandro told me to go and consult a history professor and read up on the Magna Carta to understand the meaning of democracy.

In the weeks that followed, D'Alessandro made other unhelpful comments – about Olympic sponsorship becoming 'radioactive'. The IOC, he suggested was caught up in an enterprise killing scandal. Combined with challenges from *Business Week* that corporate America should grab the Olympic torch and take it back from the IOC, these remarks did little to bolster confidence in corporate board rooms.

D'Alessandro had his own agenda. He wanted to provide impetus for change, giving the Olympic Movement a nudge. The trouble is that his nudges felt like full-bodied heaves from a line-backer. His views didn't go down well with other sponsors and, from the IOC's point of view, noone enjoys having a gun put to their head.

The bullets kept on flying. The *Wall Street Journal* became particularly aggressive. 'Sponsors consider new Olympic Event: Jumping Ship,' it reported, noting that the Olympics were 'one of the costliest, most restrictive and tightly regulated sports sponsorships in the world.' Most sponsors tried to ensure that their comments remained neutral, but it was not easy. 'We won't be fully satisfied until this is completely put to rest,' was Coca-Cola's communication director, Ben Deutsch's response.

With unceasing and unfavourable media coverage and a vocal and negative sponsor in John Hancock, calls for Samaranch's resignation continued unabated. *The (London) Times* reported 'Olympic sponsors want Samaranch to step down'. Anonymous sponsor quotes began to appear in the media. 'If there was news that Samaranch was going to resign, there would have been great relief around the room,' one TOP sponsor marketing director was quoted as saying after an IOC–sponsor meeting. *The Herald Tribune* wrote that if 'Juan Antonio Samaranch falls on his sword next month when the tottering IOC weighs its bribery habits, it will have been Mr. D'Alessandro who furnished the blade'.

Sydney Team Millennium Partner, automobile maker Holden, part of General Motors, spoke for many sponsors when its spokesperson said: 'It's difficult for a sponsor in the current environment to maximise its association with the Games for as long as these revelations keep coming to the surface.'

Michael Knight, president of the Sydney Organising Committee, and 'Minister for the Olympics', in the New South Wales Government, began to worry that the crisis could have a serious negative impact on ticket sales, and scare away additional companies from supporting the Games. Concerned with how to balance the budget, Knight also turned his attention to the IOC, demanding that the IOC agree to cutbacks in operations, and even consider making up any shortfall in finances from IOC resources.

## Not a resigning matter

Some of the coverage was as humorous as it was hysterical. Investigative journalists like Craig Copetas of the *Wall Street Journal* piled in, thinking perhaps that this was their ticket to a Pulitzer prize. Conspiracy stories were rife, with talk of dark, hidden forces trying to bring down the overly powerful IOC.

I will never forget when Copetas called me with the latest, confirmed story coming out of China. This was that, during Beijing's bid for the 2008 Olympic Games, the Chinese had given Samaranch one of the priceless 2000 year-old Terracotta warriors from Xian. Samaranch, so the story went, had spirited the diminutive stone warrior out of the country. Copetas wanted to know what Samaranch had done with it – as the warrior was not on show at the Olympic Museum. The implication was that it had been sold. I asked Copetas where he came by this information – only to be told that someone had seen Samaranch on the plane with it! I told Copetas I would check with the IOC accounts to see if we had an airline ticket receipt for a warrior from Beijing to Geneva.

Against this hysterical background, Samaranch wasn't going anywhere. I tried to explain to sponsors and the media that if we changed president now, we would be up the creek without a paddle. To have an election for a new president would be suicidal. The last thing we needed was more turmoil. The media accused me alternately of either flaunting my loyalty, or being scared for my job. It was the latter – not just my job, but also everyone's job within the Olympic Movement. We were perilously close to total collapse. The scandal threatened the very existence of the IOC.

If Samaranch had resigned I don't believe it would have helped. It was clear to anyone who understood the inner workings of the Olympic Movement that such a move would have simply left the IOC without a leader. The corporate model of having your CEO step down, to quickly stop the media criticism and turn a new page solving all of your past problems, just would not work for the IOC. The quick fix public relations solution, to send a signal that there had been a change in direction, would have been just that – a short term PR fix to respond to the media. It would not have dealt with the real issue: driving through a reform process and restructuring the organisation.

The IOC simply could not operate on the traditional corporate model. It had over 100 members scattered around the world, with different customs and traditions, and all of whom were volunteers who normally only met together once a year. It would take time for consultation among the IOC membership. The last thing anyone needed at this stage was more instability with a big internal political campaign and power struggle. The level of change that was needed to fix the IOC's problems was radical. Samaranch had to stay in charge to call the shots and drive through the changes and reforms – not all of which would be popular or well received by the members. Turkeys tend not to vote for Christmas.

## The tide turns

Slowly, sponsors and the media began to accept that a Samaranch resignation would not solve the problems and that, if we wanted reform, he was perhaps the only man who could deliver. The headlines began to turn.

With Dick Pound dealing with issues through the Ad Hoc Inquiry Commission, Samaranch set about examining the broader strategic issues and putting in place a basis for reform. He called a special session of the IOC for March 17 in Lausanne to set about acting upon the recommendations of the Ad Hoc Commission, the expulsion of six members, and to discuss the necessary reforms.

Opening the session, Samaranch dropped his usual diplomatic guard and asked the Session to allow him to address them 'with the utmost frankness and to consider with the utmost seriousness what (he) had to say'. Samaranch continued, 'It is my firm conviction that unless we act quickly, decisively and unanimously at this extraordinary Session, the damage which may be done to the Olympic Movement, and to the IOC, as a result of the recent disclosures will be very, very serious. In the past, it did not matter that very few people understood what the IOC was and how it operated. Now the world expects us to be more open – the word of current choice is transparent – and more accessible.'

Concerned that some members, especially those outside Europe and North America, who were not at the centre of the crisis and having to deal with the media furore on a daily basis, might not realise how desperate the situation was, Samaranch piled it on: 'It is important, vital, that you understand the extent of this crisis. Make no mistake, however, that there has never been a crisis of this magnitude facing the IOC, and the Olympic Movement. It is our IOC that is now on trial.'

Following Samaranch's sobering address, the IOC Session turned its attention to dealing with the report of Dick Pound's Ad Hoc Inquiry Commission and the recommendation that six members be expelled from the IOC.[9] Each of the six members was given the opportunity to address the Session and respond to the case against them, after which the Session would vote on whether to expel their colleague. All six were expelled.

Next Samaranch proceeded to address his proposals for reform. He proposed a special Ethics Commission which included five members of impeccable standing and reputation from outside the Olympic Movement.[10]

Samaranch then proposed that a special commission, to be known as the IOC 2000 Commission, be established with the mandate to study just how the IOC should reform, adapt and modernise itself for the new millennium. A further special session of the IOC would be called at the end of the year to review and vote on the reform recommendations. Some 80 individuals were invited onto the Commission – less than half of them IOC members and 26 from outside the Olympic Movement. It was deliberately set up as a large group, to include all of the different stakeholders from within the Olympic Movement – the IOC members, the International Federations, the National Olympic Committees, as well as to ensure a full geographical and political representation. It was designed so that by the time the reforms were presented to the Session, they would have the maximum support from the membership.[11]

It was taking time, but the IOC was starting to show its partners that it was taking concrete actions. A road map for definitive reform was falling into place. Daily communications with the partners continued. Senior IOC executives were spending several hours each day talking to each of them, briefing them on the latest developments and reassuring them. The IOC wrote to all the partners asking for their perspective and suggestions on the reform process. The mere act of involving them directly in the process sent another strong message from the IOC, that we wanted to take full advantage of the crisis and turn it to our advantage.

All of the TOP partners took the IOC's request very seriously, with chairmen and CEOs responding in considerable detail. Several of the suggestions were subsequently adopted by the IOC 2000 Commission.[12]

As a sign of the IOC's commitment that it would never again let its guard down on the ethical standing of the Olympic Movement, it was decided to introduce a morals clause into the sponsor contracts. The clause would allow sponsors to walk away from their agreements if there was ever a further lapse in ethical standards. It was a two-way street, though, as it would also allow the IOC to drop a sponsor if the sponsor was involved in a scandal that impacted upon the Olympic brand. 'It's the kind of clause that forces the IOC in the end to pay real attention if there is a real problem,' said D'Alessandro in one of his more helpful moments. 'It's also designed so that a sponsor can't walk away on a whim.' In reality, the inclusion of the morals clause in the sponsor contracts was more symbolic than anything else. It sent a clear message that the IOC was wholly committed to operating to the highest ethical standards.

## Brand collateral

Other leading industry commentators finally began to put some perspective on the affair. 'I think companies have come to the conclusion that the American public is not as concerned about this as the media would have us believe,' noted Neal Pilson, a sports business consultant and former president of CBS Sports. 'The fact is people distinguish between the [IOC's practices] and the excitement and competition of the Games themselves. It just isn't really a big story.' A poll by US research agency Eisner & Associates noted that, in spite of the media onslaught, only about a third of Americans were even aware of the controversy and almost none blamed the sponsors.'

Another poll, by Olympic partner General Motors, which was investing over $1 billion in sponsorship and broadcast airtime buys in the Olympics through 2008, noted that although around 68 per cent of adults were aware of the scandal, double the Eisner study, 90 per cent also said that the bribery allegations would not diminish their enjoyment of the Games.

As the IOC's reform process began to gain momentum, confidence built among the sponsors, and this became a turning point in media coverage.[13] Nicolas G Hayek, chairman of Swatch, came out stating 'The IOC is a victim of its own success by, in recent years, making the Olympics such an emotional event. It is still very much there – and the IOC is doing what it has to do, and what is necessary, to address the recent problems.' Xerox's Paul Allaire continued, 'There are few, if any, institutions in the world that enjoy the respect and prestige of the IOC and the Olympic Games. This made the recent disclosures all the more tragic. I expect however, that the IOC will respond positively to the events and take this opportunity to update the IOC's governance in recognition of its success'. Coca-Cola's sports marketing boss, Scott McCune, stated that, 'Contractually, while we're committed to the Olympics through 2008, philosophically, we are committed to the Olympics forever'.[14]

Although no sponsor had jumped ship, others in the line of fire began to find the going getting too tough and the future outlook grim. John Krimsky, the United States Olympic Committee marketing chief, who had run the US marketing programmes since 1986 as his private fiefdom, bailed out. For all his bluster and directness, used to good effect over the previous 13 years to try and beat sponsors and organising committees into submission, Krimsky wanted out. 'We have presented to probably 32 companies since the scandal broke,' Krimsky announced on his resignation, 'but we have not signed any new sponsor as of today.' This was not helpful at a time when we were desperately trying to build confidence among the US local sponsors.

## Fuelling the fire

Partners were also beginning to tire of D'Alessandro's negative commentary in the media. Most felt he was not helping by continually throwing oil on the fire and that it was better to stay quiet and let the IOC get on with the task of reform. No sponsor had until now publicly challenged D'Alessandro's outbursts, although in private, several insinuated that he had a hidden agenda.

D'Alessandro saw things very differently, comparing the Olympic situation to Watergate and the Monica Lewinsky scandal. In his view, it was not so much the initial reports of scandal that were the cause of the problem, but the slow reaction and perceived attempts at a cover up. For D'Alessandro, the question was not why he was so outspoken, but why the other sponsors remained silent.

'The others scream and yell at these meetings about how there's not enough reform, and some sponsors have tried to use this to try to get a discount, but they won't do it publicly,' complained D'Alessandro. 'Had those sponsors spoken their minds in a public forum, it would be over. It would be done ... Sponsors did not push for reform when they had a chance, and they've done a terrible job of insulating themselves. The problem is that without significant reform, there's a good chance you'll continue to get hit, if not by this scandal, then another one.'

One partner did finally break ranks and speak out, not against the IOC, but against D'Alessandro himself. Dick Ebersol, NBC Olympic and Sports chairman, had finally had enough, and launched into a blistering public attack. 'I am sick of watching this two-bit bully get on his soapbox. His actions demand a response – and that response is shut up ... D'Alessandro's tongue lashing will only hurt American athletes. His controversial seeking of front-page publicity, for no other reason than to get his name in the paper, is a tragedy. (He should) spend more time managing his own company.'

D'Alessandro quickly responded, accusing Ebersol of 'a desperate, unprofessional attack – [he] has a problem justifying a $3.5 billion purchase.' Ebersol was right, though. D'Alessandro did have his own set of problems back at John Hancock. *The New York Times* had earlier run an in-depth article detailing how Hancock had settled a $350 million lawsuit from policyholders 'for having sold policies that they did not need. The company had also had to pay $1.1 million to settle Federal and Massachusetts state charges that its lobbyists illegally gave state lobbyists golf outings and other gifts in the 1980s and 1990s'. *The New York Times* went on to note that the original policy action suite revived 'questions about the integrity and management of John Hancock, striking at the core of the company's own values of trust ... With policyholders demanding the resignation of D'Alessandro,' and claiming back more than $4 million in legal expenses.

Journalists noted that whilst D'Alessandro demanded a squeaky clean image for the Olympics and the IOC, his own company had struggled to remain untainted itself, after having admitted to illegally providing gifts to elected officials. D'Alessandro was fighting to win back the trust of his own customers. Questioning the integrity of the Olympics allowed him to take the high ground.

IOC members were now calling on a daily basis urging us to cancel the John Hancock TOP contract. Their anger was prompted by outbursts that were becoming ever more personal. 'The news media may be right when they compare the IOC to royalty,' D'Alessandro remarked. 'The IOC is like a royal family, one in which the cousins have been marrying each other so long it's no wonder that their ideas of what means what are a little daft.' The name-calling was getting out of hand. But I knew that cancellation of our contract with John Hancock would achieve nothing positive, only cause more media furore.

Thankfully, few at the IOC were aware of Hancock's own problems. If they had, it would only have added to the demands that the IOC drop the company as a sponsor. Tempting as it might have been at the time, I knew we had to try to keep the company on board. Doing so had become a key factor in showing the world that the IOC was prepared to take criticism and to reform itself. Within a few months D'Alessandro went from being the IOC's biggest critic to being one of its biggest and most public supporters.

The IOC 2000 Commission held its first full plenary Session in June 1999, at the Olympic Museum in Lausanne. Over the next few months a number of working groups thrashed out some 55 reforms. By December, a full package of reforms had been worked out and the IOC Session reconvened again on 11–12 December, to discuss the reform package. All 55 recommendations were approved unanimously. These ranged from fixed terms of office for members, which had to be renewed every eight years; through to the age limit for new members being reduced from 80 to 70 years. It was agreed that the active members of the IOC Athletes Commission be co-opted onto the IOC, which led to 15 athletes, with a number of gold medals between them, joining the IOC, including Sergei Bubka, Olav Koss, Manuela di Centa and Alexander Popov.[15]

It was also agreed that visits by individual members to candidate cities, the cause in large part of the Salt Lake crisis, be abolished. In a few short months, the IOC had pushed through a reform programme that under any other circumstances would have taken over 30 years to implement. By the Sydney Games support and recognition for the sponsor role was at an all time high.

## New shoes

On Sunday, December 12, 1999, as Samaranch was closing the press conference for the session and reviewing the extent that the reforms would have on the Olympic Movement, I passed him a scribbled note that made him smile. It advised him that 72 hours of round the clock negotiations between the IOC, Nike and the Sydney organisers had led to a deal that would see Nike becoming a sponsor of the Sydney Games – replacing Reebok, which had suddenly withdrawn.

With all that had gone on with the crisis over the year, Reebok's announcement would have been devastating – the first sponsor to actually withdraw. Instead, we were able to announce a new deal with Nike. The former bad boy of Atlanta was joining the Olympic family. The tide was turning. The IOC's *annus horribilus* was nearing its end.

Despite the Olympic reforms, however, the US Congress continued to chastise the IOC. Like a terrier that won't release its grip, the US legislatures were locked on to the Olympic Games. There was still a risk of legislation to undermine the Movement's financial and legal basis. After the adoption of all the reforms by the IOC, Samaranch decided to accept the invitation of the House Commerce Subcommittee on Oversight and Investigation.

On December 15, 1999, Samaranch faced the chairman of the sub-committee, Fred Upton. A Republican Congressman from Michigan, Upton opened the proceedings with a series of inflammatory remarks. His comments seemed designed to provoke a response from Samaranch, and ensure that he, Upton, made the network news that night. Samaranch, though, refused to be riled. In a masterstroke of media management, the IOC president elected to only speak in his native language, Spanish, and therefore through a translator. This promptly killed off any attempt by Upton to give the news networks their 30-second sound bite.

The sub-committee went on to question the power and independence of the IOC Ethics Commission with its five independent members. When two members, Congresswoman Diane DeGette from Colorado and Fred Upton, noted that, just like the US Senate Select Committee on Ethics, 'the US Congress has a self-policing ethics committee,' it failed to recognise any hypocrisy. As Olympic historian Dr Bill Mallon later commented, this was a classic example 'of the pot calling the kettle black'.

Former US Senator Howard Baker told Upton and his committee that, 'While I was initially sceptical about whether the IOC would undertake serious ethical and structural reforms in a fairly short period of time, it is now my distinct impression that the IOC – its leaders and its members – fully recognise the need to restore the Movement's credibility'.

## Crisis over

If there were any doubts that the crisis was over, an announcement a few weeks later put paid to them once and for all. The IOC Executive Board was holding its final meeting before the Games in Sydney. Samaranch decided to hold his press briefing on the field of the main Olympic stadium. As he completed his review of the issues discussed at the Executive Board, he concluded with an announcement that, for once, literally left the press corps speechless. 'Today, I am pleased to announce that we have completed discussions with one of our TOP partners for them to continue on through TOP V, to the Olympic Games in Athens in 2004. I am pleased to confirm that John Hancock will be renewing their Olympic partnership for another four years.'

The media had expected that, with the Olympic crisis now slowly drawing to a close, the IOC would re-sign many of the TOP partners. But they were convinced that we would never ever bring John Hancock back into the fold. D'Alessandro, who had been one of the strongest critics of the IOC, had once again become one of our biggest supporters: 'We made no secret of the fact that, in order for the IOC to regain our confidence, as well as that of the public, it had to become a more democratic, transparent and accountable institution. We believe that with its reform vote in December, the IOC has addressed these issues. Its members listened to voices for change from inside and outside the organisation. The IOC leadership deserves credit for this progress.'

John Hancock was putting the rings back on its annual reports and buying more than $10 million of Olympic airtime from NBC. The media took note.[16]

Other sponsors began to come forward and express their confidence in the IOC and the future of the Olympic Movement. Visa renewed its sponsorship through Athens. 'We are pleased with the reforms enacted by the IOC,' commented Coke sports marketing boss Scott McCune. 'We believe that there is a serious effort underway to bring about real reform and we commend the IOC for working to protect not only our business interests as a sponsor, but the interests of millions of people around the world who are passionate about the Games – which is the basis for Coca-Cola's continuing commitment to the Olympic Movement.' Rod Eddington, chairman of Sydney Team Millennium Partner, Ansett Airlines, noted '[The controversy] has in no way impacted on our commitment to the Olympics or our support for it. It is a distraction ... But we don't think it undermines the perception of the Olympic sponsorship we're involved in'.

Dick Pound, who with Samaranch had led the IOC through the crisis, commented: 'I believe that our sponsors understand that the IOC took the crisis very seriously, that it acted quickly to address the governance issues and went far beyond solving the crisis – putting in place a more open and modern organisation reflecting best practices. This together with the global marketing strategy developed by the IOC to add more value to Olympic sponsorship, has generated increased confidence among the sponsor group regarding their Olympic investment.'

It has been interesting to look back at the crisis and why it generated such a media frenzy and ferocious onslaught from investigative journalists. The Salt Lake crisis had revolved around a potential $400,000 – $500,000 of misappropriated funds and questionable contributions, and dominated the global media for close to a year.

The same week as the Olympic crisis broke, the European Commission in Brussels revealed that auditors estimated some five per cent of it annual budget of $100 billion went missing through fraud. In other words, over $5 billion was being lost to fraud – an amount thousands of times greater than the IOC was accused of misplacing. Yet it hardly gained a mention in the press outside of Europe, while in Europe the story soon died down. The morale? People have lower expectations of bureaucrats and politicians than of the stewards of the Olympic Games. It is the IOC's job to make sure they are never disappointed.

## Putting things in perspective

It took some time for everyone at the IOC to appreciate that the media outrage should be taken as a compliment. It didn't seem that way at the time, but the concerns underline how much people truly care about the Olympic Games, and why the Olympic brand is unique. With an almost magical aura going back to the earliest Olympic Games, the modern Games had traded on its illustrious past of idealism, fair play and international competition of the world best athletes in the interest of excellence and global peace. Disclosures of improper payments by those lobbying for their city to be awarded the Games was a fundamental breach of the ethical principles on which the Olympic Movement was founded. It was because the Olympic Movement had founded itself on a set of values and ideals beyond any normal sports event, that the disillusionment ran so deep.

In the end, it did not really matter whether it was a $1 million or $100 that had gone astray – people's trust had been broken. They looked to the IOC to be the true trustees of the ancient Olympic ideal and to keep it on its pedestal. In a perverse sense, the crisis had validated all the brand research findings of the previous year.

After the crisis, our PR advisors Hill & Knowlton produced a report analysing 'Why the media engaged in a feeding frenzy of the IOC'. Hill & Knowlton had never seen anything like it in their corporate history. They came to five conclusions.

First, the Olympic Games are held to a higher standard and are much more than just a sports event. Anything that brings into question the Movement's integrity, risks undermining the Olympic values and damaging the brand. The IOC had frankly underestimated the huge social significance of the Games.

Second, the IOC was an unknown entity and had historically been a private and inaccessible group. It was, at times, perceived as arrogant and elitist. The general public gave little thought who actually put on the Games.

Third, the communications management was a challenge. Rather than a tightly controlled media message, as any corporation would have been able to impose, the IOC was unable to control the multiple different sources from within the Olympic Movement that were speaking out to the media. The situation was not helped when some IOC members would respond with their own attacks on the media such as 'the criticism has been exaggerated and it has done disproportionate damage' (which it had) but this only continued to feed the media coverage as journalists interpreted this as a challenge to their journalistic integrity.

Fourth, the changing nature of communications with the growing role of the internet was ready made to fuel the rumour mill. Internet search engines provided easy access to local media stories that, within a few hours, would be turned into global headlines. The story was also somewhat unique in that it was multi-phased, impacting on so many different sectors, with athlete comments on sports pages, sponsor comments on business pages, and the alleged scandal seen as hard news, on the front pages.

Fifth, and finally, various politicians also saw the scandal as a potential opportunity to try and exercise control over the independence of the IOC – independence that arguably had been the very reason why the institution had survived the twentieth century.

The fact is that, whether we like it or not, scandals sell and this story had all the ingredients to make this a front-page story everyday – and the media threw all the resources at it they could.

In the end much good did come out of the crisis. Ultimately, I believe it will be seen as the catalyst for radical change and reform. At times, back at the beginning of the year in 1999 it looked as if the IOC would not survive. There was a very real risk of the sponsors jumping ship and the whole pack of cards tumbling down. But, by the end of the year, it was clear that the IOC had come through the crisis better equipped to play its part in the modern world than before. 'There is always a positive side to a crisis,' Samaranch said in closing the Session. 'Without the crisis, the IOC would never have undertaken the massive and fundamental programme of reforms, which were approved at this historic Session. Thanks to these reforms, the IOC will enter the new millennium stronger, more modern, more democratic, more transparent, more accountable for its actions and more responsible.' Samaranch would later say, 'No revolution has been possible without scandal'.

## After the storm

On Friday December 5, 2003, just under five years after Hodler gave his first unscheduled press briefing in Lausanne, US District Federal Court Judge Tom Sam launched a stinging attack on the prosecutors who had brought the case of bribery against the bid leaders Tom Welch and Dave Johnson.

The judge said that, 'In all my 40 years' experience in the criminal justice system, as a defence and prosecuting attorney, and as a Utah State judge and United States District Court judge, I have never seen a criminal case brought to trial that was so devoid of criminal intent or evil purpose'. He said that the evidence never met the legal standard for bribery, and the case 'offends my sense of justice'.

Judge Sam then went on to ask the million dollar question: 'Now that the court has determined that enough is enough and brought this misplaced prosecution to conclusion, I would be interested in knowing how much taxpayers money was spent in investigating and prosecuting Mr Welch and Mr Johnson over the past six years.' It is unlikely anyone will ever know, although the rumours were of over $20 million, more than twenty times the amount that the bid committee was accused of misdirecting. At one stage it was claimed that there were more FBI agents working on the Salt Lake Olympic case than the Oklahoma bombing.

What are the key lessons we learnt from managing the crisis? Communicate often, openly and honestly with your stakeholders. Try not to let your partners be blind-sided by unexpected developments, and ensure that they have the facts and information to manage issues and expectations internally. Try to give them some inside track as to how things will evolve. In the end, the IOC's openness, accessibility and candour with our partners stood us in good stead. But it was a close call.

Happily, Sydney sweetened any bad taste left in the mouth by the Salt Lake scandal. Sydney, as expected, was a huge success. But what about the next Olympic venue – Athens? What would happen when the Olympic flame finally went home? It is no coincidence that crisis and chaos are both Greek words and, as we were soon to be reminded, the Greeks do them spectacularly.

## NOTES

1 The IOC Ad Hoc Inquiry Commission, chaired by Dick Pound, became known as the Pound Commission. Samaranch appointed IOC vice presidents Kebe Mbaye, (Senegal, chairman of the IOC Juridical Commission and a former vice president of the International Court in The Hague); Pal Schmitt (Hungary, Olympic Gold medallist in team épée fencing in Mexico 1968 and Munich 1972 and then Hungary's ambassador to Spain); Thomas Bach (Germany, Olympic Gold medallist in individual foil fencing from Montreal in 1976 and a lawyer) and Executive Board member Jacques Rogge (Belgium).

2 An editorial in *Sports Business* spelt out the significance of Hodler's outburst: 'Almost anybody beyond their teens will be aware that allegations of such skullduggery are nothing new. The whistle-blower was not some maverick journalist, who might be silenced by threat of court order, but one of the IOC's own. That meant the allegations were sure to be taken seriously.'

3 The city was once called the City of Saints and the press saw the 'sins of the Olympic family being revealed in more scandalous detail than ever expected'. Headlines included 'Sinful book of revelations'.

4 Coke was supportive enough to issue a press statement: 'As a supporter of the Olympics for over 70 years, we believe in and are committed to the Olympic Movement. We are very confident that they are taking the right steps'. This prompted headlines such as, 'Coke satisfied with IOC Efforts' and 'Coke sticking with the Olympics', which dampened some of the media speculation about sponsors pulling out.

5 Sydney was elected during the final round of voting by 45 to 43. It was the closest city election in recent times. The result could have been even closer, if one IOC member David Sibandze (Swaziland) had not left before the final round of voting to catch a flight.

6 Graham Stringer, the former leader of Manchester City Council, one of the defeated bid cities announced in *The Times*, that the 'IOC should take a very serious look at whether the Games can be moved from Sydney'.

7 Other US politicians who waded in included Senator Ted Stevens, who circulated draft legislation that would limit the IOC's tax-exempt

status, limit global sponsors ability to deduct payments as business expenses and transfer all rights to award the US broadcast rights from the IOC to the USOC. US Congressmen Henry Waxman and Rick Lazio tried to introduce a bill to prevent anyone from doing business in inter-state commerce in the United States from providing financial support to the IOC until the Committee adopted certain reforms. Waxman would later note in a House Subcommittee testimony, 'It was a tough bill, a controversial one, but a necessary piece of legislation'. None of the acts were passed, probably to the chagrin of Dick Schultz, the USOC executive director, who continued to quietly work the agenda to try and take control of commercial issues away from the IOC for the benefit of the USOC. Barry McCaffrey, the White House Drug Policy tsar, launched a public, and very scathing, attack on the IOC, at the World Doping Conference in Lausanne, calling the IOC a Byzantine organisation and saying the failure of leadership had challenged the legitimacy of the institution. McCaffrey's lecture to the conference about the lack of drug standards by the IOC and many NOCs was seen by some as highly hypocritical a year later, when it turned out that the USOC and the American sports system faced sports-related drug issues at least equal to the rest of the world.

8  Investigating the IOC and the bidding process suddenly became a very popular and high profile pastime. At one stage, there were four sep-arate investigative commissions – in addition to the IOC's. The Salt Lake Ethics Board was chaired by the Honourable Gordon R Hall, the former Chief Justice of the Utah Supreme Court. The five member commission released their 57 page report to the SLOC Board of Trus-tees on 8th February 1999 detailing the extent of SLOC's aggressive lobbying efforts to win the Games, but did not find any new infor-mation of substance not already dealt with in the IOC's report. The USOC established a Special Bid Oversight Commission, with George Mitchell, the former US Senator from Maine, as Chairman. The Mitch-ell Commission released its findings on 1 March 1999, in a 50-page report that took a broad look at the overall bidding process, the IOC structure and the USOC. The New South Wales Government turned to Tom Sheridan, the former Auditor General of Australia, to review the records of the Sydney bidding process.

The Georgia House Subcommittee on Oversight and Investigation turned to Griffin B Bell, the former US Attorney General to conduct a review of Atlanta's bid for the 1996 Games. The Bell report, released on 15th September, did not find any wrongdoing, noting that 'this is not a corrupt system, but is subject to abuse. We had a couple of cases where we gave gifts of $1,000, and given all the people fighting for the same thing, I'm amazed it didn't go higher'.

9　The IOC Ad Hoc Commission recommended the expulsion of six members: Agustin Arroyo (Ecuador); Zein El-Abdin Ahmed Abdel Gadir (Sudan); Jean-Claude Ganga (Congo); Lamine Keita (Mali); Sergio Santander Fantini (Chile) and Paul Wallwork (Samoa). Charles Mukora (Kenya) whose expulsion had been recommended earlier had in the interim resigned. Three members also resigned before the Ad Hoc Commission had presented its initial findings on 23rd January – Bashir Mohamed Attarabulsi (Libya); Pirjo Haeggmann (Finland); and David Sibandze (Swaziland).

10　Howard Baker, former majority leader of the US Senate and White House Chief of Staff under Ronald Reagan; Kurt Furgler, former President of the Swiss Confederation; Javier Perez de Cuellar, former UN Secretary General; Robert Badinter, the former French Justice Minister and President of the French Constitutional Court and a representative of the IOC Athletes' Commission; and five time Canadian Olympian Charmaine Crooks all joined the IOC Ethics Commission.

11　Outside members of the IOC 2000 Commission included political leaders such as US statesman Henry Kissinger; Boutros Boutros Ghali, the former UN Secretary General; and Oscar Arias Sanchez, the 1987 winner of the Nobel Peace Prize and former President of Costa Rica. Business leaders included Paul Allaire, the chairman of Xerox; Fiat's Giovanni Agnelli; Nicolas G Hayek, chairman of Swatch; Japanese sports goods manufacturer, Masato Mizuno; Peter Ueberroth, the organiser of the Los Angeles Games along with Dick Ebersol, chairman of NBC Sports and Albert Scharf, president of the European Broadcast Union to represent the interests of our broadcast partners.

12　George Fisher of Kodak noted how 'there can be few international organisations, whether governmental or businesses, that do not have some form of term limits for their governing members. Appointment of members for a life term seems to create an atmosphere that is counter to good governance and sensitivity to the constituencies represented. Effective governing bodies need to be continually refreshed with new ideas and perspectives to remain in tune with ever changing global conditions and values.'

13 Press headlines included 'Sponsor Support Steadfast' (*Washington Post*); and 'Scandal? What Scandal – Olympic sponsors aren't fazed by allegations of corruption' (*Business Week*).

14 Kodak came out with a strong statement applauding the IOC's reforms. 'Basically from the onset, we have been telling the IOC to go deep and go wide in their investigations and it appears they are now doing that,' said spokesman, John LaBella. 'The good news for the IOC is that they seem to be in a position to avoid an internal meltdown. They clearly had their ducks lined up (for the house cleaning and reform process at the Lausanne Session),' another sponsor representative told the *Wall Street Journal.* Coca-Cola commented 'We expect the IOC to continue to review other opportunities to rebuild public trust and support. Ultimately the success of this week will be determined by the IOC's ability to quickly define, embrace and enforce new reforms'; Jack Greenberg, McDonald's CEO noted: 'We're all concerned about what happened and don't want it to happen again ... but today we believe in the values, the athletes and the power of the Olympics'.

15 IOC athlete commission members co-opted onto the IOC: Roland Baar (Germany); Hassiba Boulmerka (Algeria); Sergei Bubka (Ukraine); Charmaine Crooks (Canada); Robert Ctvrtlik (USA); Alexander Popov (Russia); Jan Zelezny (Czech Republic); Manuela Di Centa (Italy); Johann Olav Koss (Norway); and Vladimir Smirnov (Kazakhstan).

16 'The IOC in a deal that suggests that sponsors are trickling back ... a deal [that] represents a mile stone for the IOC, reeling from a bribery scandal,' was how *The Wall Street Journal* finally acknowledged that the IOC had turned the corner. *USA Today* reported that 'Hancock's renewal is a major boost for the IOC in its campaign to convince the public the reforms enacted in December are real and meaningful'. 'Despite the tarnish of the Salt Lake bidding scandal, the Olympics remain good as gold for marketers and media buyers', was *Advertising Age's* perspective. And the Salt Lake media, where the whole crisis

had begun, was reporting that it was finally over: 'In what is sure to be called a turning point in the Olympic credibility crisis ... by re-signing John Hancock, the IOC can claim the recovery is complete and the power of the Olympic brand is as strong as ever.' Industry commentators like John Hoberman, an historian and long-term critic of the IOC noted that, 'There is a kind of Teflon coated appeal to the Olympics'. Professor Rick Burton noted how D'Alessandro had been the IOC's 'biggest critic and he came around. This reflects the great integrity of the Olympic property. He has been very sincere about the ethics issue almost to the point of becoming a pariah. In challenging the sacred icon that is the Olympics, D'Alessandro stood alone. He was the 12th angry juror for quite a while and a lot of people threw sticks at him, including Dick Ebersol. He could not have taken what he took without having some intuition and integrity of opinion'. Lisa Ukman in *IEG* commented that 'there was no more dramatic comeback in 2000 than the one the IOC has made on the sponsorship front. Stronger than ever financially – the negative fallout just did not happen'.

# Chapter 10

# COMING HOME

## 2004 hindsight

At just after 8.30 pm on Sunday August 30, 2004, Gianna Angelopoulos-Daskalaki, the president of the Athens Olympic Games Organising Committee (ATHOC) strode out from underneath the newly constructed Calatrava roof into the centre of the main Olympic stadium to deliver her speech for the closing ceremony.

'We can fairly claim today that Greece and the Greek people have kept their promise. A promise made to the world and to ourselves. It was a promise of success, joy, celebration, peaceful coexistence and noble strife ... And we can truthfully say that, with the Athens Olympic Games, the Olympic Movement and the Olympic ideal took a step forward.'

A crowd of 70,000 and more than a billion television viewers around the world looked on in admiration. The IOC and the rest of the international sports community breathed a huge sigh of relief.

The 20,000 representatives of the world's media in Athens could not quite believe what had happened over the previous 17 days. They scrambled to re-write their summaries and analysis of the Games of the XXVIII Olympiad. The 10,500 athletes from 202 countries had felt what it was like to walk in the footsteps of their forefathers three millennia previously. Athens was an unequivocal success. Against the odds, Athens had not only delivered, but exceeded beyond anyone's wildest imagination. At Athens in 2004, the world experienced one of the greatest and most symbolic Olympic Games ever.

It was a long, hard road. Long before the opening ceremony, a cynical press and doubting world decided that Greece was not capable of organising so much as a children's tea party let alone the Olympic Games. The country was far too small – and far too laid back. On more than one occasion, it looked as if the Games would have to be withdrawn from Greece.

At Athens, we knew all the elements of the IOC's marketing agenda would be put under pressure. It was the acid test of the strategy developed over the previous 20 years. Aside from the sheer logistical challenge of staging the world's largest event in the smallest country to host the Olympic Games since Finland in 1952, how would the IOC's carefully honed marketing strategy cope with a country that was so full of contradictions?

Chief among the contradictions was the Greek attitude to Olympic sponsorship. Greece had been vitriolic in its criticism of the IOC for commercialising the Games. Yet, Athens offered the most liberal commercial environment of any Olympic host city.

As the Games approached, we wondered whether the Olympic sponsors and the international business community would be welcomed or treated as pariahs? Would the outdoor advertising industry, dominated by illegal billboards due to the government's total lack of willingness to control them, prompt ambush marketing on a scale that would make Atlanta look like a paragon of best practice? And would the licensing industry plummet to new depths in cheap trash, found throughout so many of Greece's souvenir stalls? Or could a new brand image be created? Would the world watch, or switch off, having lost confidence that the Games would happen? Would the broadcasters set new records in financial losses, or new ratings highs? Would there be any attempt to co-ordinate the Olympic brand image across the 35 venues scattered across different precincts of the city council, or would everyone treat it as a free for all?

While the stakes were high for Greece, in many ways they were even higher for the IOC and its overall Olympic marketing strategy. We always knew the Athens Games had the potential to enhance two decades of Olympic marketing and showcase the evolution of a quiet business strategy. But as they came closer, it increasingly looked like they might destroy everything that had been achieved over the past two decades.

It's easy to be wise after the event. Hindsight, as we all know, is a marvelous thing. But I was convinced from the outset that not only would Athens pull it off, but it would do so in style. The Greeks would show what could be achieved and what the Olympic brand really stands for. They had to. There was too much riding on it for them not to pull it off. Failure was not an option. For me personally there was also a lot at stake. It was my last Olympic Games at the IOC. Athens was the culmination of more than twenty years work.

## High stakes

I understood what it meant to the Greek people for the Olympics to return to their birthplace. I also knew what it could mean for the Olympic brand.

Athens offered a unique opportunity to see the Games in their original light. But I also knew that there were real risks involved.

In the late 1970s and early 1980s, I was involved in the staging of a number of international athletic events in Greece. I'd seen first hand the power of the symbolism and potential imagery of one of the world's richest visual cultures. Unfortunately, I also saw first-hand how it could all go very, very wrong.

The IAAF Golden Marathon in 1982, for example, assembled one of the greatest fields of long-distance runners ever. In spite of numerous challenges in the preparation for the race, everything finally came together and the race got off to a smooth start. Everything was proceeding according to plan right up until the 37 km marker. At that point, things began to unravel. The Greek police had forgotten to close the last five kilometres of the marathon course to traffic. As I sat with local race director, George Courmousis, overseeing the race from the lead car, I slowly made out the red brake lights of the traffic jam ahead. Forty of the world's best marathon runners were rapidly catching up with the rush hour traffic. A Japanese television producer, responsible for sending the live images back around the world, looked on aghast.

It was one of those moments you never forget. Slowly, we came to a grinding halt, behind a large, dirty bus, belching out thick fumes. It presented a unique broadcast image, runners piling past a now stationary broadcast truck. The camera crew filmed them as they disappeared into the distance and out of sight for the final two kilometres of the race. The television commentators were faced with the challenge of commenting on a blank screen for the next five minutes, until the runners finally entered the stadium. A few months later when athletes arrived in Athens for the European Athletics Championships, the track in the main stadium still had to be laid. Back then, I feared I would never see the day when Greece was allowed to stage the Games.

## Vote of confidence

Athens won the right to host the Olympic Games on September 5, 1997. This was less than 12 months after the Atlanta Games and the IOC was still smarting from the media onslaught provoked by the crass over-commercialisation allowed by the city authorities. The IOC had to show the world that in selecting a host city for the 2004 Olympic Games, it could exercise sound judgement. It had to demonstrate that it understood the dynamics of hosting the Games and what was needed to perpetuate the Olympic ideal. Most of all, it had to show beyond all doubt that the Olympic ideal had not been surrendered to the commercial agenda.

Eleven cities set out to bid for the 2004 Olympic Games: Athens, Cape Town, Istanbul, Lille, Rio de Janeiro, Buenos Aires, Rome, San Juan, Seville, St. Petersburg, and Stockholm. Although there was much talk of Athens as a potential front runner, the Greeks' previous performance in front of the IOC Session in Tokyo in 1990 had ended in humiliation. On that occasion, they had arrogantly demanded to host the Games as their birthright. There was little to inspire confidence that things would be any different this time around.

But things were very different. For a start, the Greek government had the foresight to ask Gianna Angelopoulos-Daskalaki, a 41-year old former national politician, married to a billionaire ship owner and industrialist, to lead the bid. Angelopoulos-Daskalaki accepted, but there was one condition: she would control everything. There was to be no interference from anyone, least of all from the Greek government. If Greece wanted the Games, she and her husband, Theodore, would go and get them – but with her team and on her conditions. She refused to be hamstrung by a set of bureaucratic dictates from ministers and their civil servants. Fearing humiliation for a second time, the Greek government accepted her demands.

Over the course of the 12 month bid, Angelopoulos-Daskalaki and her executive team – led by Marton Simitsek, a gruff no-nonsense former vice president of the Greek National Olympic Committee – charmed the IOC membership. The Greek delegation convinced the IOC, and a cynical media, that Greece was ready this time to stage the Games. They argued that they had learnt from their failings in the previous bid and that, in the intervening period, Greece had built much of the promised, and sorely needed, infrastructure. Most importantly, they no longer arrogantly claimed that the Games were theirs by birthright. Instead, they said, they wanted to prove that Greece could not only keep its promises and deliver, but add its own magic to the Olympics, by returning the Games to their original creators.

Proving that Greece could add its own special magic to the Games, was the easy part. Proving that Greece could stage them without stretching its national resources to breaking point, bungling the job, or compromising the country's finances in the process, was another matter.

There was clearly some guilt within the IOC that Greece had been passed over seven years previously, in favour of Atlanta. The fact was that the original Athens bid was ill-conceived and unrealistic. The IOC would have been irresponsible, and in dereliction of its duties as trustees of the Olympic ideal, if it had awarded the Centennial Games to Athens. And yet Atlanta had not been a great vindication of the IOC's judgement either.

In the end, Athens won the right to stage the 2004 Olympic Games, beating Rome by 66 votes to 41 in the fifth round of voting. (The voting process continues until one city has a 51 per cent majority. The city with the least number of votes in each round is dropped. A new vote is then held with the remaining cities hoping to collect the votes of the city which has just fallen by the wayside.)

Victory was a major boost for national morale, fulfilling the country's psychological need for international recognition. But no sooner had Angelopoulos-Daskalaki and her bid team returned home, than the politicians unceremoniously dumped her. The IOC was not amused. We had received specific commitments from the Greek government and clear promises from Prime Minister Simitis that the bid team would also lead the Olympic effort for the next seven years.

With Gianna sidelined, Greece quickly returned to its bad old ways. The Olympic effort deteriorated into internal fighting and bickering. Everyone involved wanted to rest on their laurels. Officials procrastinated over every decision. They discussed at length what needed to be done, but very little happened.

ATHOC, the Athens Organising Committee, was established with a competent management team, but it was paralysed by a Greek government that refused to take any decisions. The government simply did not comprehend the true magnitude of the task ahead. Valuable preparation time slipped away, with no minister focusing on the real issues. Venue construction had not even begun. Collectively, there seemed to be a total lack of urgency. Despite repeated pleas from the IOC, the Greek government was not listening. Samaranch appointed Jacques Rogge to head the IOC's oversight commission for the preparation of the Games, but Rogge was simply not getting through.[1]

# Seeing red

By early 2000, with three years already lost, the IOC was increasingly concerned that it might have made a terrible mistake. If Greece maintained its current pace, there would not be enough time left to build all the venues. Hosting the Olympic Games is a colossal task for any nation; Greece was now faced with the challenge of doing it in half the normal time. Greek companies were not falling over themselves to support the Games either. With four years to go, Greece did not have a single national sponsor on board. The IOC's carefully structured step by step approach to preparations, with detailed time lines, had somehow got lost in translation.

The word crisis comes from the Greek word for decision. It became clear to Samaranch that he was facing one of the most serious organisational crises of his presidency. If dramatic action was not taken, the Games were in jeopardy.

On April 20, 2000, in a surprise press conference at the Olympic Museum in Lausanne, and with no advance notice – not even to his closest advisors – Samaranch issued a warning to Athens. He explained that the planning for the Olympic Games was like a traffic light. Green and it was all go, and everything was running smoothly. Yellow and there were problems and delays. And then there was red. Red meant everything had stopped and the Games might have to be withdrawn. For the preparations of the Athens Games, Samaranch warned, the colour was now very dark orange.

You could have heard a pin drop in the auditorium. The Olympic press pack, used to Samaranch's diplomatic and carefully worded statements designed to avoid offence, were shocked. They were unsure if they had heard the seasoned diplomat correctly.

A few short questions quickly confirmed that there had been no misunderstanding. The magnitude of what Samaranch had really said was fully understood. The media corps scrambled to write their headlines – translating the coded message of a bright orange traffic light into a clear statement that nobody could misunderstand. The Athens Games were in grave danger of being withdrawn.

Greece understood the global embarrassment and national humiliation that would ensue from losing the Games. Lest there be any doubt, the Greek stock market tumbled in the 24 hours after Samaranch's pronouncement.

The government was left with only one choice – bring back Gianna and her original bid team and give them back their 'blank cheque'.

Finally, we could begin to execute on the Olympic marketing strategy.

## Marketing in motion

Gianna understood that she could not deliver the Games alone, and immediately began courting the Greek business community. I advised her that a re-launch of the marketing plan for the Athens Games was needed. We had to explain to Greece's business leaders the power of Olympic marketing. They needed to understand what could be achieved – both for Greece and for their own companies and brands – if they became Olympic partners and joined in this unique adventure.

We invited over 1,000 business people for a dramatic audio visual presentation in Greece's national theatre and made the pitch. The ATHOC marketing team was led by George Bolos, a larger than life former supermarket executive. Together, we began the long, slow process of creating a competition, between multiple players in each of the potential key national sponsor categories.

Bolos quietly and methodically worked the potential sponsors. The predicament facing ATHOC and the need for positive headlines made it sorely tempting to grab the first deal that appeared. I counselled Bolos to hold back, to nurture the big deal – a deal which would establish the market value.

When ATHOC announced its first national sponsor, it was Alpha Bank, with a record $70 million offer. The deal was worth nearly twice what any bank had previously paid to support the Summer Games. At the time, it was the highest national Olympic sponsorship fee ever. ATHOC pledged to its partners that it would restrict the number of sponsors and suppliers to a select number of companies, to maintain a clean and uncluttered marketplace.

Nobody really believed it. History suggested they would be unable to do so. Every organising committee, under pressure from their financial directors and government officials, embarked on a last-minute fire sale. There was nothing to make anyone think the Greek committee would be any different. But the sceptics were wrong.

To ATHOC's and Bolos' lasting credit, they remained true to their word. They stuck with a limited number of partners, who enjoyed one of the most tightly controlled Olympic marketplaces to date. As evidence that less is more, the ATHOC marketing programme generated nearly twice the original financial forecasts.[2]

## Chaos is a Greek word

Preparations on the ground were still not going so well. From the moment Greece was elected to host the Games, right up until the Opening Ceremony, Gianna Angelopoulos-Daskalaki, ATHOC, and the Greek government struggled under the global media spotlight. The preparations for Athens became the most scrutinised of any Olympics, with a relentless barrage of international media criticism. Newspaper headlines predicted chaos and questioned whether Greece would ever be ready. Articles speculated on whether the IOC really had a secret contingency plan to move the Games, and whether Greece would fall flat on its face.

Athens was slammed by the media – and especially the Anglo-Saxon media – like no previous Olympic host city. The Greeks were found wanting long before the Games had even begun. The media predicted that the 37 sports venues would never be finished and described them as the new Greek ruins. Athletes, they said, would collapse in searing heat; traffic would be grid locked and security would fail. 'Everybody knows that the Summer Olympics in Athens will be a mess at best – or a disaster at worst. A remarkable case of self denial ... A bad idea that has gotten worse with each passing year,' was how one Canadian media commentator put it, capturing the prevailing mood. (Critics would have been further encouraged by the fact that in 1896, the local organisers faced similar problems with the construction of the main stadium. Short of funding, they had to turn to private benefactors to help. The main stadium was only apparently fully completed in 1898 – two years after the event.)

As the final countdown began, the world's media warned people to stay away, predicting impending disaster against a continual back drop of political bickering and impossible construction deadlines.[3] The Australian government even issued a formal travel advisory about travelling to Greece.

In the post-September 11 climate, there were heightened security concerns for the 2004 Games. Greece had long been considered the sick man of Europe in battling terrorism. By 2000, Paul Bremer, the chair of the US National Commission on Terrorism, was slamming the Greek government for its ineffectiveness and recommending a US arms embargo against the country.

Other US politicians soon joined the bandwagon, with Senator John Kyle publicly stating that the safest place to watch the Olympics was on television. These concerns added to the sense of uncertainty about whether Athens would be allowed to stage the Games. The IOC itself didn't offer much reassurance. Dr Jacques Rogge, who had now been elected IOC president, announced that the IOC would be taking out Games cancellation insurance for the first time in its 108 year history. The fact that the IOC had been studying the subject for years did not matter. The timing, and the manner in which it was announced helped convince an already cynical media that the Athens Games were out of control and that even the IOC had lost confidence. Broadcasters, desperate to sell their remaining Olympic advertising, were appalled that the IOC could score such a public relations own goal.

Faced with this global onslaught, even the Greeks began to have second thoughts. Not wanting to embarrass themselves in front of four billion people, the local population became increasingly nervous. They convinced themselves that there was no way that they could get it right. Many felt that some kind of terrorist attack was inevitable.

Some members of the Greek government also decided that it might be politically wise to distance themselves from the impending debacle. Some challenged the wisdom of Greece embarking on the Olympic adventure. With less than ten weeks to go before the opening ceremony, Georgios Souflias, the Greek minister for public works, announced to a parliamentary committee that he had 'to question whether our country should have undertaken the organisation of the Games'.

Greek journalists, who might have been expected to defend the pride of their country, also decided that disaster was imminent. George Kassimeris wrote in the UK's *Independent* newspaper, 'the Olympics were meant to reverse negative stereotypes that have followed Greece for decades. But it has been instead, a public relations disaster'.

But the PR disaster never materialised. So how was a Greek tragedy averted and turned to triumph? The answer lies, in part, with a Herculean last-minute effort by all those involved.

In the end, history was always on Greece's side, even if time was not. The Ancient Greeks gave the world the Olympics and the modern Greeks have a greater sense of Olympic ownership than any other nation on Earth. The Athens Games were probably more important than any previous Games have been to a host nation. Shame of failure would have been too much to bear. The Games provided a unique rallying call for a Hellenic revival. They also provided the motivation to mount a colossal last push that saved the day.

But the success of the Athens Games also lies with the earlier groundwork put in place by the IOC. Gilbert Felli, the IOC's executive director of the Olympic Games, had built up a strong operational department, and team of core advisors with multiple Games experience to transfer knowledge from one Games to the next. Other experienced IOC directors and advisors, including Pere Miro (NOCs), Patrick Schamash (medical), Thierry Sprunger (finance), Howard Strup (legal), Philippe Verveer (technology) and Manolo Romero (host broadcasting) helped guide ATHOC through the final operational hurdles. In particular, on the marketing front the lessons we had learned about ambush marketing and managing the Olympic image were critical.

## Keeping it clean

The Athens Games presented many challenges. From an image standpoint, there was the very real risk that the world would not see a city full of heritage and classical monuments. Aside from being one of the most environmentally polluted cities in Europe, Athens had allowed its outdoor advertising industry to take over the skyline. Legal, and often illegal, bill-boards were erected on every roof top and scrap of spare land. It was a major eyesore.

After Atlanta, the IOC had made steady progress in extending the Olympic look and imagery to the wider host city. Control over outdoor advertising is a vital element in maintaining that visual identity. Athens looked like it might be a major backward step.

Shortly after the city's election in 1997, I met with the local Greek politicians and organisers to begin the long planning process. After the over-commercialisation of Atlanta, and its out of control street vending programmes, it looked like Greece had the potential to lower the bar still further. Rather than the IOC and the Olympics gaining from the symbolism of the Games returning to their birthplace, we risked adding to the perceptions that the Olympic commercial agenda was out of control.

I pointed out to the local organisers that since 1984, Greece had lectured and repeatedly attacked the IOC for commercialising the Olympic ideal. Wouldn't it look somewhat hypocritical for Athens to become the most visibly polluted city to ever host the Games? The authorities, I suggested, might consider pulling down all the illegal advertising and taking control of the remaining official billboards for the duration of the Games. This would allow Athenians and the rest of the world to rediscover the beauty of their ancient city.

The city officials thought I was mad. Why would they give up such a money spinner? For years, it had been one of the major sources of political funding. Members of ATHOC, though, saw things differently. They immediately understood the potential, the challenge and the risks if Athens did not embrace the IOC's suggestions.

Over the course of the next seven years, the IOC kept the pressure on the Greeks to deliver a 'clean' city. Slowly but surely, the local authorities began to understand the longer term benefits of what might be achieved by cleaning up the city. By the time the athletes and the world's media arrived in Athens for the Games, all of the illegal billboards had been pulled down. The few remaining boards were offered to sponsors and used for specific messages promoting the Olympic ideal. Athenians themselves began to rediscover the beauty of their city that for so long had been hidden behind a screen of advertising hoardings.[4] Sponsors enjoyed a whole new level of protection against ambush marketing.

The Greek government, too, eventually caught the spirit of the Olympics. It decided to use the Games as a catalyst for the regeneration of Athens. A city that had been paralysed and starved of infrastructural investment for nearly half a century was given a new lease of life. Greece embarked on the biggest capital infrastructure programme the country had ever known, building a new airport, a new subway system capable of carrying 530,000 people per day, 20 miles of light suburban railway and 130 miles of new highways. Athens, for the first time in 50 years, was opened to the sea.

## Passing the Olympic flame

In some areas, too, the Greek organisers pushed the IOC to innovate. The decision to expand the route of the Olympic torch relay, for example, proved a stroke of genius. The Greeks had decided that rather than stage the shortest Olympic relay ever – from Olympia to Athens – they would stage the longest. They proposed a global relay of over 78,000 km, taking 33 days and 3,600 runners to visit 33 cities in 26 countries, across all five continents.

The IOC leadership was not enthusiastic about the idea of a global torch relay. Soon after taking over the presidency, Jacques Rogge, as part of his Games cost control programme, decided to forbid future organising committees from embarking on what many saw as an expensive distraction from the core mission of staging the Games. He had a point. The last thing the Greeks needed at the time was another major Olympic project. They had their hands more than full with the responsibility of putting on the Games.

But the Greeks were adamant. They wanted to take the Olympic relay to the four corners of the Earth, to Africa, South America, and China where the torch had never been before.

Rather than try and dissuade the Greeks from their ambitious programme, I felt that we should help them achieve it. I have seen first hand how the magical flame inspires people. I also knew what a global relay can do to promote the Olympic brand. Twenty years earlier, Peter Uebberoth, the Los Angeles Games organiser, successfully used the relay to ignite the Olympic message in the host country. With the help of the IOC, the Greeks had an opportunity to expand the concept onto the global stage.

I recommended to Rogge that we allow the Greeks to proceed – but on two conditions. The first was that we find sponsors to fund the $50 million budget for the relay so that it did not put a strain on the operation of the Games. Coke and Samsung were quickly persuaded to back the project.

The second pre-condition was that the Greeks outsource the operation of the global relay and getting the Olympic flame back to Greece on time to an experienced operator. It was not that the Greeks could not do it themselves, but every capable executive was required back in Athens to prepare for the Games.

I gave the organisers the names of two executives who had successfully staged previous Olympic relays. The ATHOC team understood the complexity of the task at hand and fully accepted the IOC's dictate. The Greek parliament was not so sure. It spent days arguing about my personal interference in the Greek procurement process.

George Bolos, who had by now proved himself highly effective at delivering the Athens marketing programme, was tasked with taking over the management of the torch relay. From the IOC's shortlist, he selected Steve McCarthy and his company ALEM, which successfully ran the operations of both the Salt Lake City and Atlanta torch relays.[5]

The torch was lit on March 25, 2004, and travelled around Greece before setting off for its international tour. On June 3, it began its global journey. The world's media quickly became enthralled by the daily images of the torch being carried by personalities such as the Brazilian soccer hero Pele and Nelson Mandela against stunning back drops. The news images created a nightly preview to the Games. They provided broadcasters with the perfect platform to begin the count down to their Olympic broadcasts, and gave rise to a series of newspaper stories that provided an alternative to the barrage of negative headlines about the preparations in Athens.[6]

ATHOC's adoption of the Games slogan 'Welcome Home' was also inspired. It captured the essence of what the Athens Games stood for (and what the Olympic brand gained from returning to its roots). The world's athletes competed under the shadow of the 2,400 year old Parthenon, the symbol of Greek civilization's golden age and where the Olympic torch rested on the final night of its global journey.

The Greek organisers understood the symbolic significance and used it to full effect. They added to the symbolism by restoring the ancient tradition of crowning all Olympic medalists with an olive wreath which sat halo-like on the head of each athlete.

At Athens, athletes walked in the footsteps of their forefathers nearly three millennia before to the original stadium in Olympia. For the first time since 393 AD, they came in homage to the birthplace of sport – the mythological home of the gods. They returned to the marble ruins and cypress trees of the remote Peloponnese peninsula. Athens 2004 also rewrote history. For the first time ever at the temple of Olympia, male athletes were joined by female athletes.[7]

## The final sprint

The preparations for Athens were reminiscent of a traditional Greek dance, the *syrtaki*. It starts very slowly and gradually builds momentum, accelerating so that in the end it is difficult to keep up with the pace. The Greek mental worry beads eventually worked. The 18,000 tonne Calatrava roof to the main stadium, was a prime example. The Greeks were given a cut off date by the IOC. They were told that the roof must be in place by then, or the project would be dropped – and it would have to be installed after the closing ceremony. Miraculously, the roof was moved into place on the very day the IOC set as a final deadline.

Sport also played its part. On July 4, the Greek national soccer team won the 2004 European Championships. Greece entered the tournament as an 80 to 1 outsider. Before the tournament began, not even the most ardent Greek soccer fan gave their team any realistic chance of making it through the first round, never mind winning the trophy. Victory gave the Greek people a new sense of national pride and sporting confidence. It was just the boost they needed to help carry them over the line to the opening ceremony.

The venues finally came together. Not only were they ready on time, but the venue and city operations actually worked. The technology did not collapse. The much vaunted traffic grid lock did not materialise. Athletes did not collapse in the searing heat and smog. Athens looked better than perhaps at any time in its recent history. It was transformed from a polluted traffic jammed city into the most delightful of venues.

In the last few weeks leading up to the opening ceremony, some of the media began to recognise they had been rushing to judgement. The self appointed doomsayers, who only a few weeks earlier had been predicting disaster, finally realised that it was all working. More than that, Greece was on track to stage one of the greatest Olympic Games ever. The Athens communications team slowly began to relax. They even began to 'spin' the story of the mad dash to the finish as if it was something that had been planned all along so that the country could showcase its efficiency and ingenuity at the last minute. There was talk of 'just on time' delivery.

## The underdog has its day

The Opening Ceremony of each Games sets the mood for the 17 days that follow. Athens was no exception. Gianna Angeloppolous came out fighting. In her opening speech, in front of the world, she declared that 'No country has been more underrated than Greece'. Even if the athletes did have to march in under the aroma of fresh paint, they and the rest of the world were stunned as Greece staged a classical spectacle, fusing its rich history and mythological past with its promising future.

The apologies soon began to flow. *The Times*, which had been perhaps the most critical of all the Anglo-Saxon media was the first to apologise. 'From Tragedy to Triumph' ran the front page headline following the opening ceremony, to be followed 17 days later by 'Shame on us for having little faith – Greeks pulled it off with style'. The day after the closing ceremony, *The Times* ate more humble pie: 'To Athens an apology. The world media has let you down. What we in the media have done was to make completely the wrong call.'

*Sports Illustrated* in the US continued the apology. 'Sorry about the way we acted. We were paranoid and stupid and just flat out wrong. It was all done and it was beautiful'. 'Let's give these Games a Gold Medal,' continued the *Washington Post*, 'the first order of day is to extend a big sorry to the Greeks. Nothing collapsed, and nothing less has been accomplished than the full restoration of Athens as a splendid world capital. The Greeks have proved a very pointed point. There is more than one way to throw an Olympics'.

The press were right about one thing. They referred to 'The greatest race of the Olympics producing the most unlikely winner' – Athens. Greece had under-promised and over-delivered. It was the exact opposite of Atlanta eight years previously. According to one leading US commentator, it was 'One of the greatest upsets in sports history'. But, as their national soccer team had just proved, the Greeks knew something about sporting upsets. The nail biting finish to opening the Athens Games in the end only added to the self congratulatory mood.

Athens succeeded in dispelling its image as a smoggy Third World Argian backwater. It redefined the country as a 'can do' place, instead of a poor European relation.[8] Only Barcelona achieved so much and, in so many areas, so quickly.

The successful delivery of the Games was a confidence builder for a whole new generation.[9] Theodore Couloumbis, the director of the Hellenic Foundation for European and Foreign Policy, declared that 'the Games will be decisive in terms of finalising our transition to self-esteem ... Finally we can create the impression we are a normal European country'.

The images and media reports from the Games transmitted around the world, helped to re-brand Greece as a country. The world ended up discovering a new Greece – mythological and traditional images combined with modern, dynamic designs. The Games became the catalyst to completing infrastructure projects that otherwise would still remain just an architect's dream. Athens, the city that gave the world the Olympic Games, was saved by them.

All of this came at a price but, once again, financial meltdown simply didn't happen. The last-minute scramble to complete the array of projects did increase costs. But, through diligent financial management and a larger than expected contribution from IOC broadcast and sponsorship revenues, ATHOC not only balanced its books but is expected to declare a surplus. In addition to the costs of actually staging the Games was substantial investment in essential capital infrastructure and sporting venues. These came in at 37 per cent over the original plan – not disastrous considering the scale and nature of the projects. In addition, Athens incurred extra security costs in the wake of September 11, much of it imposed by a nervous international community and aggressive American lobbying. Even so, Games spending helped to spur Greek GDP to a four per cent annual increase.

The pay-off is clear: Greece was re-branded and much of its crumbling infrastructure rebuilt. What other event could have made this happen?

## Strategy delivered

The Olympic marketing strategy also received a boost. Sponsors got what they signed up for. Our efforts to control ambush marketing paid off, with no incidents of any note. The Olympic look and imagery also set a whole new standard. The technology, delivered through a consortium of providers, worked (and at less than half the previous cost). And the world tuned in to watch the Athens Games in record numbers. An estimated four billion people watched across 220 countries – the largest television audience for any event in history.

The Athens Games set a number of new broadcast records – a testament to the changing nature of broadcast technology and the IOC's strategy of expanding coverage to provide more choice to the viewer. Broadcasters produced more hours of Olympic coverage than ever before.[10]

NBC saw its prime time audience share increase by more than 14 per cent over Sydney's coverage. It was a remarkable achievement and an indication of the true pulling power of Olympic programming, especially when set against a general and ongoing decline in audience levels. Since 2000, US households have added an average 25 additional TV channels to each home, only serving to further reduce the dominance of the networks.

Other broadcasters achieved equally impressive results, with countries like Chile establishing further broadcast records, as nations won their first ever gold medal.[11]

In the end, then, the Athens Games provided a fitting showcase for the Olympic homecoming. The national resolve of the Greek people triumphed over the cynicism of the doomsayers. The Greeks showed their mettle – and in doing so drew immense satisfaction and national pride from hosting the world. The Olympic Movement, too, drew sustenance from the homecoming. It left Athens far stronger than when it arrived – propelled forward on its journey towards Beijing, China. Athens also saw a 25-year marketing strategy come to fruition – a strategy that all those involved knew would be tested to destruction. I took enormous personal satisfaction from the fact that all the hard work paid off. At Athens, the lessons of Atlanta and other Games were put to work. The results vindicated our approach, and took the Olympic franchise to a new level. But the Olympic Movement cannot afford to rest on its laurels. Looking forward to Beijing and beyond, new tests and challenges are already clear. It is to these that we turn our attention in the final chapter.

## NOTES

1  The Athens Organising Committee built up a solid management team, led by a highly respected Greek lawyer, Stratis Stratigis, and an experienced international executive Costas Bakouris. They hired many of the key executives – from George Bolos, head of marketing, through to Theodora Mantzaris-Kindel, who were critical to the successful delivery of the Games.

2 Throughout the years of negative publicity counting down to the Games, the Athens marketing programme was identified by the media as one of the few genuine success stories.

3 Had they but known it, the media's pre-Games reporting was very similar to the coverage 108 years earlier for the first modern Olympics. In 1896, Athens had only had 100,000 inhabitants, rather than the four million today. But that didn't stop the *New York Times* observing: 'Athens is a dump, the transport system is on a par with the provincial cities of Algeria, the democracy is bogus. The Games will be crooked, and the Greeks know as little about amateur sport as the Chinese.' Neither did the Greeks initially embrace the first Games with much enthusiasm, burdened as they were under heavy foreign debt and a costly canal project.

4 For the Games, the city covered up construction sites with large building wraps with Olympic imagery, dressing the city with 20,000 celebratory Olympic banners, using 23,000 metres of fabric with Olympic-themed messages for bridges and another 8,000 metres for entrances to venues.

5 McCarthy set about the complex task of planning a global relay. It took on many of the traits of a US Presidential campaign, with all of its incumbent media and security apparatus. Two jumbo jets – 747s – were chartered and one repainted in Olympic colours. A large team was assembled to manage the logistics. The Olympic torch was guarded around the clock, as if it was the nuclear suitcase carried by Airforce One.

6 The relay was presented under the theme of 'Pass the Flame, Unite the World' and became a platform for Greece to promote the ancient tradition of the Olympic truce. The original vision of the relay had been for it to cross the various borders of conflict and dispute around the world; from North Korea to South Korea, India to Pakistan and the US to Cuba. Unfortunately, this idea had to be dropped. The operations team and ATHOC diplomats had their hands full just delivering on the Games, and getting the torch back home, without opening up a new front. The Greeks, never short of ideas, were soon petitioning the IOC to create a permanent centre to promote the idea of the truce, as another Olympic legacy of their Games. George Papandreou, the eloquent Greek Foreign Minister, championed the cause and eventually

succeeded in persuading a reluctant IOC to sign up. Fani Palli Petralia, the deputy Greek Cultural Minister, talked of how the Olympic truce was man's first attempt to make peace between nations. Peace is a core part of the Olympic DNA, but many of the sports administrators saw initiatives in this area as a diversion of resources, and that the IOC was stepping beyond its remit and mission.

7 Kirstin Heaston of the US became the first women ever to compete in Olympia. The shot putt was not actually part of the ancient Olympics – it was invented by the Celts – but was deemed to be the only event that could be held without archaeological damage.

8 The Athens economy was not the only one to receive an economic injection. The Games provided a major boost to the world's flat screen makers, with sales in Japan in July 2004 up 70 per cent for one manufacturer. Corporate results like these prompted Dentsu, the Japanese advertising giant, to forecast that the Olympics would generate additional direct spending of more than 400 billion Yen ($3.6 billion) 75 per cent of which came from electronic products.

9 It was often the simplest of incidents that would surprise people. One journalist wrote that the 'most significant Olympic moment happened on a shuttle bus. A European passenger, late for a game, was hassling the Greek driver to leave. It was 8.28pm. "Tell him, I have a schedule," the driver told the journalist. He pulled it out and showed the guy. "We leave in two minutes ..." Schedule? Greece? For those of us who know it, the Athens of the Olympics has been an alternate universe; a grown-up, modern efficient, businesslike place ... Greece decided to give the Swiss lessons in timekeeping and, in the process, change whole perceptions of how the nation was viewed around the world'.

10 NBC's Athens coverage of 1,210 hours was nearly triple its Sydney coverage of 441 hours and covered seven platforms: NBC, cable channels, MSNBC, CNBC, Bravo and Telemundo, along with NBC HDTV affiliates. Coverage included 399 hours in high definition and, for the first time, broadcasts in a second language, with 226 hours on NBC's newly acquired Spanish language channel Telemundo. Advertising revenue exceeded $1 billion, with an estimated 13–14,000 commercials and prime time spots selling at around $740,000 each.

11 Chile won its first Olympic gold in the tennis men's doubles.

# Chapter 11

# THE FUTURE OF THE RINGS

## The Olympics now

In July 2001, Jacques Rogge succeeded Samaranch, becoming only the eighth President of the IOC. Rogge is a Belgian surgeon and former Olympic sailor. He immediately embarked on consolidating the IOC's position, focusing on the operation of the Games and taking a zero tolerance policy towards doping. An accomplished communicator, Rogge quickly won over the media with his open and relaxed style.

Rogge inherited a very different IOC from his predecessor 21 years previously. The IOC was no longer facing bankruptcy; politicians no longer saw the Olympics as a political football. The Olympic Movement today is probably stronger than at any time in its history. The Games of Athens, Salt Lake City and Sydney were among the most successful ever – both athletically and financially. Interest in the Games is at an all-time high, with record broadcast audiences and frenzied bidding for future Olympic rights.

Broadcasting rights for the major territories of North America and Europe are all sold through to 2012. Sponsors remain highly committed to their involvement with the Olympic brand. Strong marketing revenues have allowed the IOC to significantly increase revenue support for NOCs, Sports Federations and athletes. Add in fierce competition among the world's leading cities to host future Games, and the Olympic brand, and all it stands for, continues to resonate around the world.

As we have seen, none of this happened by chance. There are, I believe, eight key lessons from the Olympic turnaround. The future success of the Olympic Games rests on these. Together, they provide a new marketing framework for sports franchises as well as broader lessons in leadership and management.

## 1   Leadership is multi-dimensional

The Olympic turnaround was driven by leadership. Although it was sometimes misunderstood by those outside the IOC, Samaranch's leadership – long-term and strategic – was fundamental to saving the Games. It helped the IOC seize the agenda. Instead of being constantly on the back foot, the IOC began to dictate terms. Samaranch offered a clear vision. He wanted to modernise the Olympics while remaining true to its ideals; to commercialise without compromising. It also helped that, according to one observer, Samaranch had the strategic skills to play chess in three dimensions.

Samaranch understood the special attributes of the Olympic franchise and he was patient. The Olympic Movement works to long-term plans. It is not driven by quarterly results. At the same time, clarifying what constitutes success for the Olympics is an important element in its resurrection. The key measures of the Olympics' success are: whether the Games is still the ultimate prize for athletes; whether it is true to its values, philosophy and brand; and the size of the broadcast audience (as the unequivocal test of the public's interest).

Samaranch's focus on getting the IOC to stand on its own feet financially and to act as a united body was crucial in the early years.

The entire Olympic Movement faced a crisis, he explained, and it was only by working together that we could get out of it. In this simple plea lay the insight that the Olympic brand is bigger than any one person or group.

## 2  Financial independence buys freedom of action

It was clear that the Olympic Movement had no future unless it could break its political dependency and become financially independent. This financial imperative led to the creation of what became the most successful global marketing programme in the world.

TOP represents a marketing strategy that, over time, has come to provide companies with a unique platform to fast track their development, enhance their brand and motivate their employees.

All this was achieved with less commercial association, not more. There was a dramatic reduction in the number of marketing partners and a strategy was developed to avoid compromising some of the basic tenets that helped make the Olympic Games unique and special.

## 3  Higher values set the commercial value

Maintaining the values and ethical principles of the Olympics, and not selling out to Mammon, is a fine balancing act.

But there is a paradox here. Over the years, it has become increasingly clear that the non-commercial values provide the Olympic brand with its true commercial value to marketing partners.

The Olympics possess a set of attributes that are undeniably valuable to any marketer. The Olympic Games value honour, integrity, determination and commitment to excellence, all qualities that most companies aspire to. The Olympic Games possess attributes such as dignified, worldly, global, modern, multi-cultural and dynamic – all of which reflect well on sponsors and project a positive image.

As David D'Alessandro, chairman and CEO of John Hancock Life Insurance, observed 'the Olympic Games may be the biggest marketing opportunity on earth, but only because they were something else first'.

And that is the crux of the proposition. The Olympic Games are far more than just another sporting event. The unique value proposition of the Olympic Movement, carefully nurtured over the past century but able to trace its roots back nearly 3,000 years, is what has driven the value of the partner association. The Olympic franchise is built on the Olympic values. It can only be sustained though carefully managed and long-term relationships.

This then is the benign paradox at the heart of the Olympic brand. Any erosion of the Olympic ideals would also erode the value of the brand. Contrary to what the critics say, the Corinthian values and the commercial value are intrinsically linked. Safeguarding the Olympic principles relies on the brand stewards being prepared to communicate this – and fight to protect it.

## 4   Zero tolerance – 'sorry' doesn't work

Greater clarity about what matters for the Olympics has been matched by greater assertiveness about what the commercial success of the Games depends on. Defending its rights, its image and what it stands for is central to the Olympic turnaround. Exclusivity is key. Sponsors need to know that they can invest in the Olympic Movement and be certain that they are not going to be undermined by a last-minute surprise promotional campaign by their competitor.

If the IOC had sat back and taken the easy option, turning a blind eye to the occasional borderline promotion or partner presence marketing indiscretion, the marketplace would have rapidly been cluttered and sponsorship fees would have stagnated at 1980 levels.

## 5 Hold the torch aloft

It is not enough, though, to simply protect the Olympic brand – unless that brand is truly cherished. The Olympic heritage is the Olympic brand's greatest asset and that should never be forgotten.

In the centre of Lausanne, overlooking Lake Geneva, is a museum dedicated to the Olympic spirit. It is a permanent reminder of what the Olympic brand really stands for. It was built in 1994 and houses a wealth of Olympic memorabilia, much of it donated by former Olympic athletes. To the uninitiated it looks like a curious assortment of vintage sports clothes and outdated equipment. But to the Olympic aficionado – and that's most of us in some way or other – it is an Aladdin's Cave.

Here, for example, are the very shoes that Jesse Owens wore when he won the gold medal for the long jump in front of Hitler at the Berlin Games of 1936. Here, too, are the medals that have been produced for every Games of the modern era. The museum also houses an archive of some of the most memorable sports footage ever filmed – from American swimmer Mark Spitz winning seven gold medals at Munich in 1972 to British rower Sir Steve Redgrave capturing his fifth gold medal in Sydney.

Managing this heritage and making people – internally and externally – aware of its importance is crucial to creating a sense of belonging in the organisation, a sense of meaning among other stakeholders and a sense of permanence and magic in the brand.

## 6 Manage the grey areas

There are two aspects to this element in the turnaround. First, is the simple fact that you cannot nail down every detail of a long-term relationship in a contract. There will always be grey areas. You have to be prepared to deal with the inevitable issues these create as and when they emerge. Flexibility is essential if you are to build long-term relationships. At times, it comes down less to what the contract says but whether an action enhances and supports the Olympic brand and strengthens the partnership for the future.

The second grey area is that the Olympic brand will always attract people with their own agenda. Beijing will be no exception. Every Games brings its own ethical challenges. Burying your head in the sand is not a viable strategy. The long-term protection of the Olympic brand requires its custodians to engage with the grey areas. This is the nitty-gritty of brand management. Failure to do so is an abdication of responsibility.

There are times, too – not often but occasionally – when it is necessary to bend the rules. The key to this is recognising that rules are not the same as principles. Rules can be bent, but you must never break the fundamental Olympic principles.

## 7   Develop fast reflexes – use crises as a catalyst

Crises happen. It is the mark of an organisation's management and leadership as to how it responds. It is the mark of its resilience as to how it emerges from the crisis.

Surviving a crisis requires leadership. When the IOC was threatened with the Salt Lake crisis, Samaranch dropped the diplomatic niceties, acted quickly and decisively, and, perhaps most importantly, drove through further changes. The crisis was used to totally reform the IOC – pushing through changes that under normal circumstances would have taken decades, in under six months. These actions not only saved the IOC from the immediate crisis, they also ensured its long-term credibility.

## 8   Appeal to the highest common denominator

When times are tough it is tempting to compromise standards, to forget founding principles. The Olympic turnaround, however, was built around cherishing the Olympic principles and bringing them into the lives of more people. It was founded on the highest common denominator rather than surrendering to the needs of short-term commercialism.

In the 1990s, the IOC was not seduced by higher offers from private broadcasters. It took the view that the Olympics stand for equality of access to opportunity and should be open to all. As a result, it kept the broadcast on free-to-air broadcast so that anyone in the world could watch. Money must never become a barrier to following the Games. Similarly, the Olympic stadiums and athlete bibs are free of any form of advertising – and tobacco and spirits sponsorship are prohibited.

## Always better

As strong and healthy as the outlook is today, it is essential for the Olympic Movement to continue to reach forward, push the agenda – not sit back, and become overly bureaucratic. It must continue to push for the big ideas, realise the full potential and power of the Olympic ideal – like the athlete, always aspiring to do better.

Success tends to have easily disturbed foundations. In the case of the Olympics it is always one flawed Games away from trouble. Another Atlanta could see the IOC on the defensive, fighting to keep sponsors on board and trying to ensure the Olympic brand image is not compromised. Nor can the IOC legislate in an increasingly fragile world for security, medical or other events which have the potential to disrupt the Games – or even prevent them happening.

Performance-enhancing drugs will remain an issue. There is always the potential for drug taking to erode the ethical basis of sport. If competition is tarnished by drug users the Games could be seen as a cynical deceit. Victor Conte, the Balco chemist, and advisor to many leading US sports stars, talks of the child-like gullibility of the public. 'The Olympic Games are a fraud,' he has said. 'It's almost like what I am here to tell you right now is that not only is there no Santa Claus, but there's no Easter bunny or tooth fairy either in the world of sport. The whole history of the Olympics is full of corruption, cover-up, performance-enhancing drug use.'

The IOC's stance has always been unequivocal. Jacques Rogge has made tackling drug users a core part of his presidency, and Dick Pound now leads the worldwide anti-drug body. Both advocate a zero tolerance policy and together they have made major inroads into the fight against doping, finally persuading governments around the world that they must also share in the responsibility – that the sports movement cannot solve the problem alone.

Success in the future requires the Olympic Family to remain both vigilant and credible in these areas. On the commercial side, too, there are a number of issues that the Olympic Movement must address in the next few years. Failure to do so could damage, or even destroy, it.

- **Decisive leadership.** There must be clear and decisive strategic leadership. There is a danger of retreating into the comfort zone. The IOC is not a savings bank, nor a simple administrative body where the management of the process is more important than the result. It must seek out opportunities, be able to react quickly, while remaining true to a long-term strategic vision. It must be exceptional rather than accepting of mediocrity. It must also understand that decisive leadership requires long-term vision.
- **Revenue distribution.** Few spectacles are as unbecoming as different members of the Olympic Family squabbling over money. If they are allowed to, these squabbles will continue to threaten and undermine the overall unity of the Olympic Movement, and place marketing programmes like TOP at considerable risk.

  Sooner, rather than later, the political leadership of the IOC needs to grapple with the problem. It will need to develop a clear and transparent revenue distribution formula for all members of the Olympic Family. With the economies and sporting performance of countries like China and Russia continuing to grow, they will soon be demanding a much larger share of the revenue cake. The question will be where to take it from. Something will have to give. Always taking money from the organising committee share is not necessarily the solution. The IOC must also focus on ensuring that the actual product – the Games themselves – are properly funded and continue to set new standards.
- **Multi-city bids.** The third issue is maintaining a healthy climate for cities to bid for the privilege of hosting the Games. The host cities are the lifeblood of the Olympic Movement. No host, no Games. It really is as simple as that. Twenty years ago, the IOC had to beg and plead with cities to host the Games. Today, too many people have forgotten those dark days. We have become used to seeing cities falling over themselves in their desire to bring the Games to their city.

Following the Salt Lake scandal, the IOC introduced tight guidelines on the bidding process, overseen by an energetic and, supposedly, independent IOC ethics commission. However, the guidelines have become so suffocating and, at times, petty, that there is a very real risk that cities and their governments will begin to question whether it is worth the hassle of bidding at all. Cities must be able to promote their candidatures – and benefit from just being a candidate. Politicians should be encouraged to support their bid, and speak out for the Olympic ideal. Balance must be found between ensuring a fair playing field and preventing a repeat of the ethical problems and excesses of past campaigns.

The Olympic ideal is best served by having multiple bidding cities competing against each other. The day when the number of cities falls to one or two candidates is the day the IOC will no longer be in the driving seat. When that happens, as Los Angeles showed in 1984, the city will dictate its own terms. That could threaten the integrity of the Olympic brand.

- ***Managing new technologies.*** In the coming years, there is no doubt that new technologies will present exciting new opportunities. The fourth challenge will be to find the right balance – making sure that the end result is really enhancing the viewer experience – giving the viewer greater choice of when to watch, what to watch, how to watch, in which language to watch and so on. Effectively this will allow everyone to create their own customised Olympic viewing experience. But in the rush to embrace new technology, we need to be careful not to undermine one of the critical elements of the Olympic presentation – the family viewing experience. The Olympics are about a shared experience.

New technology will also challenge the existing commercial advertiser-based models. In time, the only commercial message that the sports viewer will see will be the messages he or she wants to see. The viewer will be in control. This is already happening. TiVo and other video recorders allow viewers to delete advertising messages. If advertiser-supported television is slowly eroded over time, how will commercial rights fees be funded?

- ***Avoiding political interference.*** Samaranch spent much of the first decade of his presidency engaging with the political leaders of the world so that the Olympic cancer of boycotts could be banished. Although boycotts now seem a distant memory, there is a new and growing political threat on the horizon, and the IOC leadership must continue to engage with the world's political leaders.

  The European Commission is already trying to use sport and sports broadcasting as a vehicle to facilitate technological development across the continent. Whether the IOC, and other sports bodies, should be used to promote the development of 3G telecom and other technologies, is a cause of much debate. If there is no real demand yet for the service, is it right that the sports bodies be forced to license their rights, to create such demand? Especially when doing so might undermine the broader economic model on which sports broadcast rights had been founded?

  During the bidding for the European broadcast rights to the 2010-2012 Olympic Games, conducted in 2004 prior to Athens, the IOC was required to separate the tenders for mobile and new media rights from broadcast rights. This the IOC reluctantly did – only to find that not a single company wanted to bid for the stand-alone mobile rights. In the end, everyone realised – everyone except the offices of the EEC in Brussels, that is – that it only made sense if there could be one overall gatekeeper to co-ordinate all rights and maximise the potential promotion for the viewer.

  The EEC came to the rescue of the Athens Games by providing financial support for infrastructure development. But the IOC and all sports leaders must stay alert to ensure that the sports agenda is not once again captured by political leaders for their own ends.

- ***Risk management.*** Would another ethical scandal among the IOC membership create the same furore and confusion as the Salt Lake scandal did? Probably not. For one thing, there is now a mechanism to deal rapidly with such issues. The IOC president, Jacques Rogge, has both the authority and the will to act.

  The broader issue, though, is the overall question of security of the Games in today's global environment. One of the most worrying developments of the Athens Games was the enormous cost of bringing the security infrastructure up to a satisfactory level and responding to the global media's onslaught to find holes in the armour. And for all the security at Athens, a defrocked Irish priest was still able to disrupt the men's marathon. But this paled in significance next to media speculation. There was talk of sabotage, chemical and biological attacks, poisoning of the food supply to the athletes village, and cyber attacks to close down the Games information system.

Some commentators have begun to ask who can afford the security costs now necessary to protect the Games. Who, for example, should foot the bill for the cost of F16 fighters patrolling over the host city 24 hours a day? Insurance premiums have spiralled in the last decade and the insurance market is no longer anywhere near big enough to cover all the Olympic market needs, never mind the added pressures of other major events like the soccer world cup.

The threat is not just at the event itself but also in the lead up to the Games. Would the Salt Lake City Games have been able to take place, if September 11 had taken place on January 11, one month before the Games? Would the Beijing Games take place if the SARS epidemic were to break out for the first time in the summer of 2008?

Olympic Games have been cancelled three times over the past 100 years. It is not unreasonable to assume that, at some stage in the future, the schedule of the Games will again be compromised by events outside of the IOC's direct control. The IOC has moved to try and in part cover such an eventuality by building up a set of financial reserves that could carry the organisation through a quadrennial without an Olympic Games.

- ***Realising the full potential of the Olympic brand.*** Finally, the Olympic Movement has a responsibility to develop and use the Olympic brand to its full potential. The power of the Olympic Games is potentially awesome. The IOC has a duty to be more than simply the Olympic administrator. The question the Olympic Movement must ask itself is whether the IOC is using its resources to carry forward its mission beyond the Games themselves?

The danger is that if too much attention is focused on the operational aspects of the Games – creating multiple reporting systems, excessive focus on cost control – other aspects may be neglected. The

Olympics celebrate humanity's highest aspirations. The most diverse congregation on the planet meets to pay homage – not to one God, but to a wider faith in human ability and aspiration. The Olympic Games are a microcosm of global civilisation.

The three pillars of the Olympic ideal are sport, culture and respect. The five Olympic values are: sportsmanship; education; exceeding one's expectations; solidarity; and peace and happiness. Those who serve it are charged with advancing that agenda. These values are the foundations upon which the Olympic franchise is based. They are immutable. They are the reason why athletes are prepared to dedicate years of their lives to pursuing the Olympic dream. And we, like them, are elevated by the spectacle of their endeavour as they strive to live up to the Olympic ideals. That must never change.

As Baron Pierre de Coubertin, the founding father of the modern Olympic Movement, put it, the objectives of the IOC are: 'To celebrate the Games regularly. To make this celebration evermore worthy of its glorious past and in keeping with the lofty ideals that inspired those who restored it. To instigate and organise all events and … take all measures to ensure that modern athletics develops in the desirable manner.'

Higher, faster, stronger is the Olympic motto. It continues to inspire athletes to compete for the honour of being called Olympians, but it must also be the aspiration of those who manage and safeguard the future of the Olympic Games. The Olympic brand is one of the most powerful brands in the world. To remain so, its future stewards will have to be vigilant in defending its honour, and yet also have the courage to grasp new opportunities as they present themselves. It is only by constantly reinventing itself – and by striving for greater glory – that the Olympic Movement can remain relevant and vital in a changing world. In an era when cynicism seems to have reached epidemic levels, it is inevitable that the Olympic ideal is constantly being challenged – whether it is through attitudes to doping in sport or inappropriate attempts to exploit the Olympic brand. But the Olympic dream is also more sorely needed now than at any time in its history. It is the responsibility of the Olympic leadership to serve mankind. We owe it to future generations not only to defend the Olympic ideal but to advance its agenda into every sphere of human endeavour.

# APPENDIX

# THE RINGS AND THE SMALL SCREEN

To understand how the scorpion wars of Calgary, and the general frenzy surrounding modern TV rights, came about you need to rewind to the first recorded transmission of the Olympic Games. This was at the 1932 Los Angeles Games, when NBC radio broadcast short late-evening news summaries of the day's events. Even then there were concerns. The Los Angeles organisers worried that radio broadcasts would impact on their primary source of revenue – ticket sales.

Four years later, the organisers of the 1936 Berlin Games introduced the medium of television to the Olympics, with 138 hours of coverage of some 175 events. This was perhaps the first and only time that television audience ratings would be totally accurate – as the organisers were able to count literally every single viewer. The signal was distributed to viewing rooms, typically beer halls, provided they were within 15 km of the centre of Berlin. The 162,228 viewers watched what was effectively the first ever closed-circuit television broadcast.

The German state broadcaster had three cameras for the event. Each weighed over 200 kg and required four people just to change the lens. Only one camera would actually work for live transmissions and then only if the sunlight was strong enough. The other two cameras had a 65 second delay before broadcasting. The overall result was less than spectacular. *The Times* reported that the pictures 'resembled a very faint, highly underexposed photographic film and were so much worse than ordinary transmissions from a studio that many turned away in disappointment'. It was not a very promising start – though the sporting action in the venues was highly memorable – Jesse Owen winning four gold medals while Hitler looked on disapprovingly.

The 1948 Games in London witnessed a number of firsts. The first use of starting blocks and the photo finish, and the first time the Olympics were broadcast into viewers' homes. When the Olympic Games returned to London 12 years later, after World War Two, the organisers were faced with the challenges of how to finance the Games, and looked to the new medium of broadcasting as a potential revenue source. With remarkable foresight, the BBC was anxious to avoid what it saw as a potentially very dangerous precedent, namely having to pay for the right to cover the event. After all, print journalists and photographers did not have to pay. Nevertheless after a long debate the London organisers were eventually able to persuade the BBC to pay 1,000 guineas (a guinea was a pound and one shilling).

Television was still in its infancy. Only 80,000 homes throughout the United Kingdom were able to receive any form of coverage. Live broadcasts were restricted to an 80 km radius around London. Yet, the Games attracted an average television audience of around 500,000 viewers each day in the UK. (There was no broadcast outside the UK.).

The London Organising Committee ended up with a small revenue surplus, as a result of better than forecast ticket sales. Being true English gentlemen, they elected not to cash the BBC's cheque! The BBC saved its 1,000 guineas, but the precedent of paying a fee to gain the broadcast rights to an event had been established.

The next two Olympics in Helsinki in 1952 and Melbourne in 1956 remained fraught with negotiations over rights fee payments. The rest of the broadcast industry was far from willing to follow the precedent established by the BBC in London. Both Helsinki and Melbourne were virtually boycotted by the broadcast industry due to a combination of technical issues and arguments over rights payments and exclusivity.

Broadcasters and cinema newsreel companies were deeply concerned about having to pay for the right to cover an event. Roger Tartarian of the United Press Association wrote to Avery Brundage, the then IOC president: 'I think you will agree that the whole world would be aghast if the right of newspapers and other news media to cover the Games would ever be put on the auction block, yet this is apparently being contemplated (by the Organisers) in the case of television coverage of the Melbourne Games ...

despite the fact that television is only another arm of the press.' Tartarian concluded: 'It would certainly be a contradiction to that principle for another branch of the press to be denied the same privilege, just because it is a newer branch.'

## Free press

Ironically, it was NBC and the BBC, both current rights holders, who led the charge for an international TV boycott of the Melbourne Games over arguments about rights fees and exclusivity. The broadcasters claimed that an exclusive rights deal 'was exploitation and would have a calamitous effect' on them. They appealed to the constitutional rights of the free press and demanded free and equal access to news sources. NBC sent an indignant telegram to the Melbourne Organisers protesting that: 'The Olympic Games is a news event; television news-film is the newest and most dramatic method of visual reporting ... We insist on free and equal access to that event!'

The Australian Consul-General in New York was advised by NBC executives that no network would break ranks and that, if the Melbourne Committee did not back down, they would refrain from any positive publicity about the Games and Australia generally. The issue quickly began to escalate, with the Australian Prime Minister, Robert Menzies being advised in a briefing note that 'every endeavour should be made to get good press and as much international goodwill from the Games as possible'.

Meanwhile, the Melbourne Committee had sold exclusive rights to the Games to Britain's principal commercial broadcaster, Associated Rediffusion for £25,000. Britain's newly licensed independent channels had won over viewers from the BBC with an aggressive policy of acquiring sports rights. The head of Rediffusion, Roland Gillett, also secured a $500,000 exclusive sponsorship deal with Westinghouse to show Games footage as a series of nightly specials in the US.

Under a non-stop barrage of threats and political intervention, the Melbourne Organisers were forced into a humiliating climb-down. They cancelled their exclusive agreement with Rediffusion and announced that they were still seeking a buyer for television rights. The Melbourne Committee offered overseas broadcasters up to three minutes of free footage on a daily basis for news access. The networks held out for a minimum five minutes. But with the backing of the IOC, the Organisers refused. With hindsight this proved to be a fatal mistake for the broadcasters.

The organisers lobbied a local Liberal MP and Minister, Kent Hughes, who forced an amendment to the Australian Broadcast and Television Act. This gave sports organisers protection against television channels claiming automatic rights for free coverage of events.

The organisers nevertheless also recognised that they needed to find a solution for the evolving local broadcaster industry. Channel 9 put together what was probably the first ever sports broadcast sponsorship agreement, whereby Ampol paid £1,000 to the Organisers and a further £8,000 to Channel 9 for commercial announcements during its coverage of the Games.

International broadcasters, paranoid about the further precedent of rights fees and exclusivity for an international event, refused to concede. The upshot of all this wrangling was that the Melbourne Games went ahead with no international television coverage whatsoever. This prompted *New York Times* columnist Jack Gould to observe: 'The Olympic Games as an institution, Australia as a nation and television as a medium of the free world all have suffered as a consequence of the extensive blackout.'

But an important milestone had been passed – sports, and Olympic rights in particular, would no longer be free. It is interesting to reflect what the current status of the global sports scene would be if the IOC and the Melbourne Organisers had backed down and accepted that broadcasters receive the same free access right as their colleagues in the print media.

## Another sixty years

The 1956 Winter Games in Cortina, Italy were held shortly before the Melbourne Games. While Melbourne was a broadcasting blackout, Cortina was the first Winter Games to accept broadcast cameras. Unfortunately, this began with farce. During the Opening Ceremony, at one of the most critical moments of Olympic protocol, the final Olympic torch-bearer, Italian skater Guido Caroli, tripped over TV cables laid out along the ice. As Caroli fell he dropped the torch. Luckily it did not go out – even though some reports suggested it had to be re-lit by a spectator's match.

Against this background, it was perhaps no surprise that IOC president, Avery Brundage was less than enthusiastic about the medium. Addressing the IOC Executive Board later in 1956, he observed: 'The Olympic Movement has done perfectly well without television for the last 60 years, and believe me, we are going to manage for another 60.'

Brundage's confidence – or complacency – was quickly proved outdated. As television expanded, the IOC began to look seriously at the potential and how relationships with this new medium should be managed.

In 1960 the Olympic Movement returned to the USA with the Winter Games in Squaw Valley, beside Lake Tahoe on the border between California and Nevada. ABC, accepting the principle of some form of local payment, bought the rights for $50,000 but then suddenly backed out. Bill Paley, the ruthless and brilliant CBS president was eventually persuaded to step in by Walt Disney, who was involved with the organisation of the Games. Paley agreed as a personal favour to Disney, rather than because of any love for the Games. This was reflected in the coverage. CBS provided cursory news coverage and refused to send a single sports anchorman to Squaw Valley.

The Rome Olympics, four years later marked the true beginning of broadcasting's love affair with the Olympic Games. The Rome Games were the first to be televised live with 18 countries across Europe taking live coverage and the first to see the introduction of video recorders. The US networks did a complete about-face over their refusal to pay the organisers for broadcast rights. CBS offered $0.4 million for the US rights.

The broadcast momentum continued with the Games in Tokyo in 1964 with the introduction of satellite transmissions. However, the Games had still not established itself as a dominant force within American television. NBC refused to move the Johnny Carson *Tonight* show on the West Coast for the Olympics.

In one of the opening salvos in the on-going debate between print and electronic media over live and not-so-live coverage, the *New York Times* wrote: 'For the sake of a few thousand dollars ... what will be the effect of an opinion of American values when the rest of the world hears that this country makes a moment of history subordinate to the fate of a cluster of advertising spot announcements in California?'

## Close up and personal

It was not until 1972 that the Games finally made their mark on global television audiences. Although ABC had paid $7.5 million for the US rights, the Olympic broadcast still only garnered relatively small audiences and 'the advertising community could barely stifle a yawn'. It took the tragic kidnappings of the Israeli team by eight Palestinian terrorists at Munich, to wake up an otherwise sleepy US audience, into riveted and near obsessive viewing. Ultimately, it was through the tragedy at Munich that the Olympic Movement entered the modern media age. After Munich, the American networks began to slowly recognise that the intensity of the Olympic viewing could not be matched by any other programming, and competition between networks to acquire Olympic rights heated up.

Roone Arledge approached the Montreal 1976 organisers with a $25 million offer – over three times what ABC had paid for Munich. There was one catch: the organisers were given 24 hours to accept. This brazen technique of offering a quantum increase coupled with strict deadline pressure, became known within the industry as the ABC, or 'Arledge closer'. Ebersol who referred to Arledge as 'the master' obviously watched this technique closely, because in later years, when he was leading NBC's Olympic negotiating team, he embraced the same process with similarly effective results.

The other US networks looked on enviously as Arledge and ABC parlayed their Olympic telecasts into significant increases in their Neilsen ratings and used it as a promotional tool for their Autumn programming schedule. ABC reported a profit of $1 million from its Innsbruck broadcast in 1976 against a rights fee of $10 million.

The other networks were far from happy with ABC's negotiating tactics. NBC's vice president and general counsel telexed the IOC president, Lord Killanin, complaining that 'the bidding procedure [for Montreal] had been a sham'. Arledge responded by criticising NBC for 'playing the wounded party ... Bidding is simply not the way rights are granted for most sports ... and that not a single sports event on NBC's schedule was gained through competitive bidding.' Newspaper reports later commented on reports of kickbacks over the broadcast rights of $5 million to the provincial Government of Quebec.

Lake Placid in 1980 saw a new and even more worrying development for the IOC. The United States Olympic Committee tried to lay claim to a share of the broadcast rights. It argued for a 30 per cent tax on US network payments whenever the Games were staged outside of the US. This prompted screams of blackmail from the IOC director Monique Berlioux. Such claims became a recurring theme throughout the 1980s and 1990s, as the USOC tried to leverage its position by threatening Congressional legislation as a means of first claiming and then increasing its revenues.

## Politics and vodka

For the rights to Moscow, all of the networks were beginning to wake up to ABC's negotiating tactics and started their own direct courtship with the Soviet organisers. The broadcasting opportunities were obvious: American athletes striving for gold medals behind the mysterious and ideologically distant Iron Curtain engaged the imagination of the US network executives.

The various attempts to curry favour and influence with the Soviets had little effect on the overall process. According to one report, the Moscow organisers considered 'the whole episode as a chance to tweak the Americans a bit, watch them squirm and dump on them a bunch of worthless productions gathering dust in some Ministry of Culture film library.'

The IOC was still reluctant to take a leading role in any rights negotiations, fearing that it would be criticised for engaging directly in business, a hangover from Avery Brundage's oft-expressed views on the evils of commercialism. Instead the IOC delegated the responsibility to the Organising Committee, with the IOC reserving the right to approve the final contracts.

The first round of negotiations were held aboard the *Alexander Pushkin*, a Soviet vessel moored in Montreal's harbour during the Montreal Games. The Soviets laid on a feast. 'Tables groaned beneath platters of cracked lobster, sliced sturgeon and caviar ... and the decks were awash with gallons of Stolichnaya vodka and Armenian cognac,' reported *Sports Illustrated* on the first formal negotiating encounter of the Soviet organisers and US network teams. During the course of the banquet, the Soviets advised the US networks that they would be looking for a rights fee of $210 million – a nine-fold increase over what ABC had paid for Montreal. The Organising Committee president, Ignati Novikov also requested a change in attitude by the networks in their news telecasts with their political coverage of the Soviet Union.

The ensuing months brought intrigue and double crosses, lawsuits and counter suits, broken handshake agreements and secret agents, collective walk-outs by the US network presidents and threats from the Soviets that they would never be allowed to ever again return to Soviet soil. Roone Arledge reflected that 'the intrigue surrounding these Olympics would have suited John le Carré.'

At one stage, concerned about Moscow's demands, all three networks got together to explore whether they might pool resources and approach the US Justice Department about an exemption to the Sherman Anti-Trust Act that prohibited any form of collective bidding. In the end, in a last-minute secret bidding session, NBC ended ABC's long run as the Olympic network.

Of course, in the end, NBC never televised the Games. Kremlin leaders, concerned that Afghanistan's President Hafizullah Amin was working to move his country away from the Soviet sphere of influence, invaded on 27 December 1979, less than seven months before they were scheduled to host the 22nd Olympiad.

US President Jimmy Carter immediately sought means to respond to the Soviet action and deemed that 'a boycott of the Moscow Olympics would be a severe blow to Soviet prestige.' The US Department of Commerce, as part of the overall agenda to lead a boycott of the Moscow Games, placed an embargo on further rights payments by NBC to the organisers.

President Carter subsequently extended this embargo to also cover payments to the IOC. Just as it looked as if the IOC might begin to gain some form of financial stability, the organisation was thrown into disarray. NBC eventually paid the IOC its share of revenues, even though it did not broadcast a single hour of coverage from Moscow. NBC succeeded in recouping some of its payments through insurance coverage taken out with Lloyds of London and elsewhere. Even so, it still lost around $30 million as a result of advertising expenses and other operational costs.

# SOURCES

Multiple sources were relied on when writing this book – from the library of the Olympic Museum, through to the press archives of the IOC studies centre, as well as many late nights with Google. Book research ranged from an extensive list of publications on Olympic history, including the official reports published by each Organising Committee from 1896 onwards; the biographies of former IOC presidents and OCOG presidents, through to various books on corporate marketing and broadcasting. Over the years, the IOC, and its agencies have published a number of specialist marketing publications – including a regular newsletter, initially known as the *TOP Bulletin*, and then with a broader remit, as *Marketing Matters* as well as a comprehensive post-Games Marketing Report.

The press archives of a broad range of publications from the wire agencies Reuters, AP, AFP and Kyodo; the *New York Times, Wall Street Journal, USA Today, Fortune, Business Week* and *Advertising Age* in the US, along with local publications in Atlanta, Los Angeles, Salt Lake City and Sydney; international publications such as the *International Herald Tribune,* the *Financial Times* and *The Economist,* through to the *Guardian,* the *Daily Telegraph* and *The Times* in the UK, all provided valuable reference points, to help tell the story, and place critical issues in context. The sports marketing publications *Sports Business Journal* (US), and *Sport Business* (UK) were particularly helpful in this regard. The search through media archive encompassed a broad selection of publications, outside of the classic Anglo Saxon media, from the *China Daily,* and *South Chinese Morning Post* in China through to *L'Equipe* and *Le Monde* in France, *Frankfurter Allgemeine* in Germany to the *Asahi Shimbun* in Japan. All quotes and references contained in the book, other than my own direct conversations are from previously published sources.

A list of the key sources is provided below.

# Chapter 1 – Rings Side Seat

### Beijing, August 8, 2008

'Olympics to lift firm's fortunes', *China Daily*, 27 May 2004.
*South China Morning Post*, 30 July 2001.
Miller, David, *Athens to Athens: The Official History of the Olympic Games and the IOC, 1894–2004*, Mainstream Publishing, 2003.
Clarke, Liz, 'For China, Future is both now and later: Plans for 2008 are ahead of schedule', *Washington Post*, 19 August 2004.

### Starting at the finishing line

Weinberg, Herb, 'The Olympic selection process, Baden-Baden, 1981', *Journal of Olympic History*, Winter 2001.
Rodda, John, *Guardian*.

### Running on empty

Bose, Mihir, 'Why Host the Games?', *Sports Business*, March 1997.
Siddons, Larry, *The Olympics at 100: A Celebration in Pictures*, Macmillan General Reference, 1995.
Boulongne, Y.; Landry, F.; Lennartz, K.; Müller, N.; and Schantz, O., *The International Olympic Committee – One Hundred Years*, IOC.
Lawrence, Robert; and Pellegrom, Jeffrey, 'Fool's gold. How America pays to lose the Olympics', *The Brookings Review*, 7 (4) Fall 1989.
'Montrealers identify with Athens's challenges', *Canadian Press*, August 5, 2004.

### Mission impossible

*Marketing Matters*, Issue No. 15, International Olympic Committee.
Miller, David, *Olympic Revolution: The Olympic Biography of Juan Antonio Samaranch*, Pavilion Books, 1992.
Levin, Richard; Ueberroth, Peter; and Quinn, Amy, *Made in America: His Own Story*, Morrow, 1985.

### Gentlemen amateurs

Lyberg, Wolf, Fabulous *100 years of the IOC. Facts – figures – and much, much more*, International Olympic Committee, 1996.


### Any takers?

Weinberg, Herb, 'The Olympic selection process: Baden-Baden 1981', *Journal of Olympic History*, Winter 2001.

Hill, Christopher R., *Olympic Politics: Athens to Atlanta, 1896–1996*, St. Martin's Press.

Dwyre, Bill, '1984 Olympics – The legacy', *Los Angeles Times*, 25 July 2004.


### Hostage to ill fortune

Samaranch circular letters to IOC Members, 14 August 1980.


### Less is more

Larson, James F.; Rivenburgh, Nancy K.; and de Morgas Spa, Miquel, *Television in the Olympics*, John Libbey & Co., 1995.

# Chapter 2 – Scorpion Wars

### Lausanne, January 23, 1984

Johnson, William Oscar, 'A contract with the Kremlin', *Sports Illustrated*, February 21 1977.

Arledge, Roone, *Roone – A Memoir*, HarperCollins, 2003.

Spence, Jim; and Diles, Dave, *Up Close and Personal: The Inside Story of Network Television Sports*, Atheneum, 1988.

Pound, Dick, *Inside The Olympics*, John Wiley, 2004.

Wenn, Stephen, 'A turning point for IOC television policy: US television rights negotiations and the 1980 Lake Placid and Moscow Festival', *Journal of Olympic History*, Spring 1998.

### The TV deal

*Business Week*, 4 February 2002.
Bellamy, RV., 'The evolving television sports marketplace', in LA Wenner (ed.), *MediaSport*, Routledge Kegan Paul, 1998.


### Sting in the tail

Kavanagh, Gerard, 'Gifted story teller finds happy ending', *Sports Business Journal*, 21 December 1998.
Barney, Robert K.; Wenn, Stephen R.; and Martyn, Scott G., *Selling the Five Rings: The International Olympic Committee and the Rise of Olympic Commercialism*, University Of Utah Press, 2002.
Arledge, Roone, *Roone – A Memoir*, HarperCollins, 2003.
Klatell, David; and Norman, Marcus, *Sports for Sale: Television, Money, and the Fans*, Oxford University Press, 1988.


### Sucked dry

Arledge, Roone, *Roone – A Memoir*, HarperCollins, 2003.
Kim, Un-Yong, *The Greatest Olympics*. Si-sa-yong-o-sa, 1990.
Taafe, William, *Sports Illustrated*.
IOC TV Workshop 1987- Conference Proceedings.


### Lessons learned

IOC TV workshop, 1987.
Christopher, R., *Olympic Politics*, Manchester University Press, 1992.
*Wall Street Journal*, 26 May 1988.


### Barcelona 1992: NBC's triple jump

Lewyn, Mark.; Landler, Mark, 'Why NBC's triple-cast never made a run at the gold', *Business Week*, August 17 1992.


### Europe becomes competitive

Bailey, Eric, 'The big fight for the big matches', *Daily Telegraph*, 23 February 1990.

### Split decision

Saatchi & Saatchi Media Bulletin, February 1994.


### Building a dream

'Games could provide biggest ad blitz ever', *USA Today*, 15 July 1996.


### Implausibly live

Manning, Jeff, 'Olympic produce wins and profits', *Portland Oregonian*, August 4 1996.


## Chapter 3 – Shock and Awe

### Two's company

Kavanagh, Gerard, 'Gifted story teller finds happy ending', *Sports Business Journal*, 21 December 1998.


### The pre-emptive strike

Kavanagh, Gerard, 'Gifted story teller finds happy ending', *Sports Business Journal*, 21 December 1998.
Martzke, Rudy, 'NBC parlay sound investment', *USA Today*, 8 August 1995.
Sandomir, Richard, 'For $1.27 billion NBC accomplished an Olympic sweep', *New York Times*, 8 August 1995.


### Out-foxed

*IOC Marketing Matters*, Issue No 8.
'Olympics safeguarded for BBC TV viewers until 2008', BBC Press Release, 30 January 1996.
Poulter, Sean, 'BBC strikes Olympic Gold', *Daily Mail*, 31 January 1996.
Salter, David, 'Pay TV plays dirty pool. Robber Barons: Do Rupert and his fellow pay–TV moguls really own the wide world of sport', *The Bulletin*, 1 March 1996.

### Signed and sealed

Bernstein, Andy, *Sports Business Journal*, June 2003.

Lawrence, Robert; and Pellegrom, Jeffrey, 'Fool's Gold: How America pays to lose the Olympics' *The Brookings Review*, 7 (4) Fall 1989.


### The tail wagging the scorpion

Cardona, Mercedes M., 'Ad-spending soothsayers optimistic on year ahead', *Advertising Age*, 15 December 2003.


## Chapter 4 – The Shoemaker's Vision

### Dazzling

Abrams, Bill, 'Adidas makes friends, then strikes deals that moves sneakers', *Wall Street Journal*, 24 January 1986.


### Solving the puzzle

Miller, David, *Olympic Revolution: The Olympic Biography of Juan Antonio Samaranch*, Pavilion Books, 1992.

*TOP Bulletin*, Issue No. 10.

Schmitt, Eric, 'Revamping the Olympic franchise', *New York Times*, 16 February 1986.

Lord Luke, Vice Chairman of IOC Finance Commission to the IOC President, February 1984.


### Seoul searching

Cosell, Howard, *New York Daily News*.

Eisenberg, Jerry, *New York Post*.


### Spinning TOP

'Price of gold', *Guardian*, 24 September 1988.

*Financial Times Supplement*, 11 June 1988.

McThomas Robert G., 'Games on sale at TOP prices', *International Herald Tribune*, 17 December 1987.

'Here comes Fuji', *Newsweek*, 19 July 1982.

Levin, Richard; Ueberroth, Peter; and Quinn, Amy, *Made in America: His Own Story*, Morrow, 1985.

Schmitt, Eric, 'Revamping the Olympic franchise', *New York Times*, 16 February 1986.

Macleod, Ian, 'Ideal of excellence redundant in the Games with no soul', *Daily Telegraph*, 25 February 1992.

### Visa accepted here

*Marketing Communications*, January 1989.

Chuktow, Paul, 'Visa the power of an idea', *Going for Gold*, Visa Publication.

### The end of the beginning

'Top gets good reviews', *Sports Marketing News*, 14 March 1988.

### Membership is a privilege

Bernstein, Andy, 'Brand building is the name of the Games', *Sports Business Journal*.

'Visa Olympic research results', *Marketing Matters*, Issue No. 6.

*Fortune*, 24 July 2000.

*Guardian*, 26 February 1994.

*Wall Street Journal*, 14 October 1998.

### That dog won't hunt

Greising, David, *I'd Like The World To Buy A Coke: Life & Leadership of Roberto Goizueta*, John Wiley, 1997.

Barnes, Simon, *The Times*, 21 September 1990.

Collins, Glenn, *Advertising Age*, 28 March 1996.

### Blink and you might lose

'Here Comes Fuji', *Newsweek*, 19 July 1982.

Zampetakis, Helene, 'Samsung A$310 million for Olympics', *Australian Financial Review*, 7 September 1999.


## Connecting with customers

D'Alessandro, David; and Owens, Michelle, *Brand Warfare: 10 Rules for Building the Killer Brand*, McGraw-Hill, 2001.
*Atlanta Journal*, 18 September 2000.
*Business Week*, 9 February 1998.
Rivera, Nancy, 'McDonald's bruised winner at Games', *Los Angeles Times*, 9 September 1984.
'Sydney diary', *The Times*, 24 September 2000.


## The world's largest stage

*IOC Marketing Matters*, Issue No. 16.
*Salt Lake Marketing Report*, IOC 2002.
'Olympic notebook', *International Herald Tribune*, 28 February 1994.
*USA Today*, 26 September 2000.


## Jockeying for position

'Greenpeace attacks promotion by Sydney 2000 Olympic sponsor', *Advertising Age*, 9 March 1998.


## Invitation of a lifetime

*IOC Marketing Matters*, Issue No.6
Kolah, Ardi, 'How to develop an effective sponsorship programme', *Sports Business Information Resources*.
'UPS nurturing Olympic hopefuls with equipment and time to train', *Atlanta Constitution*, 5 October 1995.


## The results

Grenville, Andrew, 'Do sponsors benefit? Sponsorship awareness: a bad answer to a good question', Ipsos-Reid.

Ludwig, S.; and Karabetsos, J.D., 'Objectives and evaluation processes utilised by sponsors of the 1996 Olympic Games', *Sport Marketing Quarterly*, 8(1), 1999.

'Interview with Carl Pascarella', *CNNfn*, 21 February 2000.

*Fortune*, 1998.

*IOC Marketing Matters*, Issue No.6.

'Marketers view the Olympics as a commercial bonanza', *Media Advertiser*, 6 February 1998.

# Chapter 5 – Beyond a Brand

## *Lillehammer, Norway, February 9 1994*

Powell Jeff, 'Do not mock the Games that care', *Daily Mail*, 28 February 1994.

## *Ring ritual*

*Olympic Review*, Issue No. 13.

Lennartz, Karl, 'The story of the rings', *Journal of Olympic History 10*, December 2001/January 2002.

## *Yin and yang*

UN Secretary General, Kofi Annan to the UN Assembly, February 1998.

'Selling world peace at $55 million a pop', *Business Week*. *IOC Sydney Marketing Report*.

Collins, Glen, *Advertising Age*, 28 March 1996.

*Fortune*, 24 July 2000.

*Wall Street Journal*, 14 October 1998.

*Fortune* 1998.

## *Sceptical sponsors*

Barney, Robert K.; Wenn, Stephen R.; Martyn, Scott G., *Selling the Five Rings: The International Olympic Committee and the Rise of Olympic Commercialism*, University Of Utah Press, 2002.

Guttman, Allen, *The Olympics: A History of the Modern Games*, University of Illinois Press, 1992.

'Javelins are already flying at Billy Payne', *Business Week*, 22 July 1996.

### Celebrate humanity

Garfield, Bob, 'Surprisingly humanity wins over scandal in Olympic ads', *Advertising Age*, 28 February 2000.

### Something unusual and unplanned

Levin, Richard; Ueberroth, Peter; and Quinn, Amy, *Made in America: His Own Story*, Morrow 1985.

Malcolm, Andrew H., 'More than Olympic flame crosses America', *New York Times*, 10 June 1984.

MacNamara, Kate, 'Big oil may light Olympic Torch. Tough bidding expected; Petro Canada, Imperial Oil may vie for sponsorship', *National Post*, 21 July 2003.

Heath, Thomas, 'Sponsors warm up for the run to Olympic profit', *International Herald Tribune*, 15 March 1996.

'Carrying a torch for the heartland', *Business Week*, 24 June 1996.

### The greatest

Birch, Ric, *Master of Ceremonies*, Allen & Unwin, 2004.

*South Morning Post China*, 19 September 2000.

Barney, Robert K.; Wenn, Stephen R.; and Martyn, Scott G., *Selling the Five Rings: The IOC and the Rise of Olympic Commercialism*, University of Utah Press, 2002.

## Chapter 6 – Beating the Ambushers

### IOC Marketing Operations Centre, Marriot Marquis Hotel, Atlanta; July 1996.

Woodward, Steve, 'Silver campaign – Nike's guerrilla in the midst of the Olympics', *Sports Business Journal*.

'Going for gold cashing in', *Globe & Mail*, Canada, 20 July 1996.

Aspden, Peter, 'Nike accused of trashing the Olympic ideal', *Financial Times*, 27 July 1996.

### *Keeping the Olympics clean*

Letter from Steve Jones to Francois Carrard, 15 December 2000.

### *Off message*

'Interview with Craig Singer', *New York Post*, 14 February 2002.

### *The battle of the credit card giants*

Meenaghen, Tony, 'Ambush marketing – a threat to corporate sponsorship', *Sloan Management Review*, 1 September 1996.

### *The PR battlefield*

Coker, Darby, 'A disease strikes Olympic athletes', *Olympic Message*, Summer 1996.
Wheatley, Keith, 'Parasites on the piste', *Financial Times*, 14 February 1994.


# Chapter 7 – Operation Perfect Hosts

### *The world's longest commercial*

'Evoking the images of the Games', *IOC Museum Catalogue*.
*Olympic Review*, Sept/Oct 1990
Larson, James F.; Rivenburgh, Nancy K.; and de Morgas Spa, Miquel, *Television in the Olympics*, John Libbey & Co., 1995.
Radford, Paul, 'Barcelona remembered for peace and harmony', Reuters, 2 July 2004.
Bruce, Peter, Berlin, Peter, 'Games prove a runaway success for Spain', *Financial Times*, 10 August 1992.
'Homage to Barcelona', *The Times*, 10 August 1992.
'Homage to Barcelona', *The Japan Times*, 11 August 1992.
Vescey, George, 'The real winner is Barcelona, not the athletes', *International Herald Tribune*, 11 August 1992.
Johnson, William Oscar, 'Barcelona was pure gold', *Sports Illustrated*, 17 August 1992.
Weir, Tom, 'Commentary', *USA Today*, 11 August 1992.

## Arctic circles

Rowbottom, Mike, 'Games touched heights and hearts', *Independent*, 1 March 1994.

Mihoces, Gary, 'Norwegian warmth knows no boundaries', *USA Today*, 1 March 1994.

Miller, David, 'Clear message from winter wonderland', *The Times*, 1 March 1994.

'Lillehammer was a success and wants another bite of the cake', *Guardian*, 1 March 1994.

Vecsey, 'George, "'Bland games" would be nice', *New York Times*, 5 February 2002.

'When Norway was heaven's gate', *VG*, February 1994.

Barry, Dave, 'Cowbells, salmon jerky: Is this skiing or insanity?', *Seattle Times*, 18 February 1994.

Montville, Leigh, 'Once upon a time', *Sports Illustrated*, 7 March 1994.

Thompson, Ian, 'The Olympics: Not just surviving but better than ever', *International Herald Tribune*, 1 March 1994.


## Atlanta shoots itself in the foot

'Gold medal for chaos', *Sports Business Journal* 1996.

'Atlanta has blown it big time', *France Soir*.

'The Greed Games', *Los Angeles Times*.

'Greed eclipses Olympic creed at Olympic flea market. Atlanta promised the greatest Games of all time, but never mentioned that they would be the tackiest too', *Atlanta Constitution*, 19 August 1996.

Main editorial, *The Times*, 6 August 1996.

Letts, Quentin, 'Greed eclipses Olympic creed at Atlanta flea market', *The Times*, 3 August 1996.

'Ideals left behind in the Atlanta gold rush', *Independent*, 6 August 1996.

*International Herald Tribune*, 1 March 1994.

IOC Director General, Francois Carrard to Atlanta Mayor Maynard Jackson, 12 February 1993.

Barney, Robert K.; Wenn, Stephen R.; and Martyn, Scott G., *Selling the Five Rings: The International Olympic Committee and the Rise of Olympic Commercialism*, University Of Utah Press, 2002.

'Why Atlanta missed out on Olympic glory', *Daily Telegraph*, 6 August 1996.

Yarborough, C Richard, *And They Call Them Games*, Mercer University Press, 2000.

Thompson, Ian, 'Atlanta rates only a silver medal for its Games' *International Herald Tribune*, 6 August 1996.

Korporaal, Glenda, 'Atlanta City of corporate clutter' *Sydney Morning Herald*, 22 July 1996.

Aspden, Peter, 'The end of a golden dream. Man in the News: Billy Payne – the Olympic organiser under fire for excessive commercialism', *Financial Times*, 3 August 1996.

Copetas, Craig; and Thurrow, Roger, 'Atlanta blues: Commercial clutter irks Olympic leaders', *Wall Street Journal*, 2 August 1996.

Cummings, Jeanne, 'Preparing for the 1996 Olympics', *Atlanta Constitution*, 9 January 1991.

### A play in three acts

*Atlanta Constitution*, 19 August 1996.

Yarborough, C Richard, *And They Call Them Games*, Mercer University Press, 2000.

Aspden, Peter, 'Nike accused of trashing the Olympic Ideal', *Financial Times*, 27 July 1996.

### The wake-up call

'Ideals left behind in the Atlanta gold rush', *Independent*, 6 August 1996.

Copetas, Craig; and Thurrow, Roger, 'Atlanta blues: Commercial clutter irks Olympic leaders', *Wall Street Journal*, 2 August 1996.

CNN.Com 22 September, 2000

### Lessons learned

*Wall Street Journal*, 2 August 1996.

'A game plan', *Advertising Age*, 12 August 1996.

Vecsey, 'George, '"Bland games" would be nice', *New York Times*, 5 February 2002.

Hillenbrand, Barry, 'Thanks a million and sayonara', *Time*, 2 March 1998.

### Raising the bar in Sydney

Bryson, Bill, 'A city under starter's orders', *The Times*, September 2000.

*Look of Games* Sydney video, IOC.

Longman Jerry, *New York Times*, 29 September 2000.


## Party time

*Daily Mirror UK*, 3 October 2000.
Horovitz, Bruce, *USA Today*, 29 September 2000.
*Independent*, 2 October 2000.


## Lighting the fire in Salt Lake

Keating, Steve, 'Salt Lake ready to toast Winter Olympics', Reuters, 29 January
     2002.
Mackay, Duncan, 'Tainted Games hailed a success', *Guardian,* 26 February
     2002.
Fisher, Eric, '2002 Winter Olympics were as good as gold', *The Washington Times*,
     26 February 2002.
Gorrell, Mike, 'SLOC organisers submit final report', *Salt Lake Tribune*, 17 December 2002.


## The tourism dividend

Truno, Enric, *The Political Legacies of the Olympic Games: Barcelona 1992.*
Morse, John, Speech given to the IOC organised symposium on the 'Legacy of the
     Olympic Games', Lausanne 14–16 November 2002.

# Chapter 8 – Making it Happen

## The blues

Lyberg, Wolf, *Fabulous 100 Years of The IOC: Facts, Figures And Much, Much More,*
     International Olympic Committee, 1996

## Hot technology

Dodge, John, 'IBM has quite a bit riding on the Olympics', *Atlanta Constitution*, 25
     February 1996
*Business Week*, 22 January 1996
IOC Marketing Matters. No. 17
*Advertising Age*. 15 July 1996

'IBM saw it's golden opportunity go up in flames', *Independent*, 6 August 1996.

## Crash test dummies

Miller, David, *Athens to Athens: the official history of the Olympic Games and the IOC, 1894–2004*, Mainstream, 2003
'IBM's Olympic fiasco', *Fortune*, 9 September 1996
'IBM's frenzied race to save face', *USA Today*, 5 August 1996
Johnson, Bradley, 'IBM spotlights little guys for the Olympics', *Advertising Age*, 9 September 1998
'The risks and rewards of going for gold', *Business Week*, 9 September 1998

## Twice shy

DiCarlo, Lisa, 'IBM, Olympics part ways after 40 years', *Forbes*, 23 August 2000
Copetas, Craig, 'Divorce is never a pretty sight', *Wall Street Journal*, 14 October 1998
'Glitches to gold', *Washington Post*, 25 September 2000.

## The integrated mousetrap

Copetas, Craig, 'Sema takes Olympic business jump to become global technology sponsor', *Wall Street Journal*, 7 December 1998 'European firm picks up IBM's torch', *International Herald Tribune*, 8 December 1998
*Sports Business*, January 1999
'European group Sema replaces IBM as Olympic technology provider', *Associated Press*.
Jobbers, Ross, *Wall Street Journal*, 7 December 1998.
*Wall Street Journal*, 19 March 1999
*Sports Business*, January 1999
Thomaselli, Rich, 'SchlumbergerSema – The invisible sponsor', *Advertising Age*, 11 February 2002
CNBC Interview, 21 February 2002

## New media, false dawn

Church, Rachel, 'Sport on the internet', *Screen Digest*, June 2000
Maney, Kevin, 'Little net firm rocks TV giants', *USA Today*, 8 February 2000
Haverson, Patrick, *Financial Times*, 4 August 2000.

*Chicago Tribune*, 4 September 2000.


### Discovering the internet

Poole, Mel, 'Until the IOC learns to deal with internet rights, web is shut out at the Olympics', *Sports Business Journal*


### Sink or surf

Poole, Mel, 'Until the IOC learns to deal with internet rights, web is shut out at the Olympics', *Sports Business Journal*
*New York Times*, 25 September 2000
'IBM admits to cyber misdirection', *San Francisco Chronicle*, 28 September 2000


### Casualties of hype?

Copetas, Craig, *Wall Street Journal*, December 2000
Roberts, Kevin, 'Glimpse of a brave new world', *Sports Business*, January 2001
The 1st World Conference on Sport and New Media took place in Lausanne, 4–5 December 2000. Quotes from speakers at the Conference are taken from the proceedings published by the IOC, in association with Sports Business Group
Woodward, Steve, 'Subject of internet delivery divides room at IOC conference', Sports Business Journal


### New media, new mission

'The Swiss accomplish an Olympic first: live web-casts', *International Herald Tribune*, 12 February 2002
'Salt Lake 2002 overview', *Marketing Matters*, June 2002, Issue 21

# Chapter 9 – To the Brink and Back

### The city of saints

Miller, *David, Athens to Athens, the official history of the Olympic Games and the IOC, 1894–2004*, Mainstream, 2003

Packer, Lynn, 'Did Sen. Orrin Hatch and his LDS Mission friend Judge David Sam foil the government's case in the Olympic Bid scandal?', *City Weekly*, 24 January 2002.

Fantin, Linda, 'Ex SLOC Secretary defends actions', *Salt Lake Tribune*, 12 December 2001.


## The loose cannon

'Salt Lake apologises for bribery scandal', *CNNSports Illustrated.Com*, 13 December 1998.


## Bunny business

Labi, Nadya, 'The Olympics turn into a five ring circus', *Time*, 11 January 1999.

Haverson, Patrick, 'Olympic torch gutters', *Financial Times*, 23 January 1999.

Hayward, Paul, 'Olympic Games: Bribes scandal reveals sham of Olympic ideal', *Daily Telegraph*, 25 January 1999.

Gorrell, Mike; and Boulton, Guy, 'SLOC confident goals to be met', *Salt Lake Tribune*, 12 January, 1999.

Raboin, Sharon; and Allen, Karen, 'Calls for resignation, threat of IOC lawsuit add to scandal', *USA Today*, 13 January 1999

'Salt Lake should pay, Swedish rival says', *USA Today*, 21 December 1999.


## Who pays the piper?

Longman, Jerry, 'Corporate backer tells the IOC to come clean', *New York Times*, 13 January 1999.

*Economist*, 'Saving the Olympic spirit', 30 January 1999.


## Next up

Fatsis, Stefan, *Wall Street Journal*, 11 February, 1999

Headline, *The Times*, 16 February 1999

Siddons, Larry, 'Corporate sponsors give IOC an earful', Associated Press, 13 February 1999

Nyhan, David, 'This Olympic sponsor isn't happy', *International Herald Tribune*, 15 February 1999

### The tide turns

Opening address to the 108th IOC Session, Lausanne by Juan Antonio Sama-
    ranch.
Letter from George Fisher, chairman and CEO Kodak, to IOC. 10 May 1999.


### Brand collateral

Farhi, Paul, 'Article sponsor support is steadfast', *Washington Post*, 17 March
    1999.
Echikson, William; and Siklos, Richard, 'Scandal? What scandal', *Business Week*,
    22 March 1999
'Backers leery of Olympic probe', *USA Today*, 15 February 1999.
Hayek, Nick, quoted in *Olympic Marketing Matters*, Issue 15, 1999.
Mullen, Liz, 'Coke backs IOC, proceeds with Games plans',
*Sports Business Journal*
'Kodak applauds IOC for actions against corruption', *Associated Press Report*,
    March 1999.
Fatsis, Stefan, 'Reform is not going to happen overnight', *Wall Street Journal*, 18
    March 1999.
'McDonald's still committed to Olympics', *Reuters Wire Report*.
Mullen, Liz, 'USOC moneyman Krimsky moves on', *Sports Business Journal*


### Fuelling the fire

Bernstein, Andy, 'D'Alessandro wages lonely war on IOC', *Sports Business Jour-
    nal*.
Sandomir, Richard, 'Ebersol defends his investment from scandal-induced criti-
    cism', *New York Times*, 2 June 1999.
Treantor, J., 'Monitor of the Olympic mettle', *New York Times*, 28 March 1999.
Hughes, Duncan, 'Sponsors urge Olympic clean up', *Sunday Business*, 4 April
    1999.


### New shoes

Mallon, Bill, 'The Olympic bribery scandal', *Journal of Olympic History*, May
    2000
'Hearings on the Olympic site selection process and review of the reform effort',
    *United States Congressional Testimony*, 15 December 1999

### Crisis over

*Olympic Marketing Matters*, Issue 16
'Hancock Olympic buy with NBC said to top $10million', *Sports Business Journal*
*Wall Street Journal*, 15 February 2000.
*USA Today*, 16 February 2000.
*Advertising Age*, 11 September 2000.
Fantin, Linda, 'IOC scores PR coup – re-signs John Hancock as Olympic sponsors', *Salt Lake Tribune*, 15 February 2000.
*Los Angeles Times*, 23 July 2000.
*Salt Lake Tribune*, 15 February 2000.

### Putting things in perspective

Closing remarks, Juan Antonio Samaranch IOC 110th Session, Lausanne, December 1999.
Dodd, Mike, 'IOC's reform path at crossroads', *USA Today*, 8 December 1999

### After the storm

'Sam's rebuke', *Desert Morning News*, 6 December 2003

# Chapter 10 – Coming Home

### Chaos is a Greek word

'Knight rider', *The Vancouver Province*, 16 April 2004
Price, S.L., 'Hello Athens', *Sports Illustrated*, 26 January 2004
'*The final sprint*', *Wall Street Journal*, 20 May 2004.
Kassimeris, George, 'We should not be hosting the Olympics',*Independent*, 3 August 2004.
Nicholas, George, 'Greek myths', *New York Times*, 24 July 2004

### The underdog has its day

Barnes, Simon, 'From tragedy to triumph', *The Times*, 14 August 2004.
Corrigan, Peter, 'The ideal home', *Independent on Sunday*, 29 August 2004.
*New York Daily News*, 30 August 2004.

'Panasonic sales up 70% in July on Olympics', Reuters, 21 July 2004.

Twaronite, Lisa, 'Japan flat screen makers are already Olympic winners', *Investors.Com*, 16 August 2004.

Fatsis, Stefan, 'Greeks bearing success', *Wall Street Journal*, 27 August 2004.

Mossop, James, 'Proud Athens emerges in triumph', *Sunday Telegraph*, 29 August, 29 Auguat 2004.

Wilson, Steve, "Efharisto', AP, 29 August 2004.

*St Louis Post*, 29 August 2004.

Goodbody, John, 'Greece gets it right to defy doubters', *The Times*, 31 August 2004

Slot, Owen, 'Shame on us for having so little faith', *The Times*, 31 August 2004.

Reilly, Rick, *Sports Illustrated*, 30 August 2004

Jenkins, Sally, 'Let's give the Games a gold medal', *Washington Post*, 30 August, 2004

*Reuters*, 30 August 2004

Brennan, Christine, 'Athens the comeback kid of Olympic host cities', *USA Today*, 30 August 2004.

Sachs, Susan, 'On time Athens wins first medal of Games', *New York Times*, 9 August 2004.

'Olympics and the unexpected winner', *The Times*, 9 August 2004.

# Appendix

*Los Angeles Organising Committee Official Report*, 1932.

*The Times*, 3 August 1936.

Letter from Roger Tartarian, United Press Association, to Avery Brundage, IOC President 23 January 1956.

Cahill, Shane, 'The battle over Olympic television rights return to Australia, where it all began', ABCzine, Spring 2000.

Gould, Jack, 'Nobody was first', *New York Times*, 9 December 1956.

Barney, Robert Knight; Wenn, Stephen R; and Martyn, Scott G, *Selling the Five Rings: The International Olympic Committee and the Rise of Olympic Commercialism*, University of Utah, 2002.

Arledge, Roone, *Roone – A Memoir*, HarperCollins, 2003.

Kavanagh, Gerard, 'Gifted story teller finds happy ending', *Sports Business Journal*, 21 December 1998.

McMillan, John, 'Bidding for Olympic broadcast rights: The competition before the competition', *Negotiation Journal*, 7, July 1991.

*New York Times*, 18 October 1964.

Klatell, David; and Norman, Marcus, *Sports for Sale: Television, Money, and the Fans*, Oxford University Press, 1988.

*New York Times*, 4 January 1973.

*New York Times*, 16 January 1974.

Johnson, William Oscar, 'A contract with the Kremlin', *Sports Illustrated*.

Carter, Jimmy, *Keeping Faith: Memoirs of a President*, Harper Collins, 1982.

## Additional reading, not directly referenced

Aris, Stephen, *SportsBiz*, Hutchinson, 1990

Barr, Steve; Poppy, John, *The Flame*, William Morrow and Company, 1987.

Borgers, Walter, *Olympic Torch Relays*, Agon SportVerlag, 1996.

Duffy, Neil, *Passion Branding*, Wiley, 2003.

Gaddy, Charles, *An Olympic Journey. The Saga of an American Hero Le Roy Walker*, Griffin Publishing Group, 1998

Gordon, Harry, *The Time of Our Lives, Inside the Sydney Olympics*, University of Queensland Press, 2003.

Gosper, Kevan; Korporaal, Glenda, *An Olympic Life*, Allen and Unwin, 2000.

Greenspan, Bud, *100 Greatest Moments in Olympic History*, General Publishing Group, 1995.

Guttmann Allen, *The Games Must Go On. Avery Brundage and the Olympic Movement*, Columbia University Press, 1984.

IOC Publications: Symposium of International Sports Media, Novemeber 1984; Television in the Olympic Games. The New Era. International Symposium, Lausanne 1998; Broadcasting and the Olympics, the Olympic Museum, Lausanne 1999; Olympic Ceremonies, Historical Continuity and Cultural Exchange.

Killanin, Lord; *My Olympic Years*, Secker & Warburg, 1983.

King, Frank, *It's How You Play The Game, The Inside Story of the Calgary Olympics*, Script, 1991.

Lucas, John, *Future of the Olympic Games*, Human Kinetics Books, 1992.

McGeoch, Rod, and Korporaal, Glenda, *The Bid: How Australia Won the 2000 Games*, William Heinemann, 1994.

Moragas, de Miquel; Botella, Muquel, *The Keys to Success: The Social, Sporting, Economic and Communications Impact of Barcelona 1992*, Centre d'Estudis Olympics, Barcelona, 1995.

Naber, John, *Eureka: How Innovation Changes the Games (and everything else)*, Xerox, 2004.

*The Olympic Century, Volumes 1–24*, World Sport Research and Publications.

Pendergast, Mark, *For God, Country and Coca-Cola: The Unauthorised History of the World's Most Popular Soft Drink*, Weidenfeld and Nicholson, 1993.

Perelman, Richard, *Olympic Retrospective*, LAOC, 1985.

Pound, Richard, *Five Rings Over Korea: The Secret Negotiations Behind the 1988 Olympic Games in Seoul*, Little Brown and Company, 1994.

Preuss, Holger, *Economics of Staging the Olympics: A Comparison of the Games 1972–2008*, Edward Elgar Publishing, 2004

Preuss, Holger, *Economics of the Olympic Games. Hosting the Games 1972–2000*, Walla Walla Press, 2000.

Puijk, Roel, *Global Spotlights on Lillehammer. How the World Viewed Norway During the 1994 Winter Olympics*, John Libbey Media, University of Luton, 1997

Romney, Mitt; and Robinson, Timothy, *Turnaround, Crisis, Leadership and the Olympic Games*, Regnery Publishing, 2004

Samaranch, Juan Antonio, *Memorias Olimpicas*, Planeta Singluar, 2002.

*Share the Flame: The Official Retrospective Book of the Olympic Torch Relay*, Murray Love Productions, 1988.

Shell Pat, *Olympic Babylon: The True Story of the Olympic Games*, Macmillan, 1998.

Zyman, Sergio, *The End Of Marketing As We Know It*, Harper Business, 1999.

*100 Years Olympic Design*, Quon Editions, 1994.

# INDEX